THE IDENTITY
THEFT

THE IDENTITY
THEFT

THE RETURN OF THE
1ST CENTURY MESSIAH

5 REASONS WHY WE HAVE A
ROMAN CHRIST INSTEAD
OF A JEWISH MESSIAH

AUTHOR OF *THE HEALING POWER OF THE ROOTS*
DOMINIQUAE BIERMAN, PHD

ZIONS GOSPEL
PRESS

Unless otherwise identified, all scripture quotations are from the Tree of Life Version (TLV) and the New American Standard Bible (NASB). Tree of Life Version. © 2015 by the Messianic Jewish Family Bible Society. Used by permission of the Messianic Jewish Family Bible Society. New American Standard Bible. © 1995 by the Lockman Foundation. Used by permission, all rights reserved.

Words such as Jesus, Christ, Lord, and God have been changed by the author back to their original Hebrew renderings, Yeshua, Yahveh, and ELOHIM.

E-Book ISBN: 978-1-953502-01-8
Paperback ISBN: 978-1-953502-00-1

First paperback edition June 2020
Published by Zion's Gospel Press
shalom@zionsgospel.com
52 Tuscan Way, Ste 202-412,
St. Augustine, Florida 32092, USA

First Printed June 2020
Published in the United States of America

ZIONS GOSPEL
PRESS

Can a virgin forget her ornaments, or a bride her attire?
Yet My people have forgotten Me, days without number.

— *Jeremiah 2:32*

Truly, You are a God who hides Himself,
O God of Israel, Savior!

— *Isaiah 45:15*

DEDICATION

At Yad Vashem, the Holocaust Museum in Jerusalem, outdoors, there is a particular lane lined up with trees. Under each tree, there is a sign with a name and a country. This lane is called the Avenue of the Righteous Gentiles. Each tree represents a brave person in Europe that risked their lives to rescue Jews from the Nazi extermination. Among them are some Christians of both Catholic and Protestant faith.

With their righteous and just actions, they overcame the monstrous anti-Semitic theologies that were the fertile soil of all the persecution, humiliation, and murder of Jews in the name of Christ during the Nazi *Shoah* (Holocaust).

I dedicate this book to all these known and unknown Christians who were greater than their theological upbringing.

I salute them all.—Archbishop Dr. Dominiquae Bierman, president of *Kad-Esh MAP Ministries* and *The United Nations For Israel.*

FOREWORD

I have been in full-time ministry for 54 years. I have traveled all over this world and have read what seems like myriads of books and study courses. I have read books with encouraging historical facts, and many, many books on our beloved Israel, our people's plight, and the plans our Yah has for His people. As you read this incredible book by Archbishop Bierman, you will discover shocking truths that have been shuttered and hidden by historians and theologians for generations. She has uncovered and boldly declares these truths that very few ministers and would-be scholars have been afraid and reluctant to openly discuss, not wanting to make waves. This book is a tsunami of revelation of our past, present, and future of the people of Yah.

The betrayal of the memory and current condition of God's chosen people seems to be overlooked by and in what is called the Church of today.

One cannot read through this book and then lay it aside. It is captivating to the pure in heart and those who so sincerely desire to please the heavenly Father.

I applaud you Archbishop for your courage, your tenacious faith, and boldness as the prophetess you are — taking such a firm stand historically with such vibrant revelatory writing that can and should become a study guide to all who seek pure truth.

Over the years, I have ministered with and to multitudes of Yah's men and women — servants who are considered cutting edge — but I can say without reservation none so far have pursued to recover and restore our true identity without compromise.

Archbishop, Prophetess, I am so very thankful for your dedication and your passion. I am blessed to call you "friend" and fellow servant in the faith.

Shalom be multiplied with unending blessings and favor upon you;

— **Archbishop General Dr. Lawrence Langston, Th.D. Ph.D.**

CONTENTS

THE PROPHECY OF THE ROSE

I received this prophecy in 1993. While on board an El Al flight from Zurich to Tel Aviv I asked the Holy Spirit, "So, what's the 'big deal' about ministering the 'roots' to the Church?" I wanted to understand the purpose of my traveling to so many nations. "God, what are you saying?"

Still very vivid in my mind were the testimonies of miraculous healings and deliverances that were shared after we finished our first *Back to the Roots* seminar in Herisau, Switzerland. Hans Peter and Anita Vogt had welcomed us, and all the Jews, with open arms. "The Church needs to repent," they said.

One testimony shared by a youthful woman was very touching.

"I had mental problems," she said, "I could not find my *identity*. They had cast many demons out of me, but I never got free. As you explained about the roots of our faith and the unbreakable connection between the Jews and Gentiles, peace came into me, and I was reconciled with my roots. I am free now!"

I pondered all of these things on that El Al flight from Zurich to Tel Aviv. As the plane was landing, the Spirit of God answered my original question, "What's the big deal about ministering the roots to the Church?"

"It is a matter of life and death," He said. *"The Church is like a beautiful rose that has been cut off from its roots in the garden. It has survived*

1

for two days in a vase with water. But on the third day, it will die unless it is planted and connected back to its roots."

I started weeping. It pierced my heart through and through. If it's a matter of life and death, I will pay the price for the sake of THE LORD and His children. The Scriptures say that a day is like a thousand years to THE LORD. It has already been two thousand years since THE LORD Yeshua (Jesus) was revealed to Israel, and the Church came into being in Jerusalem. They were all Jewish then. Now we are entering a new era of history. Being reconnected to our roots is a matter of life and death!

For I do not want you, brethren, to be uninformed of this mystery—so that you will not be wise in your own estimation—that a partial hardening has happened to Israel until the fullness of the Gentiles has come in...

— ROMANS 11:25 NASB

The Divine Call to a Church Like Esther

"In 2016 the Archbishop of Canterbury, Justin Welby, likened anti-Semitism to a 'virus,' adding that 'it is a shameful truth that, through its theological teachings, the church, which should have offered an antidote, compounded the spread of this virus.'" (Telegraph.co.uk)

This book is a wake up call to every Christian, church, and denomination to rise as Esther in this generation. The defeat of anti-Semitism in all Christian ranks is vital as we prepare for the return of the Jewish Messiah to Jerusalem.

... and he said, "THE LORD has sworn; THE LORD will have war against Amalek from generation to generation."

— EXODUS 17:16 NASB

Anti-Semitism is Again on the Rise!

The WZO's (World Zionist Organization's) annual report on global anti-Semitism finds that the coronavirus pandemic has led to a resurgence of anti-Semitic activity and beliefs:

By Lauren Marcus, World Israel News, April 20, 2020:

On the eve of Holocaust Remembrance Day, the World Zionist Organization (WZO) released its annual report on the state of global anti-Semitism. This year's report details a spike in global anti-Semitism, partially attributed to the coronavirus pandemic.

The report found an 18 percent increase in violent anti-Semitic incidents worldwide from 2018 to 2019. Both the Poway synagogue shooting in California, in which one woman was killed and several worshippers were seriously wounded, and the attempted Halle synagogue attack in Germany, which led to the deaths of two bystanders and wounding of two others, occurred in 2019.

Since the outbreak of the coronavirus pandemic in 2020, anti-Semitic activity has increased online, with "Jews, Zionists and Israelis, as individuals and as a collective, being accused of causing and spreading the coronavirus." However, the practice of blaming Jews for the world's ills is hardly a new phenomenon.

"Blaming Jews for 'why things go wrong' is a common practice as old as anti-Semitism itself," says the report, prepared by veteran anti-Semitism researcher Eli Nachum. (World Israel News)

3

Many years ago, I stood outside the massive walls of a church near the Auschwitz-Birkenau death camps in Poland, asking the Almighty the following question.

How could the Shoah (Nazi Holocaust) have been prevented?

His answer to me was, "There was no Esther Church."

Had there been an *Esther Church,* then six million of my people would not have been exterminated.

This answer placed the responsibility for the protection and wellbeing of His Jewish people on the Church, one called an *Esther Church.*

Historically, the Church has not been the protector of the Jewish people, but the persecutor. Events such as the kidnapping of Jewish children to raise them as Christians, the Christian Crusades, Spanish and other Inquisitions, anti-Jewish murder orgies held at Easter, New Year, and Christmas in Europe and Russia, and the Nazi mass murder (Holocaust). They did these persecutions in the name of Christianity and Jesus Christ: it seemed very doubtful that the Church can ever be the protector of the Jewish people.

I set myself to facilitate the formation of such an Esther Church to prevent another anti-Semitic, Amalek and Haman outbreak for murdering more Jews.* This timely book is part of this endeavor, as anti-Semitism has escalated to proportions similar to what happened before World War II. We cannot, and we *must* not remain silent.

To my delight, today, there are a few Christian organizations that are showing the marks of an Esther Church, but it is not enough.

So, you may ask, "What is an Esther Church?" and what distinguished Esther to become the heroine of an entire book in the Bible?

---

* Amalek, in the Bible, is an enemy of Israel (see Exodus 17:8-16 for an example). Haman is another enemy of the Jewish people and tried to exterminate the Jews in the book of Esther (see Esther 3:6 for an example).

If I had to sum up the one crucial factor that made Queen Esther the uncontested savior of her people, it would be *identity*.

When she was first called to task by her cousin and adoptive father, Mordechai, she said 'no,' and was not willing to risk her life for the Jewish people. Esther had forgotten her *identity* as a Jew. She was comfortable and protected in the king's harem*, and she was willing to see her people murdered rather than lose her comforts.

Mordechai also gave Hathach (Esther's eunuch servant) a written copy of the decree which had been distributed in Shushan for their annihilation, to show to Esther and to explain it to her. Mordechai instructed Esther to go to the king, to beg his favor, and plead before him on behalf of her people. Hathach reported to Esther what Mordechai had said. Then Esther spoke to Hathach and gave him instructions for Mordechai:

> "All the king's servants and the people of the king's provinces fully understand that for anyone, man or woman, who approaches the king in the inner courtyard without being summoned, he has one law—that he be put to death, unless the king extends his golden scepter permitting him to live. But I have not been summoned to come to the king for 30 days." So they conveyed Esther's words to Mordecai.

> — ESTHER 4:11–12

Most of the Church has also forgotten her *identity*, days without number. She has considered herself a Romanized Christian with Roman feasts and traditions, and she is comfortable that way.

---

* *Harem* is the separate part of a household reserved for wives, concubines, and female servants.

Anti-Semitism is rising to the highest proportions since World War II, but she is comfortable. She is not Jewish, or is she?

When Gentiles receive the New Covenant in the Blood of a Jewish Messiah, they get grafted into a Jewish olive tree, thus becoming *one* with Israel.

> **But if some of the branches were broken off and you—being a wild olive—were grafted in among them and became a partaker of the root of the olive tree with its richness, do not boast against the branches. But if you do boast, it is not you who support the root, but the root supports you.**
>
> **— ROMANS 11:17**

God does not call Gentiles to replace or usurp Israel, but to join Israel like Ruth joined with Naomi.

> **Ruth replied, "Do not plead with me to abandon you, to turn back from following you. For where you go, I will go, and where you stay, I will stay. Your people will be my people, and your God my God. Where you die, I will die, and there I will be buried. May ADONAI deal with me, and worse, if anything but death comes between me and you!"**
>
> **— RUTH 1:16**

However, the Church today (mostly) is not grafted into the olive tree but into a Roman, pagan Christmas tree. Thus, she has lost her true identity. And not only the identity of the Jewish Messiah has been replaced for a Romanized Christ, but the identity of the Church has been stolen as well. That is why there was no Esther Church to prevent the Shoah (Nazi Holocaust) from happening during World War II.

Will there be one today? It depends on us restoring the true *identity* of the Jewish Messiah and with it the *identity* of His bride.

Recovering from this age-old *identity theft* is the order of the hour; if not, it will release a great judgment on the Church and the nations—the signs are already here!

> **Rescue those being dragged off to death, hold back those stumbling to slaughter. If you say, "Look, we didn't know this." Won't He who weighs hearts perceive it? Won't He who guards your soul know it? Won't He repay each one according to his deeds?**
>
> — **PROVERBS 24:11–12**

Mordechai's reply to his comfortable and compromised niece was,

> **For if you remain silent at this time, relief and deliverance will arise for the Jews from another place—but you and your father's house will perish. Who knows whether you have attained royal status for such a time as this?**
>
> — **ESTHER 4:14**

Notice that Mordechai separated Esther and her father's house from the rest of the Jews who would be delivered by YHVH in another way. If Esther remained silent, she and her father's house would not be saved, though all the other Jews would be saved.

However, Esther was an orphan since the Babylonian exile; Mordechai was the only father she had. Was Mordechai dooming himself? Or was Esther's father's house another house?

> **There was a Jewish man in the Shushan palace whose name was Mordecai, son of Jair son of Shimei, son of Kish, a Benjamite, who had been taken into exile from Jerusalem with the captives that had been carried away with King Jeconiah of Judah, whom King Nebuchadnezzar of Babylon had taken away. He had raised Hadassah—that is Esther—his uncle's daughter, for she had neither father nor mother. The girl was attractive and had a beautiful figure. When her father and mother died, Mordecai took her to him as his own daughter.**
>
> **— ESTHER 2:5**

Esther had no father, no mother, and no father's house. She was now married to the King of Persia who had become her husband, and by default all the king's father's house became her father's house. If the father of the king was alive, then Esther might have had a father-in-law.

Could it be that Mordechai said that if she did not help her own people, the God of Israel would judge her and her family in-law, the Persian Royal family whom she belonged to? They regarded the King of Persia as the father of his nation. So, he also was Esther's father and husband.

So Mordechai's warning to her could be paraphrased: If you do not fight for the Covenant Jewish people that birthed you and raised you, we will be delivered anyway—for God has a covenant with us. But you, that became *one* with the King of Persia and his people, will perish. And not only you will perish, but your king, father, and all the Persian people.

Esther apparently got the picture. She repented and went to fast before she interceded with her king. For the first time she embraced her forgotten identity as a Jew.

> So Queen Esther answered, "If I have found favor in the eyes of the king, and if it pleases the king, grant me my life—this is my petition. And spare the life of my people—this is my request! For we have been sold, I and my people, for destruction, slaughter and annihilation. If we had simply been sold as male and female slaves, I would have remained silent, for such distress would not be worth disturbing the king."
>
> — ESTHER 7:3

Her act of intervention was risky, but she was not intervening only for the Jewish nation. No! She was rescuing Persia from annihilation, as she was now a Persian. This is a principle repeated throughout the Scriptures: Any person or nation that comes against Israel would incur the wrath of the God of Israel.

> "For thus says ADONAI-Tzva'ot, He has sent me after glory to the nations that plundered you—because whoever touches you touches the apple of His eye—'For behold, I will shake My hand against them and they will be plunder to their servants.' Then you will know that ADONAI-Tzva'ot has sent me."
>
> — ZECHARIAH 2:12

The rest is *His*-Story. Wicked Haman hung on the gallows he had prepared for Mordechai the Jew, as also were his ten sons.

So they hanged Haman on the gallows that he had prepared for Mordecai. Then the king's rage subsided.

— ESTHER 7:10

With those dangerous "snakes" eliminated, the Jews could now defend themselves and overcome their enemies. They elevated Queen Esther in prominence and Mordechai became the advisor of the king instead of the Amalekite Haman.

Then Mordecai went out from the king's presence in blue and white royal robes, with a large gold crown, and also a purple robe of fine linen. The city of Shushan shouted and rejoiced. For the Jews, there was light and gladness, joy and honor. Throughout every province and throughout every city, wherever the king's edict and his law went, the Jews had gladness and joy, banquets and holidays. Many peoples of the land became Jews, because the fear of the Jews had overcome them.

— ESTHER 8:15

Queen Esther's identity was fully restored and the name of her Jewish father's house is now remembered. She became identified as the daughter of Abihail again. In Hebrew, Abihail means "a mighty father." She was now a full daughter of the Most High God. Her orphanhood and her misplaced identity were things of the past.

Then Queen Esther, the daughter of Abihail, and also Mordecai the Jew, wrote with full authority to confirm this second letter of Purim.

— ESTHER 9:29

All is well when it ends well.

The question is this: Will it end well for the Church and the nations that the Church represents? It will only end well if an Esther Church arises to intervene with their governments and authorities to crush the hideous rise of anti-Semitism.

> **I will bless those who bless you, but whoever curses you I will curse, and in you all the families of the earth will be blessed.**
>
> — **GENESIS 12:3**

For such an Esther Church to arise, she must restore her identity as one who is grafted into the Jewish olive tree and as a worshipper of a Jewish Messiah. Only a Jewish Messiah in her can overturn anti-Semitism and the impending judgment on the nations because of the cause of Zion (Isa. 34:8). A Roman Christ won't do!

For an Esther Church to arise, we must recover the stolen identity of the Jewish Messiah Yeshua, who, like Mordechai the Jew, is knocking at our door.

> **You worship what you do not know; we worship what we know, for salvation (Yeshua) is from the Jews.**
>
> — **JOHN 4:22**

Today is not a moment too soon for an Esther Church to *arise*!

> **For ADONAI is enraged at all the nations, and furious at all their armies. He will utterly destroy them. He will give them over to slaughter. So their slain will be thrown out, and the**

stench of their corpses will rise, and the hills will be drenched with their blood. For ADONAI has a day of vengeance, a year of recompense for the hostility against Zion.

— ISAIAH 34:2

As you continue reading, you will discover the five major reasons why the Church has lost its Jewish identity. You will also learn how to take it back! In gate one (chapter one) we will unveil the fruit due to THE IDENTITY THEFT of the Messiah.

For the Lion of Judah—Archbishop Dr. Dominiquae Bierman, President of *Kad-Esh MAP Ministries* and *The United Nations for Israel*

POISON FRUIT FROM THE IDENTITY THEFT

**Yes, just as you can identify a tree by its fruit,
so you can identify people by their actions.**

— MATTHEW 7:20 NLT

I t is widely understood in Christian circles that much of the Jewish nation has not been acquainted with their Messiah and Savior. But how many people realize that most Christians in the world do not know Him either? Christendom, at large, has met a Roman Christ— not a Jewish Messiah. The outcome of this identity theft has been despicable acts of humiliation, murder, and prevalent anti-Semitism in many Christian circles. The fruit of communing with a Roman Christ rather than a Jewish Messiah is bloodshed and cruelty.

Events such as the kidnapping of Jewish children to raise them as Christians; restricting and discriminatory laws against Jews; the Christian Crusades, Spanish Inquisition, and other inquisitions, *pogroms*;* the Nazi Holocaust and much of the anti-Zionism of today is the

---

* The definition of *pogrom*: An organized massacre of a particular ethnic group, in particular that of Jews in Russia or eastern Europe." Oxford Dictionary Definition.

terrible legacy of this age-old identity theft that has lasted over 18 centuries. Emperor Constantine solidified it through the Council of Nicaea in AD 325, which called for a complete divorce from the Jews—which included a separation from the Jewish Messiah.

The following paragraphs are from what I call *The Act of Divorce* from the Jewish people and everything Jewish. This separation has affected Christians until this day and has been the culprit for all Christian anti-Semitism.

The Council of Nicaea

From the letter of the Emperor (Constantine) to all those not present at the council. (Found in Eusebius, Vita Const., Lib III 18-20)

When the question relative to the sacred festival of Easter arose, it was universally thought that it would be convenient that all should keep the feast on one day; for what could be more beautiful and more desirable than to see this festival, through which we receive the hope of immortality, celebrated by all with one accord and in the same manner? It was declared to be particularly unworthy for this, the holiest of festivals to follow the customs (the calculation) of the Jews who had soiled their hands with the most fearful of crimes, and whose minds were blinded. In rejecting their custom we may transmit to our descendants the legitimate mode of celebrating Easter; which we have observed from the time of the Savior's passion according to the day of the week.

We ought not therefore to have anything in common with the Jew, for the Savior has shown us another way; our worship following a more legitimate and more convenient course (the order of the days of the week): *And consequently in unanimously adopting this mode, we desire, dearest brethren to separate ourselves from the detestable company of the Jew.* For it is truly shameful for us to hear them boast that without their direction we could not keep this feast. How can they be in the right, they who, after the death of the Savior, have no longer been led by reason but by wild violence, as their delusion may urge them? They do not possess the truth in this Easter question, for in their blindness and repugnance to all improvements they frequently celebrate two Passovers in the same year. We could not imitate those who are openly in error.

How, then, could we follow these Jews who are most certainly blinded by error? For to celebrate a Passover twice in one year is totally inadmissible. *But even if this were not so it would still be your duty not to tarnish your soul by communication with such wicked people (the Jews).* You should consider not only that the number of churches in these provinces make a majority, but also that it is right to demand what our reason approves, and that we should have nothing in common with the Jews. (Percival)

From then on, they adopted the Roman Christ as the all-prevalent Savior of Christians. This Roman Christ came with a Roman name, Roman pagan feasts and traditions, and Roman hatred of everything Jewish. The outcome of this is nothing short of devastating. Today the younger generations are at a crossroads of what to believe, and millions are exiting the churches feeling empty and deceived. The Holy Spirit has been knocking on the doors of all churches for repentance and restoration of the identity of His Jewish Son, who is the only Savior of the world.

Before writing my first book on the subject (known worldwide as *The Healing Power of the Roots*), I asked the Almighty, "Why is it so important to administer the Jewish roots to the Church?" His answer to me was loud and clear, and it has kept me running with this message for nearly three decades: "It is a matter of life and death. The Church has been like a rose that has been cut from its roots and placed in a vase with water for two days. But on the Third Day, if she is not *replanted* back, she will surely die." One day is like one thousand years to THE LORD (2 Pet. 3:8). This is the Third Day, the Third Millennium – and the Rose is dying.

Recently my team and I took part at the National Religious Broadcasters Convention (NRB) held in Nashville, Tennessee, for Americans and those of other nations in media. This was my third time attending the convention with them.

This important association has been established since 1944. They have fought like a lion for the freedoms of Christian radio, TV, and media. It has influenced many prominent ministries and even governments, being a great resource of training for all media ministries. Upon our arrival, I noticed that, contrary to previous years, the attendance was very low, and the sessions were half-empty. I also noticed that many of the spots allotted for paid advertising of media ministries were vacant. I felt that the NRB was involved in serious warfare. On top of it, Dr. Ravi Zacharias who was assigned to give the opening address, had to be rushed to emergency surgery. Unfortunately, three months later on May 19, 2020, Ravi, a spiritual mentor to many and a brilliant leader, died of cancer of the spine that was discovered during surgery. Lauren Green of Fox News wrote: "The death of Ravi Zacharias is the end of an era." Many were praying for his wellbeing, including our team.

By the last day of the convention, we attended an open meeting of the Advisory TV Board to the NRB. All participants could voice their opinion and make suggestions to improve the next year's convention. It was then that the chairman of the board confided in us that the NRB had almost ceased to exist this year of 2020 and that the mere fact that the convention even took place was a sheer miracle! I knew in my spirit that this powerful association, a veteran of many wars since 1944, was now facing a monster they had not faced before.

I spoke the following words to them:

"I suggest that in order for the NRB to experience resurrection power and to have a future, it needs to bring the Message of Israel and Jewish roots of the faith to the forefront and to center stage. This will also bring back the anointing. We must educate the broadcasters that ignorance on the streets is appalling, and anti-Semitism is rising to dangerous levels. The key for the coming revival is in Romans 11:15, *'The acceptance of the Jews is life from the dead.'*"

There was a thick silence after my words. But the reaction of this important board was to invite me to become a board member of the TV Advisory Board. I would have joined willingly; however, because of a technical mistake, I did not yet have my membership with the NRB—I was a guest only. They expressed their hope that it could happen by next year. However, I pray that they will heed my words, as the future of the NRB and all its members depend on it.

This book is all about that monster that almost killed the NRB, and is killing many good Christians, and gives us the strategy on how to defeat it.

The question is not if something *can* be done, but we need to realize that it *must* be done, even against all the odds, to restore the identity of the Messiah. The victims of this satanic plan are not only the Jews but countless deceived Christians that suffer from terrible religious confusion that leads to what I call *spiritual schizophrenia*.

Sin runs rampant: homosexuality is acceptable even among the clergy; mental sickness and suicide are at an all-time high; pornography is popular among a sizeable portion of Christians; adultery and fornication even in the pulpit have become normal; greed and the pursuit of mammon above the pursuit of God is the order of the day. The Exodus from many churches has escalated to a rate never seen before, and all this because of a broken fellowship with One Jew—One that died for us.

As you read this book, you will go through a spiritual journey, much like that of the Israelites, who were delivered from slavery in Egypt after 430 years. Your journey, however, involves exiting a carefully crafted deception running for nearly 1,800 years, which took root in the fourth century when it became established Church doctrine. Today, in theological circles, it is called replacement theology. However, this is not all you may think it is. Even if you have heard of it before and you think you do not have any of it, please keep reading – as it is much more rampant than you know, and it hides in places you may not be aware of.

Even if you are a lover of Israel, this book is for you.

Even if you are Messianic, this book is for you.

The thief of Messiah's identity is a five headed monster: The demonic principality that I call,

The Anti-MESITOJUZ

Each of its heads has a focus in which to deceive His bride into being weak, following "a form of godliness, but denying the power" (2 Tim. 3:5) that Yeshua's sacrificial death provides us. Its strategy is to twist scripture to convince us to become like this monster, in word and deed. The five areas of deception are:

- Anti-**Me**ssiah
- Anti-**I**srael
- Anti-**To**rah
- Anti-**Ju**wish
- Anti-**Z**ion

It is sly, sophisticated, brutal, and bloodthirsty. It has tried to exterminate the Jews, and now it's coming for the Christians, with plans to thrust entire nations into destruction.

Follow me as we expose this monster and dismantle it with the power of the Spirit of Truth, the Word of God, testimonies, and historical facts. Then we will recover the stolen identity of our Jewish Messiah and with it His anointing, true spiritual health, holiness, and Divine authority.

On Christian Anti-Semitism from Various Sources

Christian rhetoric and antipathy towards Jews developed in the early years of Christianity and it was reinforced by the belief that Jews had killed Christ and ever increasing anti-Jewish measures over the ensuing centuries. The action taken by Christians against Jews included acts of ostracism, humiliation, violence, and murder, *culminating in the Holocaust.* (Harries)

Christian anti-Semitism has been attributed to numerous factors including theological differences, competition between Church and Synagogue, the Christian drive for converts, misunderstanding of Jewish beliefs and practices, and the perception that Judaism was hostile towards Christianity. For two millennia, these attitudes were reinforced in Christian preaching, art and popular teachings, all of which expressed contempt for Jews as well as statutes which were designed to humiliate and stigmatize Jews. (Koyzis; Gerstenfeld)

Modern anti-Semitism has primarily been described as hatred against Jews as a race and its most recent expression is rooted in 18th-century racial theories, while anti-Judaism is rooted in hostility towards the Jewish religion, but in Western Christianity, anti-Judaism effectively merged into anti-Semitism during the 12th century. Scholars have debated how Christian anti-Semitism played a role in the Nazi Third Reich, World War II and the Holocaust. The Holocaust has forced many Christians to reflect on the relationship between Christian theology, Christian practices, and how they contributed to it. (Harries; Heschel)

The church fathers identified Jews and Judaism with heresy and declared the people of Israel to be *extra Deum* (lat. "outside of God"). Saint Peter of Antioch referred to Christians that refused to worship religious images as having "Jewish minds." In the early second century AD, the heretic Marcion of Sinope (c. 85 – c. 160 AD) declared that the Jewish God was a different God, inferior to the Christian one, and rejected the Jewish scriptures as the product of a lesser deity. Marcion's teachings, which were extremely popular, rejected Judaism not only as an incomplete revelation, but as a false one as well, but, at the same time, allowed less blame to be placed on the Jews personally for having not recognized Jesus, since, in Marcion's worldview, Jesus was not sent by the lesser Jewish God, but by the supreme Christian God, whom the Jews had no reason to recognize. (Michael)

In combating Marcion, orthodox apologists conceded that Judaism was an incomplete and inferior religion to Christianity, while also defending the Jewish scriptures as canonical. The Church Father Tertullian (c. 155 – c. 240 AD) had a particularly intense personal dislike towards the Jews and argued that the Gentiles had been chosen by God to replace the Jews, because they were worthier and more honorable. (Nicholls)

Patristic bishops of the patristic era such as Augustine argued that the Jews should be left alive and suffering as a perpetual reminder of their murder of Christ. Like his anti-Jewish teacher, Ambrose of Milan, he defined Jews as a special subset of those damned to hell. As "Witness People", he sanctified collective punishment for the Jewish deicide and enslavement of Jews to Catholics: "Not by bodily death, shall the ungodly race of carnal Jews perish ... 'Scatter them abroad, take away their strength. And bring them down O Lord.'" Augustine claimed to "love" the Jews but as a means to convert them to Christianity. Sometimes he identified all Jews with the evil Judas and developed the doctrine (together with St. Cyprian) that there was "no salvation outside the Church." (Michael)

The Fertile Ground for Hitler and the Nazi Holocaust

Other church fathers, such as John Chrysostom, went further in their condemnation. The Catholic editor Paul Harkins wrote that St. John Chrysostom's anti-Jewish theology "is no longer tenable (..) For these objectively unchristian acts he cannot be excused, even if he is the product of his times." John Chrysostom held, as most church fathers did, that the sins of all Jews were communal and endless, to him his Jewish neighbors were the collective representation of all alleged crimes of all pre-existing Jews. All church fathers applied the passages of the New Testament concerning the alleged advocation of the crucifixion of Christ to all Jews of his day, the Jews were the ultimate evil. However, John Chrysostom went so far to say that because Jews rejected the Christian God in human flesh, Christ, they therefore deserved to be killed: "grew fit for slaughter." In citing the New Testament (Luke 19:27) he claimed that Jesus was speaking about Jews when he said, "as for these enemies of mine who did not want me to reign over them, bring them here and *slay them* before me."

St. Jerome identified Jews with Judas Iscariot and the immoral use of money ("Judas is cursed, that in Judas the Jews may be accursed... their prayers turn into sins"). Jerome's homiletical assaults, that may have served as the basis for the anti-Jewish Good Friday liturgy, contrasts Jews with the devil and that "the ceremonies of the Jews are harmful and deadly to Christians", whoever keeps them was doomed to the devil: "My enemies are the Jews; they have conspired in hatred against Me, crucified Me, heaped evils of all kinds upon Me, blasphemed Me." (Michael)

Some Fruit of Christian Anti-Semitism

The following are historical Christian events of hatred and anti-Semitism. Christian history is so bloody that it is impossible to be exhaustive about it in one book. I could write many volumes with too many true cruel stories to print. But this is only a partial synopsis for your information.

> Jews were subject to a wide range of legal disabilities and restrictions in medieval Europe. They were excluded from many trades, the occupations varying with place and time, and determined by the influence of various non-Jewish competing interests. Often Jews were barred from all occupations except moneylending and peddling, with even these at times being forbidden. Jews' association to moneylending would carry on throughout history in the stereotype of Jews being greedy and perpetuating capitalism.
>
> In the later medieval period, the number of Jews permitted to reside in certain places was limited; they were concentrated in ghettos, and were not allowed to own land; they were subject to discriminatory taxes upon entering cities or districts other than their own. The *Oath More Judaico*, the form of oath required from Jewish witnesses, in some places developed bizarre or humiliating forms (e.g. in Swabian law of the 13th century, where the Jew would be required to stand on the hide of a sow or a bloody lamb). (Wikipedia Contributors)
>
> The Fourth Lateran Council in 1215 was the first to proclaim the requirement for Jews to wear something that distinguished them as Jews (and Muslims the same). On many occasions, Jews were accused of a blood libel, the supposed drinking of blood of

Christian children in mockery of the Christian Eucharist. (Avrutin, Dekel-Chen and Weinburg)

Anti-Semitism in popular European Christian culture escalated beginning in the 13th century. Blood libels* and host desecration** drew popular attention and led to many cases of persecution against Jews. Many believed Jews poisoned wells to cause plagues. In the case of blood libel, it was widely believed that the Jews would kill a child before Easter and needed Christian blood to bake matzo. Throughout history, if a Christian child was murdered, accusations of blood libel would arise, no matter how small the Jewish population. The Church often added to the fire by portraying the dead child as a martyr who had been tortured and the child had powers like Jesus was believed to have. Sometimes the children were even made into Saints (The Butcher's Tale).

Anti-Semitic imagery such as *Judensau* (Jewish pig) and *Ecclesia et Synagoga* (statues of church triumphant vs vanquished synagogue) recurred in Christian art and architecture.

Anti-Jewish Easter holiday customs such as the Burning of Judas continue to the present time. (Bachner, Polish crowd beats, burns Judas effigy with hat, sidelocks of ultra-Orthodox Jew)

---

* "Blood libels" is the false and maliciously perpetuated accusation that Jews have murdered non-Jews (such as Christian children) in order to use their blood in rituals.

** "Host desecration" is a form of sacrilege in Christian denominations that follow the doctrine of real presence of Christ in the Eucharist. It involves the mistreatment or malicious use of a consecrated host—the bread used in the Eucharistic service of the Divine Liturgy or Mass.

The **First Crusade** (1096–1099) was the first of a number of religious wars initiated, supported and sometimes directed by the Latin Church in the medieval period. The initial objective was the recovery of the Holy Land from Islamic rule. Mobs of predominantly poor Christians numbering in the thousands led by Peter the Hermit, a French priest, responded first. What has become known as the People's Crusade passed through Germany and indulged in wide-ranging anti-Jewish activities and massacres. (Wikipedia Contributors)

The **Rhineland massacres**, also known as the **persecutions of 1096** or **Gzerot Tatnó**, were a series of mass murders of Jews perpetrated by mobs of German Christians of the People's Crusade in the year 1096, or 4856 according to the Jewish calendar. Some scholars consider the massacres to be the earliest known incident of anti-Semitism. (Nirenburg)

Many Jews were expelled from most countries and most cities of Christian Europe.

In the Edict of Expulsion, King Edward I expelled all the Jews from England in 1290 (only after ransoming some 3,000 among the most wealthy of them), on the accusation of usury and undermining loyalty to the dynasty. In 1306 there was a wave of persecution in France, and there were widespread Black Death Jewish persecutions as the Jews were blamed by many Christians for the plague, or spreading it. As late as 1519, the Imperial city of Regensburg took advantage of the recent death of Emperor Maximilian I to expel its 500 Jews . (Keter

Books; Florida Center for Instructional Technology; Wood)

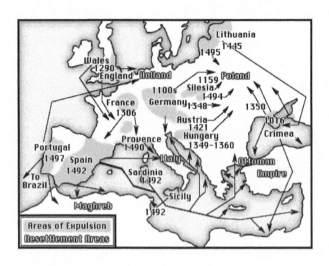

Above: Map of Jewish expulsions and resettlement areas in Europe.

The Spanish Inquisition

Over centuries, the Jewish community in Spain had flour-
ished and grown in numbers and influence, though anti-Semitism had surfaced from time to time. During the reign of Henry
III of Castile and Leon (1390–1406), Jews faced increased
persecution and were pressured to convert to Christianity.
The pogroms of 1391 were especially brutal, and the threat of
violence hung over the Jewish community in Spain. Faced with
the choice between baptism and death, the number of nomi-
nal converts to the Christian faith soon became very great. Many
Jews were killed, and those who adopted Christian beliefs—the
so-called *conversos* (Spanish: "converted")—faced continued suspicion and prejudice. In addition, there remained a significant
population of Jews who had professed conversion but continued to practice their faith in secret. Known as Marranos, these

nominal converts from Judaism were perceived to be an even greater threat to the social order than those who had rejected forced conversion. After Aragon and Castile were united by the royal marriage of Ferdinand and Isabella (1469), the Marranos were denounced as a danger to the existence of Christian Spain. In 1478 Pope Sixtus IV issued a papal bill authorizing the Catholic Monarchs to name inquisitors who would address the issue. This did not mean that the Spanish sovereigns were turning over to the church the struggle for unity; on the contrary, they sought to use the Inquisition to support their absolute and centralized regime - and most especially to increase royal power in Aragon. The first Spanish inquisitors, operating in Seville, proved so severe that Sixtus IV attempted to intervene. The Spanish crown now had in its possession a weapon too precious to give up, however, and the efforts of the pope to limit the powers of the Inquisition were without avail. ("Spanish Inquisition | Definition, History, & Facts | Britannica")

A chief inquisitor was nominated by the Spanish Monarchs who became the terror of all the Jews – Tomás de Torquemada.

At Torquemada's urging, Ferdinand and Isabella issued an edict on March 31, 1492, giving Spanish Jews the choice of exile or baptism; as a result, more than 160,000 Jews were expelled from Spain—including my Jewish family.

Let Us Meet

I am an Israeli Jew, and also an American citizen, but I was born in Chile. I have been in full-time ministry since 1988, was married and sent out in 1990 from Jerusalem. In 1991, my husband Baruch and

I were ordained at *Christ For The Nations* in Dallas, Texas and were sent out to the mission field of the nations with one prophetic word from the recognized prophet of the CFNI faculty: "Go forth, go forth, go forth." Since then we have gone forth to over 50 countries as Jewish apostles to the nations. We have had the privilege to heal the sick, cast out demons and see thousands saved. I have been a TV broadcaster since 2015, the year when the Father in heaven sent us to move from Israel to St. Augustine, Florida, the First Coast and gate of the USA. We are here to stand in the gap and fight for the life and soul of America.

I was born again in a dramatic encounter with the Messiah at the waters of the Kinneret (the Sea of Galilee), when He came to talk to me in person. He knocked me off my "horse"—much like the Jewish apostle Shaul/Paul—except it was not an actual horse, but a tourist bus (since I was then and still am today a licensed Israeli tour guide). No one preached the gospel to me; this was a Divine encounter that shook me to the core of my being. It happened inside of the Byzantine church of the Primacy of St. Peter at the Sea of Galilee while guiding Catholic-Mexican tourists. As their tour guide, I had organized their mass service.

When the Messiah started speaking to me, I felt a power trying to put me on my knees before the cross on the wall of that ancient church. I tried to oppose it, utterly panicked, but ended on my knees. Then I heard a voice saying: "Dominiquae, run for your life, get baptized and get saved." It shocked me! I am a Sephardic Jewess; Christians expelled my Jewish ancestors from Spain in 1492 through the Chief Inquisitor Torquemada lifting the cross of Jesus Christ on high - and here I am on my knees before the cross?

My first response to the voice that spoke to me was: "What are you doing with me, a Jew, if you are the God of the Christians?" I could not recognize my Jewish Messiah in Jesus Christ and Christianity. But something stronger than I had me running to get baptized, and to get saved. I knew that I was a sinner, and that I had broken God's Commandments; I needed forgiveness and salvation.

Just 24 hours earlier, after a five-month period of personal and family tragedy, I had "attacked" a canvas with crayons writing the following words:

"Light where are you lost, come to me!"

24 hours later, I was on my knees before the cross and then running for my life to get saved by the Light of the World. The question ringing in my ears was, "What does the God of Israel, on whom I called, have to do with the Christian Jesus Christ?" My journey to discover the biggest identity theft in human history had begun.

For further reading, I recommend my book, *Yes!*[*]

---

[*] www.kad-esh.org/shop/yes

KILLING IN THE NAME OF CHRIST

The thief comes only to steal, slaughter, and destroy.
I have come that they might have life, and have it abundantly!

— JOHN 10:10

If there is a theft, then by deduction there has to be a thief. According to biblical definition, the thief of all thieves is Satan. Could it be that there has been a satanic plot from the beginning to steal and replace the identity of the Jewish Messiah with that of a Roman Christ to destroy all the nations? Yes, even your nation!

I will endeavor to prove in this book that if we do not recover the Jewish identity of the Messiah, the entire world will be on its path to complete destruction. We can see it happening already with natural disasters, storms, plagues (like Ebola and the coronavirus)—but the biggest plague is the spiritual death of millions in the churches, both Catholics and Protestant Evangelicals. Then there is the danger of the escalating anti-Semitism in Europe, and in both North and South America. In the United States from 2016 to 2017, there was a 57% increase in anti-Semitism! (Anti-Defamation League)

Reclaiming the identity of the Messiah will lead to worldwide enlightening, revival, and empowerment like never before as promised in Romans 11:15, *"For if their (Jews) rejection leads to the reconciliation of the world, what will their acceptance be but life from the dead?"* The reconciliation of the Jews with Messiah will bring life from the dead to the Church and to the nations. But the Jews will never reconcile with a Roman Jesus Christ in whose name millions of Jews were murdered. They will only reconcile with a Jewish Messiah upon whose name, Yeshua, no one has ever been murdered.

Anti-Semitism will never decrease as long as Christians preach a Roman Christ. It has only increased since the Roman Christ replaced the Jewish Messiah officially in the fourth century, but if all Christian evangelists, pastors and prophets will start preaching in the name of the Jewish Messiah, anti-Semitism will break in the churches and many Jews will find their Messiah. Then there will be life from the dead, or what I call "the Revival of the Third Day." The Third Millennium will triumph.

Rejecting the Jewish identity of the Messiah will lead to a terrible judgment starting with the house of God. A loyal son or daughter of the Living God must love Him as He is, and He is a Jew, and His name is *Yeshua*, which in Hebrews means *"salvation."* How can a person claiming to belong to Him reject Him as a Jew? He is still called the Lion of Judah all the way to the Book of Revelation and this Jew is the only One that is worthy to open the Books of Judgment.

Then one of the elders tells me, "Stop weeping! Behold, the Lion of the tribe of Judah, the Root of David, has triumphed— He is worthy to open the scroll and its seven seals."

— REVELATION 5:5

For the time has come for judgment to begin with the house of God. If judgment begins with us first, what will be the end for those who disobey the Good News of God?

— 1 Peter 4:17

One day His Spirit whispered in my ears, *"My bride will love My (Hebrew) name (and thus My Jewish identity)."*

His name is Yeshua, and He is the King of the Jews—go and tell.

Facts About Identity Theft

Identity theft is the deliberate use of someone else's identity, usually as a method to gain a financial advantage or obtain credit and other benefits in the other person's name, and perhaps to the other person's disadvantage or loss. *The person whose identity has been assumed may suffer adverse consequences, especially if they are held responsible for the perpetrator's actions.* (Wikipedia Contributors)

The Jewish people assume that their Messiah is surely not Jesus Christ because in His name they have been humiliated, plundered, tormented, and murdered. The wonderful news is that no one has been murdered in His covenant name, Yeshua.

When identity is stolen, the thief can impersonate the victim of theft and pretend he is that person. Millions of Christians believe in a Roman Christ even if, in the back of their minds, they might know that He is a Jew. However, they have been taught to dismiss, suspect and even hate everything Jewish. The mere fact that people still call

Him Jesus Christ is the biggest smokescreen so that no one will relate to Him as a Jew. It defies the will of the Father in heaven who chose the name to be Yeshua, a name that is Hebrew. No one calling Him Yeshua can ignore the fact that He is a Jew. Name changes are very serious as it means a change of identity. The first fact that has stolen the identity of the Messiah for millions is His name transliteration, which is not a translation. The name was Romanized to *Iesous Christos* as it was more palatable to the masses, but this caused a loss of the Hebrew Covenant Name given by the Father.

Some scholars believe that the name itself resembled the name Zeus or Jupiter, the sun god. It sounded like *Ye-Zeus*, and as most people could not read, they only *heard* the name - it resembled Zeus, the god they worshipped. It would be easy to convince them that such a god died for them. This was especially easy when pagan Roman feasts were adapted into the Christian calendar. Feasts that worshipped Zeus, the sun god, replaced the original biblical Messianic Feasts as given to the people of Israel.

Notice also what software has been used in the 21st century for identity theft.

An October 2010 article entitled "Cyber Crime Made Easy" explained the level to which hackers are using <u>malicious software</u>. As Gunter Ollmann, Chief Technology Officer of security at Microsoft, said, "Interested in credit card theft? There's an app for that." This statement summed up the ease with which these hackers are accessing all kinds of information online. <u>The new program for infecting users' computers was called *Zeus*</u>; and the program is so hacker-friendly that even an inexperienced hacker can operate it. Although the hacking program is easy to use, that fact does not diminish the devastating effects that Zeus (or other software like Zeus) can do to a computer and the user. For example, the article stated that programs like Zeus can steal credit card information, important documents, and even documents necessary for homeland security. If the hacker were to gain this information, it would mean identity theft or even a possible terrorist attack. The Integrated Threat Assessment Centre (ITAC) says that in 2012 about 15 million Americans are having their identity stolen. (Wikipedia Contributors)

Zeus has also infected Christianity by replacing the Jewish name, biblical feasts and Jewish identity of the Jewish Messiah for a Roman Christ.

When the name was transliterated from Yeshua to *Iesous* (or Jesus) it lost its meaning which is "salvation," implying the full redemption package, including healing and deliverance. As the name lost its Hebrew character, it was much easier for pagan Christians to relate to a Roman Jesus rather than to a Jewish Yeshua, thus making it also easier to hate and persecute the Jews in the name of Christ.

The following are anti-Semitic quotes from the commonly known church fathers about the Jews.

Origen of Alexandria (AD 185 – AD 254)

Origen of Alexandria was an ecclesiastical writer and teacher who contributed to the early formation of Christian doctrines.

We may thus assert in utter confidence that the Jews will not return to their earlier situation, for they have committed the most abominable of crimes, in forming this conspiracy against the Savior of the human race... hence the city where Jesus suffered was necessarily destroyed, the Jewish nation was driven from its country, and another people was called by God to the blessed election. (Seltman; YashaNet)

John Chrysostom (AD 344 – AD 407)

John Chrysostom was one of the "greatest" of church fathers; known as "the golden mouthed." A missionary preacher famous for his sermons and addresses stated the following.

The synagogue is worse than a brothel... it is the den of scoundrels and the repair of wild beasts... the temple of demons devoted to idolatrous cults... the refuge of brigands and debauchees, and the cavern of devils. It is a criminal assembly of Jews... a place of meeting for the assassins of Christ... a house worse than a drinking shop... a den of thieves, a house of ill fame, a dwelling of iniquity, the refuge of devils, a gulf and an abyss of perdition."... "I would say the same things about their souls... As for me, I hate the synagogue... I hate the Jews for the same reason. (YashaNet; Hay)

St. Augustine (AD 354 – AD 430)

In St. Augustine's Confessions, 12.14, it is stated:

How hateful to me are the enemies of your Scripture! How I wish that you would slay them (the Jews) with your two-edged sword, so that there should be none to oppose your word! Gladly would I have them die to themselves and live to you! (YashaNet; Outler)

Peter the Venerable

Peter the Venerable was known as "the meekest of men, a model of Christian charity."

> Yes, you Jews. I say, do I address you; you, who till this very day, deny the Son of God. How long, poor wretches, will ye not believe the truth? Truly I doubt whether a Jew can be really human... I lead out from its den a monstrous animal, and show it as a laughingstock in the amphitheater of the world, in the sight of all the people. I bring thee forward, thou Jew, thou brute beast, in the sight of all men. (YashaNet; Hay)

Adolf Hitler declared the Jews to be subhuman and vermin, and, therefore, worthy of extermination based on what all Christians had been conditioned to believe by their church fathers.

We have studied the above theologians for many generations in all theological seminars and Bible schools across America and the nations. These theologians left a legacy of hatred against the Jews that is affecting Christendom until this day. By far the one that left the worst legacy is the famous Church reformer Martin Luther himself. He wrote details in his book *On the Jews and Their Lies* that we now know became "the Final Solution." Hitler would quote in his book *Mein Kampf* Luther's very plan, which he would follow to exterminate all the Jews during World War II.

Martin Luther—1543: On the Jews and Their Lies (excerpts)

> What then shall we Christians do with this damned, rejected race of Jews? Since they live among us and we know about their lying and blasphemy and cursing, we cannot tolerate them if we do not wish to share in their lies, curses, and

blasphemy. In this way we cannot quench the inextinguishable fire of divine rage nor convert the Jews. We must prayerfully and reverentially practice a merciful severity. Perhaps we may save a few from the fire and flames [of hell]. We must not seek vengeance. They are surely being punished a thousand times more than we might wish them. Let me give you my honest advice.

First, their synagogues should be set on fire, and whatever does not burn up should be covered or spread over with dirt so that no one may ever be able to see a cinder or stone of it. And this ought to be done for the honor of God and of Christianity in order that God may see that we are Christians, and that we have not wittingly tolerated or approved of such public lying, cursing, and blaspheming of His Son and His Christians.

Secondly, their homes should likewise be broken down and destroyed. For they perpetrate the same things there that they do in their synagogues. For this reason they ought to be put under one roof or in a stable, like gypsies, in order that they may realize that they are not masters in our land, as they boast, but miserable captives, as they complain of incessantly before God with bitter wailing.

Thirdly, they should be deprived of their prayer-books and Talmuds in which such idolatry, lies, cursing, and blasphemy are taught.

Fourthly, their rabbis must be forbidden under threat of death to teach any more...

Fifthly, passport and traveling privileges should be absolutely forbidden to the Jews. For they have no business in the rural districts since they are not nobles, nor officials, nor merchants, nor the like. Let them stay at home... If you princes and nobles do not close the road legally to such exploiters, then some troop ought to ride against them, for they will learn from this pamphlet what the Jews are and how to handle them and that they ought not to be protected. You ought not, you cannot protect them, unless in the eyes of God you want to share all their abomination...

To sum up, dear princes and nobles who have Jews in your domains, if this advice of mine does not suit you, then find a better one so that you and we may all be free of this insufferable devilish burden - the Jews...

Let the government deal with them in this respect, as I have suggested. But whether the government acts or not, let everyone at least be guided by his own conscience and form for himself a definition or image of a Jew. When you lay eyes on or think of a Jew you must say to yourself: Alas, that mouth which I there behold has cursed and execrated and maligned every Saturday my dear Lord Jesus Christ, who has redeemed me with his precious blood; in addition, it prayed and pleaded before God that I, my wife and children, and all Christians might be stabbed to death and perish miserably. And he himself would gladly do this if he were able, in order to appropriate our goods...

Such a desperate, thoroughly evil, poisonous, and devilish lot are these Jews, who for these fourteen hundred years have been and still are our plague, our pestilence, and our misfortune. (Luther, On The Jews and Their Lies, Luthers Works; YashaNet)

Historically, we know German Nazi troops ran over half-dead bodies of Jews and rammed them to death, while the Christian population of Nazi Europe ignored the extermination or cooperated with it—since the father of the Nation of Germany and the father of all Protestant and Evangelical Christians commanded *not to protect them.* According to Luther, protecting Jews from misery, death or destruction would incur the wrath of God. It was the duty of Protestant Christians *not* to protect the Jews. There were a few that risked their lives like Oskar Schindler from Germany and Corrie Ten Boom from Holland and numerous others whom we greatly honor, but by far the majority of people were conditioned by their own Church Father to let them be spoiled and murdered.

Hitler also said that he was following the will of God as outlined by the greatest reformer of all times. He set out to exterminate the Jews and called them, as Luther did, pestilence, plague and misfortune. Card-carrying members of Protestant and Catholic churches were now conditioned by all their church fathers to see the Jews as subhuman vermin that needed to be exterminated by all means.

No Identity Theft, No Holocaust

If identity theft would have not happened, the Nazi Holocaust would have not had a leg to stand on! Hitler murdered people one-third or one-quarter Jewish. If all Christians would have fully known that their Savior was a Jew that died for them, they would not have cooperated with Hitler. In Germany both Catholic and Protestant clergy gave the right hand of fellowship to Hitler when he came to power.

Card-carrying members of both Lutheran and Catholic churches were among the Nazi and even SS officers. Churches in Poland and Germany holding services near concentration and death camps just "sang a little louder" to drown the cries of the Jews being transported in cattle cars to their death along railroad lines. Churches in towns near death camps, such as in *Oswiecim* near Auschwitz-Birkenau, reportedly could even smell the burning flesh of Jews emanating from the chimneys—still they either cooperated with the Nazis, or did nothing to stop the mass murder.

And yet it was the Jewish Messiah Himself whom they were burning in the name of Jesus Christ. He also was burnt at the stake of the bonfires of the Inquisition, where many Jews that had been forcibly converted to Catholicism were burnt alive after horrendous tortures. They did this to them for keeping biblical Jewish traditions such as the Shabbat or the Passover. The Christian knights also burned the Jewish Messiah, Yeshua, in Jerusalem during the Crusades. They burnt the entire Jewish population in Jerusalem in AD 1099, with banners on high, singing "Christ, we adore thee."

As long as we continue calling Him by this Roman name, celebrating the Roman pagan feasts of Christmas and Easter, there is no way to reclaim the Jewish identity of the Messiah, and anti-Semitism, including anti-Zionism, will run rampart in Christian churches which will incur great judgment from the God of Israel who is very sensitive about the "apple of His eye."

For thus says ADONAI-Tzva'ot (THE LORD of the Armies), He has sent me after glory to the nations that plundered you—because whoever touches you touches the apple of His eye...

— ZECHARIAH 2:12

We cannot treat anti-Semitism superficially; we must go to the very root and eliminate it. If believers in Messiah are free from the Romanized identity of Messiah, only then will they have the power and the authority to fight it and prevail.

> **Even so, every good tree produces good fruit, but the rotten tree produces bad fruit. A good tree cannot produce bad fruit, nor can a rotten tree produce good fruit. Every tree that does not produce good fruit is chopped down and thrown into the fire.**
>
> **— MATTHEW 7:17–19**

Even if you are a Christian lover of Israel, it is mandatory that you also be willing to reclaim His full Jewish identity, including His covenant name and His covenant Shabbat and feasts. It is not enough to love Israel "romantically"; it is not even enough to fight for Israel's sake in the media. We must love Him as a Jew, including His Name, His Torah, His people and His land. This will release what I call "The Revival of the Third Day," and the *Chabod*: the weighty glory of God without measure. We will get back the Messianic apostolic, prophetic thrust and authority of the Jewish disciples of the first century and it will restore all things as promised to prepare for the return of Messiah.

> **Repent, therefore, and return—so your sins might be blotted out, so times of relief might come from the presence of ADONAI and He might send Yeshua, the Messiah appointed for you. Heaven must receive Him, until the time of the**

restoration of all the things that God spoke about long ago through the mouth of His holy prophets.

— ACTS 3:19–21

We need to tackle and defeat the five headed monster that has been ruling supremely and almost uncontested in mostly every denomination and non-denomination of what is commonly called *the Church*. To succeed, we need to first fix His identity in us—then we will be One, and nothing will be impossible.

I recommend you to further read my book, *The MAP Revolution.**

TACKLING THE FIVE HEADED MONSTER

*They overcame him by the blood of the Lamb and by the word
of their testimony, and they did not love their lives
even in the face of death.*

— REVELATION 12:11

The Thief impersonated the Savior and Messiah by replacing the essence of who He is:

- The Jewish Savior
- The Lion of Judah
- The Torah Incarnate
- The King of the Jews
- The Anointed One of God

This impersonation reminds me of the story, *Little Red Riding Hood*. She thought the wolf was her grandma because the wolf dressed himself in grandma's nightgown and it had grandma's spectacles. But it was actually the Big Bad Wolf that had stolen granny's identity. It almost caused the death of the little girl had it not been for the hunter-savior who rescued her at the last moment! There is a Big Bad Wolf that is dressed up as a Christian god, but it is more like a dragon. It has been exterminating Jews for millennia and it has caused the spiritual death of millions of Christians since the fourth century, and even before. All the nations will be judged because this "wolf in sheep's clothing" has deceived all nations, starting with the Christians.

> **For ADONAI is enraged at all the nations, and furious at all their armies He will utterly destroy them. He will give them over to slaughter For ADONAI has a day of vengeance, a year of recompense for the hostility against Zion.**
>
> **— ISAIAH 34:2, 8**

To win this battle of THE IDENTITY THEFT of the Messiah, we must know our enemy. Contrary to what most people believe, the enemy is not flesh and blood, but a demonic principality which I call the:

Anti-MESITOJUZ

Anti-MESITOJUZ comprises:

- Anti-**Messiah**—It is against the Holy Spirit's anointing
- Anti-**Israel**—It claims that the Church replaces Israel
- Anti-**Torah**—It claims that the Torah as given to Israel is obsolete (Lawlessness)
- Anti-**Jew**ish (or anti-Semitism)—It wants to get rid of all the Jews possible
- Anti-**Z**ionist—It opposes the return of the Jewish people to the land of Israel and attacking the existence of the State of Israel; this spirit refers to Zionism as "racism."

Defeating the Enemy With Our Testimonies

In the next chapters we will dismantle this five headed monster into its five components to defeat it. But, before we do this, let me introduce you to a few testimonies of Christians who have already defeated the monster, mostly after reading our books and studying in our GRM (Global Revival MAP - Messianic, Apostolic, Prophetic) online Bible School. You will see that they are from around the world and from different denominations and upbringings. These are only a very few of the testimonies that have been sent to us, but it shows that dismantling THE IDENTITY THEFT and restoring the truth about the Jewish Messiah has provoked a global move of God. Again, we call it, "The Revival of the Third Day."

Mental Healing

I left home at 16 years old. I was disappointed with God and my parents, and I made a decision to leave them and everything related to faith and religion. I moved to Helsinki and tried everything I could to find a meaning for my life. During summers I was hitchhiking around Europe and I filled my head with all kinds of drugs and alcohol. Amid all that I felt very lonely, and many times while drunk I preached to my friends about God.

I could never forget how His Presence felt. When I was a child, I used to pray for hours in the Holy Spirit. Now my life was a mess of broken relationships and addictions.

At 26, I found myself in the closed ward of a mental hospital. I had been struggling with panic disorder, anxiety and depression for months, until I completely collapsed. That was followed by seven years of hell. I was searching for help everywhere: therapy, meds, hospital, counselors and churches. Finally, one friend gave me a book: *The Healing Power of the Roots* by Archbishop Dr. Dominiquae Bierman, and through this book I learned to know God in a fresh way.

I got to know that the actual name of Jesus is *Yeshua*, which means "salvation, deliverance and healing": I was yearning for these things more than anything else! I knew that I would soon die if I could not find genuine help. I gave my life to Yeshua as a Jewish Messiah and He healed me! I started to keep the Commandments of God and was filled with the Holy Spirit. It cleansed my mind and from addictions, negative thoughts and the desire to die. I took GRM Bible School, and it provided a new foundation for my life.

—Hadassah Danielsbacka, Finland/USA

True Victory

My involvement in GRM Bible School was a monumental turning point in my life. After years of walking in Christianity, I questioned why I was not seeing more victory in the lives of those around me. I read in the Bible what was possible through faith but saw little of it.

Then my eyes were opened through the books and GRM Bible School teachings of Archbishop Dr. Dominiquae Bierman. As I continued through to graduation, it became clear that my freedom from replacement theology was necessary to enjoy pure fellowship with my Creator, my Father. This is the pathway to victory!

I thank Yahveh for allowing me to connect with this ministry tool that truly sets the captives free with the Truth! We share this same freedom around the world through our ministry team—but it would not be possible without the leadership of this dedicated couple who love us Christians unconditionally.

—Reverend Debra Barnes, Alabama, USA

Spiritual Growth

Archbishop Dr. Dominiquae Bierman played a crucial role in my spiritual growth. Her teachings are extraordinary and her tenacity in exposing replacement theology is one of the rarest blessings to the body of Messiah.

She has personally helped me in times of need, showing great compassion and sacrifice of time. The GRM Bible School is of the highest educational quality.

The Bierman's are an asset to the body of Messiah which will touch generations to come.

—Pastor Esther, New York, USA

Identity Restored

I found *my* identity in Yeshua. In Him I have inner shalom (peace), and I do not need the world to find my true identity.

I am a worshipper. If anxiety or depression tries to take over, I put my fingers on piano keys and praise Him, to get into His presence. Then all anxiety disappears.

The purpose of my life has become clear when I have understood who the Holy One of Israel is. I have also experienced new depth and power in my worship when I bless Israel. I always receive a blessing back!

—David Tuominen, Finland

Free from Lukewarmness and Immorality

Messages and teachings of Archbishop Dominiquae have set me free from the lukewarm Christian faith, adultery, fornication and rebellion that comes from religious, anti-Israel systems poisoned by replacement theology.

My journey for the last seven years, carried by the vision and mission of the Jewish Apostle Dominiquae Bierman, has been literally life from the dead (Romans 11:15).

—Eicha Lohmus, Estonia

Healing Through Obedience

I have grown stronger in THE LORD from studying the Word of God through the books by Archbishop Dr. Dominiquae Bierman. I have read *The Healing Power of the Roots, The Key of Abraham* and *Grafted In*, which were given by a friend when I started learning about the truth. I have benefited more with the guidance of God through these books. I am a recent convert—I was initially a Roman Catholic, but now I have worshipped on the Sabbath and have gotten to know the truth since last year, November 18, 2018.

Wonderful miracles have been happening and instant miracle prayers have been answered. I am joyful in THE LORD and have recovered from osteomyelitis of skull last November instantly when I said "yes" to the Sabbath and began going through the process of repentance, forgiveness, and total surrender to THE LORD.

I am an anesthetist nurse or an anesthetic scientific officer in Arawa District Hospital in Bougainville, Papua New Guinea. I am interested in pursuing God in ministering the Word of God. I have witnessed and have created a powerful growing atmosphere in spreading the Word of God. People want more of Archbishop Dominiquae's books. Together we can spread the Word of God with spiritual fire. I am very thankful for Archbishop Dr. Dominiquae Bierman.

—Alex Kehono, Papua New Guinea

From Darkness to Light

In June 2010, when I was still six months old in Jesus at an orphanage in India, I read this book *Yeshua is the Name* written by one Jew by the name of Dominiquae Bierman. That was my first encounter with a Jew, the Jewish name Yeshua, and with Dominiquae Bierman, whom I hardly knew how to pronounce. Shamefully and regretfully, I tell you now; I did not realize there are such people as Jews that existed.

Coming from a country that has completely shut the door for Israel and the Jews, I lived in ignorance for 42 years of my life, although I lived abroad in the US for five years and India for nine years. My native country is a complete example of Constantine's decree, "We ought not, therefore, to have anything in common with the Jew."

HaleluYah! I give thanks to Adonai, for He is good, for his grace continues forever (Ps. 106:1). Although I was blind for 42 years, I am grateful today and forever for this Jewish woman, Archbishop Dr. Dominiquae Bierman, and for the book *Yeshua is the Name* she wrote. I am also very thankful for the person who lent the book to me to read for two days in 2010.

Today, I have read all 19 books written by Archbishop Dominiquae, including *The Woman Factor* written by her for her husband, Rabbi Baruch Bierman. My family and I are forever thankful to this Jewish woman and her husband for living as a sacrifice on the altar of YHVH, and may she continue bringing many nations into Sheep Nations!

—Ps. Dawid Yosef Lee, Asia

The Truth Makes Me Free!

God has connected me to Kad-Esh MAP Ministries since 2011, and I am now the Norwegian Delegate for *The United Nations for Israel*. For several years, I have been closely connected with the ministry, and I am proud of their wholehearted work for the kingdom of God, something they perform with integrity. They always talk the truth in love, also directly into the lives of people, because only the Truth makes people free. I am so happy to have found a "spiritual family" who believes in the Jewish roots of the faith. This unity and love we experience in Kad-Esh MAP Ministries, where Jew and gentile are together, grafted into the Olive tree of Israel, has the unity that is described in John 17:17, 20–21. This is something I have never experienced anywhere else, except with these brothers and sisters who have received the truth in the gospel from Zion, and are willing to pay a high price for this truth, if needed.

—Pastor Hanne G. Hansen, Norway

Dramatic Increase of Anointing

I have received a major spiritual breakthrough by GRM Bible School that changed my life and my ministry. The pure, original gospel made in Zion brought me into the Promised Land. Replacement theology's ugly skin and structure left me, and today I am a purified vessel of fire. My anointing and authority have skyrocketed. I am forever thankful for Archbishop Dr. Dominiquae for her spiritual sharpness! She rebuked me for my own good, revealing my blind spot that saved my life, and lead me into genuine humility. I call this true love!

—Apostle & Prophet Sana Enroos, Sweden

Experienced Miracles

I studied Archbishop's GRM Bible School and freshly graduated on Sukkot 5780. I have experienced signs, wonders, miracles, and healing like never before. The Truth has set me free.

"You will know the truth, and the truth will set you free" (Jn. 8:32).

"I am the good shepherd; I know my own, and my own know me" (Jn.

10:14). In addition, Archbishop Dominiquae helped me to understand the Jewish roots of the faith and now I am grafted in the olive tree of Israel and have become a covenant daughter of Abraham.

—D'vora Cheung, Hong Kong

A Broken Heart Healed

In 2017, I took part in Archbishop Dominiquae's Israel Sukkot Tour, and my life changed. The truth was in front of me. It was so clear that replacement theology had been exposed. It was unbelievable that Constantine has deceived the world for over 1,600 years.

I often see Archbishop Dominiquae preach, serve, and pray full of anointing, enthusiasm, and ministering to the max of what a genuine servant of God can do. Who can run such a ministry for over thirty years? Sometimes rejected and betrayed, she is still willing to obey God and 'let go' of her own children to serve the nations.

I will not forget Archbishop's heart for the Chinese, praying wholeheartedly in deep worship in THE LORD at the Hong Kong Passover Special Conference in 2018, when she anointed everyone present. The anointing oil had finished, but Yah (God) performed a supernatural miracle that allowed the anointing oil in the bottle to multiply. ADONAI sent Archbishop as Eliyahu (Elijah) among us, to turn the hearts of the fathers to the children and the hearts of the children to the fathers (Malachi 4:6); and it healed the brokenhearted. She helped me find light in my life.

—Serena Yang, Taiwan

The Jewish Roots Sets Prisoners Free

In 2014 and 2015 we formed a team to visit the women's jail in Lima, Peru. We taught the inmates the true gospel that came from Zion to the nations—the same message preached by the Jewish apostles, the original followers of Yeshua. We based our teachings on the GRM Bible School and the anointed books of Archbishop Dr. Dominiquae Bierman. We taught them about *teshuva* (Hebrew word for "repentance"), for breaking the Commandments of Yahweh, and about the Shabbat as a day set apart, blessed by Him.

One prisoner discovered her Hebrew roots; she started obeying the Commandments and keeping the Shabbat. The prison gave her permission to use an extensive yard area to keep the Shabbat and many other prisoners joined her. They asked for help with their needs and for help to stop doing immoralities in their cells.

Over time, we could see how the women changed their behavior and attitude towards authorities, then how they found favor in their legal proceedings. Many received early release for their good behavior!

—Pastor Sonia Gotelli Gonzalez, *Peru*

From Emptiness to Fullness

I have believed in Jesus since my childhood. One day when I was listening to a sermon in the congregation, I felt a great emptiness and thought this cannot be all. I looked for something more, but I did not know what. I went to different churches, but I felt uncertain and like an orphan. I was looking for the truth of the Word among all the spiritual mixture.

Finally, I found the GRM Bible School. I understood how far replacement theology took us from the Jewish roots of the faith and the original gospel. I learned that the original name of Jesus is Yeshua, and I met him as a Jewish Messiah. I got to know the roots of my faith. The emptiness was gone, and I was not an orphan anymore—I had found the way back home!

—Pastor Terhi Laine, Finland

From Lawlessness to Obedience

Although I had been in an excellent faith-founded congregation for many years, my spiritual life was stuck. I was striving and got tired. I owe my life to this Jewish woman: All the teachings I have received from her through the GRM Bible School, books, trips to Israel, etc., have cleansed me from all Torahlessness (Lawlessness) to obedience. I have found the Hebrew roots of faith—the way of genuine joy, boldness, holiness, and compliance.

We are grateful for Yeshua and His brethren, the Bierman's!

Thank you, Archbishop Dominiquae. I love, appreciate and honor you as a mother. You are a woman of the Covenant, and I am a Finn committed to stand with you like Ruth the Moabite was committed to her Jewish mother-in-law.

—Sinikka Bäcklund, Finland

Repentance and Reconciliation

I became a believer over 40 years ago, in 1978. I was a "good Christian," reading the New Testament often, but my closest relationships were difficult. I understood nothing about the meaning of Israel, and many Old Testament passages, which were nevertheless fascinating, confused me—I could not understand why. There were so many promises, but for whom?

The Holy Spirit led me to study GRM Bible School in 2014. The first level was about Israel and soon I understood how I had despised God's own country and people, the apple of His eye. Then I attended the *Bible School on Wheels* Sukkot Tour of Israel, and there I was crying and repenting from my attitudes toward the Mother of the nations, Israel.

Later on, I also asked forgiveness from my parents for dishonoring them with my attitude towards them. As a result, my children also respected me and my husband, their parents. It restored my closest relationships. HalleluYah, Yeshua is mighty!

—Erja Lastunen, Finland

A New Bill in Life

I have been a "regular believer" since the age of ten. In later years I asked the Father often, "When will my life really begin?"

Praise to the Holy One of Israel, who prepared me already a long time ago to receive the gospel made in Zion by asking me to declare aloud daily: "I walk in the truth, and no deception has power over me."

When I received Archbishop Dr. Dominiquae Bierman's book *The Healing Power of the Roots,* the Holy Spirit reminded me of that declaration. While reading the book, it felt like everything that it contained was poured out into my heart. I was reading, crying, and repenting. How truth blesses and sets free!

Then I knew that my Savior was the Jewish Messiah Yeshua. Along with Him into my life came the Shabbat, the biblical feasts, the Commandments of the Father and the Dietary Laws, as the Holy Spirit wrote them in my heart and mind. The GRM Bible School strengthened my walk and gave me a stable foundation.

—Anneli Seppälä, Finland

> **Then I heard a loud voice in heaven saying, "Now have come the salvation and the power and the kingdom of our God and the authority of His Anointed One, for the accuser of our brothers and sisters—the one who accuses them before our God day and night—has been thrown out. They overcame him**

by the blood of the Lamb and by the word of their testimony, and they did not love their lives even in the face of death.

— REVELATION 12:10–11

For further reading, I recommend that you read my book *Eradicating the Cancer of Religion.**

THE LOSS OF THE ANOINTING

Head Number 1: Anti-Messiah

But you will receive power when the Ruach HaKodesh* has come upon you; and you will be My witnesses in Jerusalem, and through all Judah, and Samaria, and to the end of the earth.

— ACTS 1:8

———

When the Church of the fourth century rejected the Jews and all things Jewish, they also rejected the Jewish Messiah, the Anointed One with His anointing. The Holy Spirit retreated from that apostate church that slowly but surely entered the Dark Ages. Anti-Messiah or anti-*Mashiach* means "replacing the Anointed and the anointing with counterfeits."

The Importance of an Actual Identity

By having all the information, ID numbers, and details, the thief can get into the account of his victim and steal all his money and goods. The

---

* *Ruach HaKodesh* is the Hebrew word for the Holy Spirit.

first good stolen by replacing a Jewish Messiah, Yeshua, for a Roman Christ, Jesus, was the anointing and the apostolic authority.

The anointing, or in Hebrew, *meshicha* (meaning "the power of the Holy Spirit") retreated. Prophecies, signs, and wonders ceased when Constantine divorced the Church from the Jews and from all its Jewish roots. Since the Messiah is Jewish, He retreated from that apostate church. Messiah or *Mashiach* means "the Anointed One," and that means, "empowered by the oil of the Holy Spirit to rule." When in Israel, He said, "My kingdom is not of this world" (Jn. 18:36), and, "if by the finger of God I drive out demons, then the kingdom of God has come to you" (Lk. 11:20). God anointed Him to rule over the demonic powers and principalities, to heal the sick and to cast out demons. He fulfilled Isaiah 61:1, "The Ruach (Spirit) of ADONAI ELOHIM is on me, because ADONAI has anointed me to proclaim Good News to the poor. He has sent me to bind up the brokenhearted, to proclaim liberty to the captives..."

He imparted that same anointing to His Jewish disciples:

Yeshua summoned His twelve disciples and gave them authority over unclean spirits, so they could drive them out and heal every kind of disease and sickness.

— MATTHEW 10:1

But it did not stop with the twelve:

Now, after these things, THE LORD assigned seventy others and sent them out by twos before Him into every town and place where He Himself was about to go. And He was telling them, "The harvest is plentiful, but the workers are few.

Therefore, beg THE LORD of the harvest to send out workers into His harvest." Then the seventy returned with joy, saying, "Master, even the demons submit to us in Your name!"

— LUKE 10:1–2, 17

He did not intend us to gather the harvest of souls without the anointing and power of the Holy Spirit to heal the sick and to cast out demons.

The following are the last words of the Master before He was taken up. This is His will and testament for all believers, both Jews and Gentiles!

But you will receive power when the *Ruach HaKodesh* (Holy Spirit) has come upon you; and you will be My witnesses in Jerusalem, and through all Judah, and Samaria, and to the end of the earth." After saying all this—while they were watching— He was taken up, and a cloud received Him out of their sight.

— ACTS 1:8–9

After He rose from the dead, He instructed His disciples to do nothing until they were empowered by the Holy Spirit. No good religious works would do, but only those done by the anointing and empowerment of the Holy Spirit.

When the day of Shavuot (Pentecost) had come, they were all together in one place. Suddenly there came from heaven a sound like a mighty rushing wind, and it filled the whole house where they were sitting. And tongues like fire spreading out appeared to them and settled on each one of them. They were all filled with the *Ruach HaKodesh* (Holy Spirit) and began to speak in other tongues as the Ruach enabled them to speak out.

— ACTS 2:1–4

The Holy Spirit fell on those Jewish disciples, about a hundred twenty of them in an upper room of the Temple compound, where they were praying and seeking God. They were all in one accord, celebrating the biblical Feast of *Shavuot* (Pentecost). They were all on the "same page" doctrinally and they had one purpose: to get empowered by the Father through the Spirit to become witnesses of the Anointed One, from Jerusalem to Judea, to Samaria and to the ends of the earth. The following were the marks that followed all those Jewish believers that followed a Jewish Messiah:

He told them, "Go into all the world and proclaim the Good News to every creature. He who believes and is immersed shall be saved, but he who does not believe shall be condemned. These signs will accompany those who believe: in My name they will drive out demons; they will speak new languages; they will handle snakes; and if they drink anything deadly, it will not harm them; they will lay hands on the sick, and they will get well." Then THE LORD Yeshua, after He had spoken to them, was taken up into heaven and sat down at the right hand of God. And they went out and proclaimed everywhere, THE LORD working with them and confirming the word by the signs that follow.

— MARK 16:15–20

This was to never stop until the end of the age.

Go therefore and make disciples of all nations, immersing them in My name,* teaching them to observe all I have commanded you. And remember! I am with you always, even to the end of the age.

— MATTHEW 28:19–20

His disciples needed to bear the marks of the anointing and His power non-stop and everywhere they went, in every generation.

Replacement theology, through THE IDENTITY THEFT of the Messiah, stole the Jewishness of the gospel and the powerful anointing that goes with His true identity as the Anointed King of the Jews. All of us, both Jews and Gentiles, grafted into the olive tree (Rom. 11:11-24) are called to be Messianic, anointed believers to display His kingdom in holiness and power.

He gave them the authority to make disciples of entire nations, to heal the sick, to cast out demons, and to teach them to observe all He had taught them. He taught His disciples Torah all the time. He expounded upon all that had been downloaded through Moses and made it glorious, including all social and moral laws (laws of justice for the people). He brought the fullness of prophetic meaning to each one of Israel's feasts and He celebrated them all. He kept the Shabbat in the freedom of the Holy Spirit to do good, to heal and to deliver. He confronted the religious leaders of His day. He overturned the tables of the greedy money changers, and more.

---

* According to the original Hebrew text of Matthew, it says "immersing them in My name," referring to Yeshua.

This was the Jewish Messiah revealing Himself to His Jewish people. And He asked them to do the same and teach others to do the same until the end of the age.

The 21st Century, like the 1st Century!

Then before He left to fulfill His call to pour out His life on our behalf, He prayed His will to the Father in John 17. He said that others will come to believe because of their message, the message the Jewish disciples will bring. He prayed that those "others" that will come will be one with the believing Jews so that the world will believe that the Father had sent Him.

> I pray not on behalf of these (Jewish believers) only, but also for those who believe in Me through their message (other Jews and many Gentiles), that they all may be one. Just as You, Father, are in Me and I am in You, so also may they be one in Us, so the world may believe that You sent Me. The glory that You have given to Me I have given to them, that they may be one just as We are one—I in them and You in Me—that they may be perfected in unity, so that the world may know that You sent Me and loved them as You loved Me.
>
> — JOHN 17:20–23

The only prerequisite for the world to believe is for Jews and Gentiles in the Messiah, the Anointed One, to be *echad,* which is the Hebrew word for "one." This became impossible when Constantine, backed up by all the Gentile bishops of the fourth century, signed the Divorce Paper called the Council of Nicaea that commanded all Christians to "separate from the detestable company of the Jews for the Savior has showed us another way" (Percival). That "savior" that Constantine mentioned was an impostor and it had stolen the identity and usurped the calling of the Jewish Messiah. The "other way" that impostor "savior" showed is nothing less than another gospel or apostasy.

> **But even if we (or an angel from heaven) should announce any "good news" to you other than what we have proclaimed to you, let that person be cursed!**
>
> — GALATIANS 1:8

Yeshua, the Jewish Messiah was not allowed into the Church anymore. Those that wanted to follow Him needed to go outside of the camp of the mainstream church and, most times, hide underground. As anti-Semitism and hatred against the Jews and all things Jewish was the outcome, it was not safe to be a Jew in the Church anymore. The precious Holy Spirit retreated from this deceived religious system of Christianity. Signs, wonders, and miracles ceased. The Church slowly but surely drifted into the Dark Ages. Then came the Crusades, the Inquisitions, the pogroms and the Nazi Holocaust, all in the name of Christianity, in the name of Jesus Christ, leaving a trail of Jewish blood that is crying from the ground.

> **Then He said, "What have you done? The voice of your brother's blood is crying out to Me from the ground."**
>
> — GENESIS 4:10

The Light of the World, the Lion of Judah, and His anointing had been rejected, and darkness ruled for many generations. Deep darkness covered the earth through Christianity. The 21st century Church is still recovering from this deep darkness, as in many Christian circles the people are still divorced from the Jewishness of the Messiah and the anointing and empowerment of His Holy Spirit. Division is still ruling in the Church, and the struggle between those who believe in the baptism of the Holy Spirit and between those that do not still exists. In fact, very few know that even in the 21st century, the power of the Holy Spirit is sorely missing in our services, no matter how professional they appear.

This is the first outcome of expelling the Jews, cutting the Jewish roots, and with that eliminating the Jewish Messiah from our churches—The Holy Spirit and the anointing leaves

You cannot separate the Jewish Messiah from His anointing. On the other hand, in many Messianic circles, believers have fallen into the trap of self-righteousness and religiosity. Without knowing it, they have embraced replacement theology by replacing the Holy Spirit for liturgies and traditions. From the start of our life journey together, my husband and I (both of us Jews) vowed before the Almighty that whatever is anointed, we will do, and whatever is not anointed we will avoid. Without His Holy Spirit, anointing and presence, we are nothing. All our religious acts are like menstrual cloth before Him.

"For all of us have become like one who is unclean and all our righteousness is like a filthy garment* and all of us wither like a leaf, and our iniquities carry us away, like the wind" (Is. 64:5). Religious traditions and good works without true holiness and righteousness are disgusting to Him.

---

* Referring to a menstrual cloth.

When we restore the true identity of Messiah, it starts with Him being Messiah, the Anointed One, and us being anointed by His Holy Spirit and fire.

In the 21st century, just like in the fourth century, religion and professionalism have replaced the Power of God. Most times, the ministry has become a business, a career to be pursued for money or fame (or even to do something good), but not because of a Divine call, spiritual gifts, and Holy Spirit empowerment.

The Shofar Trumpet of Repentance has been sounding since Israel became a State in 1948, declaring that it is time to get reacquainted with Yeshua as a Jewish Messiah. It is also time to get acquainted with the Father's heart for Israel and to cooperate with Him for her restoration.

The Call is also to make restitution to the Jewish people for all sins committed against them in the name of Christendom. But this can all only fully occur once we reclaim the identity of the Jewish Messiah. If not, the anointing will leave, and it will be *ichabod,* which means in Hebrew, "the departure of the glory." This happened in ancient Israel when the priests were sinning, and they loved the offering but not the people. They had departed from the Torah and were worshipping a god of their own making.

Then she named the child Ichabod saying, "The glory has departed from Israel"—because of the capture of the Ark of God, and because of her father-in-law and her husband.

— 1 SAMUEL 4:21

Do You Want Popularity with God or with Man?

Today, many ministers are afraid they will lose their tithes, offerings, and popularity if they would tackle the Jewishness of Messiah. Those that are already enlightened sometimes minimize it to blend in and not make too many "waves." But, if we are to have the power and the authority that the disciples had 2,000 years ago, we must get back to the same gospel made in Zion, and to the same Jewish Messiah, Yeshua, embracing His lifestyle of holiness and righteousness. The Holy Spirit empowered and anointed these disciples, just like their Jewish Master. Nothing can replace the anointing—no money, religious tradition, or professionalism can compare with one drop of His power and one moment in His presence.

Let us remember that the Holy Spirit left after the Church's divorce from the Jewishness of Messiah and from the Jewish believers of that time. Every move of the Spirit since then has restored what identity theft and replacement theology stole.

The battle is not between the different denominations of Christianity: The battle is between every believer and the anti-MESITOJUZ principality.

> For our struggle is not against flesh and blood, but against the rulers, against the powers, against the world forces of this darkness, and against the spiritual forces of wickedness in the heavenly places.

> — EPHESIANS 6:12

The battle is not against your brothers and sisters: it is against Satan himself, who seeks to keep the Church divided and weak. The anti-Messiah or anti-Anointing head of this five headed monster must be cut off from the Church and the only way to do it is through repentance. The word for repentance in Hebrew is *teshuva,* which means "to return to be restored." This journey of returning can start with a simple prayer.

A Prayer for Restoration

Father God in heaven, forgive me for rejecting the Jewishness of Messiah, and the anointing and power of the Holy Spirit. I open my heart to You, Yeshua, as my Jewish Messiah and Savior. I ask You to fill me with Your Holy Spirit and fire just as You filled the disciples prior to THE IDENTITY THEFT of Messiah. Thank You for restoring me to the original gospel made in Zion in Yeshua's name. Amen!

THE RETURN OF THE ANOINTING

For no one can lay any other foundation than what is already laid
—which is Yeshua the Messiah.

—1 CORINTHIANS 3:11

T he Messiah is the King of Israel. All of Israel's kings needed to
be anointed by the Prophet of God with oil to rule. Then the
power of the Holy Spirit would fall on the king and he would become
"another man."

> Then Samuel took the vial of oil and poured it on his (Saul's)
> head. Then he kissed him and said, "Has ADONAI not anoint-
> ed you ruler over His inheritance?" After that, you will arrive
> at the hill of God, where the garrison of the Philistines is. It
> will come about, as soon as you enter the town, that you will
> meet a band of prophets coming down from the high place,
> preceded by a harp, a tambourine and a flute, and they will
> be prophesying. Then the Ruach of ADONAI (Spirit of THE

71

LORD) will seize you and you will prophesy with them—you will turn into another man.

—1 SAMUEL 10:1,5

Saul became supercharged and Divinely empowered to rule.

No political school of kings could empower the anointed kings of Israel or teach them how to rule by their own strength. They had to be supernaturally endowed by YHVH, the God of Israel. Then the king would be called Mashiach ADONAI or "messiah, the anointed one of YHVH."

ADONAI ELOHIM, do not reject Your anointed one (*Mashiach* or Messiah). Remember the loyalty of Your servant David.

—2 CHRONICLES 6:42

The Spirit of God anointed Yeshua king after His *mikveh* (baptism) in the Jordan River by Yochanan, who is John. "Then the Spirit rested on Him as a dove and the voice of the God of Israel declared, 'This is My beloved son in whom I am well pleased'" (Mat. 3:16-17).

The Holy Spirit always endowed the King, Mashiach ADONAI. This happened to Yeshua; His being chosen became clear because of the anointing of the Holy Spirit.

You know how God anointed Yeshua of Nazareth with the Ruach HaKodesh (Holy Spirit) and power—how He went about doing good and healing all who were oppressed by the devil, because God was with Him.

—ACTS 10:38

Being *Messianic* means *being anointed* as we become *one* with the Anointed King of the Jews and with His anointing to rule and to dethrone demonic principalities.

And they went out and proclaimed everywhere, THE LORD working with them and confirming the word by the signs that follow.

— MARK 16:20

Are We Truly Messianic or Christian?

This lofty title of Messianic is worn by many that have rejected the Holy Spirit's anointing by judging and rejecting those who carry the anointing. Skepticism, judgmentalism, self-righteousness, and plain unbelief are robbing some Messianic circles of the powerful anointing of the Holy Spirit. That is identity theft—as the anti-Messiah principality is still ruling, both in some Messianic congregations and in many Christian churches.

No one is a real "Messianic" unless we embrace, love and display the anointing. Today being Messianic in many circles means being part of another religious denomination that has some Jewish liturgies and Hebrew terminology. Many called Messianic are still deeply entrenched in replacement theology, as they have replaced the power and fire of the Holy Spirit by the traditions of men.

They have embraced only one part of the Jewish Messiah, namely that He is Jewish and that the Shabbat, biblical feasts and the Torah are not done away with, like Yeshua strongly exhorted (Mat. 5:17-22).

Do not think I came to abolish the Law (the Torah) or the Prophets; I did not come to abolish but to fulfill. For truly I say to you, until heaven and earth pass away, not the smallest letter or stroke shall pass from the Law until all is accomplished. Whoever then annuls one of the least of these Commandments, and teaches others to do the same, shall be called least in the kingdom of heaven; but whoever keeps and teaches them, he shall be called great in the kingdom of heaven.

— MATTHEW 5:17–19

But many, though calling themselves Messianic, have rejected the power, fire, and manifestations of the Holy Spirit. Thus, the anointing is grieved in many Messianic congregations—sin runs unchecked, just as in many Christian churches, and there is no spiritual growth.

Being chosen as His Messianic, anointed followers becomes clear when His Ruach (Spirit) fills us and is bestowed upon us. That is why He said to do *nothing* before we receive the Holy Spirit. We then become different—it empowers us to perform supernatural feats and to rule like He ruled over demons.

Yeshua said, "My kingdom is not of this world" (Jn. 18:36). Not once did He encourage His followers to follow a religious system of any kind, although He was very clear about obedience to His Commandments.

If you keep My Commandments, you will abide in My love, just as I have kept My Father's Commandments and abide in His love.

— JOHN 15:10

He only spoke about the Kingdom. For us to be His royal priesthood we must be royalty. The Holy Spirit must anoint all covenant and biblical royalty to rule; if not, it all becomes politics, religious politics.

He poured some of the anointing oil on Aaron's head and anointed him to consecrate him.

— LEVITICUS 8:12

Just like the Kings were anointed with oil to rule, so were the priests anointed with oil to minister. In fact, everything in the Tabernacle needed to be anointed with oil. No service to YHVH could be done without the anointing.

Take the anointing oil and anoint the Tabernacle, and everything within it, and consecrate it, along with all of its furnishings, and it will be holy.

— EXODUS 40:9

We are to be anointed kings and priests unto our God. We have also become the Tabernacle of His Presence and His vessels of worship. He must anoint us. It is the anointing of the Holy Spirit that consecrates us into service so it can separate us from the filth of this world and stay pure. No human devices, no religious traditions, nothing but His Holy Spirit's anointing empowers us to serve and walk with Him.

The Church of the fourth century established a non-anointed, Replacement religious system of Christianity because they rejected the Jewish Messiah, the Jewish roots, the Shabbat, the biblical Feasts and all Jews. Everyone must embrace the Messiah, namely the Anointed One *with His Anointing*, including Messianic groups that have embraced the Jewishness of Messiah. Our names do not define us—our fruit does.

Getting to Higher Grounds

The anointing calls us to higher grounds of obedience and accountability to the Most High, and also to a deeper level of intimacy and sacrifice. Though many people try to imitate the anointing with spiritual manipulations and professionalism, the anointing cannot be mimicked or bought. God can only bestow it on repentant hearts.

> Now when Simon saw that the Ruach HaKodesh (Holy Spirit) was given through the laying on of hands by the emissaries (apostles), he offered them money, saying, "Give this power to me, too—so that anyone on whom I lay hands may receive the Ruach HaKodesh." Peter said to him, "May your silver go to ruin, and you with it—because you thought you could buy God's gift with money! You have no part or share in this matter, because your heart is not right before God. Therefore, repent of this wickedness of yours, and pray to THE LORD that, if possible, the intent of your heart may be pardoned. For I see in you the poison of bitterness and the bondage of unrighteousness!" Simon replied, "Pray for me, so that none of what you have said may come upon me."
>
> — ACTS 8:18–24

Unbelief is also a byproduct of replacing the Jewish Messiah with a religious system. Where there is unbelief and dishonor, the Holy Spirit is grieved—and even the greatest of ministers cannot display God's power. Yeshua Himself could do no miracles in Nazareth.

And they (the people of Nazareth) took offense at Him. But Yeshua said to them, "A prophet is not without honor except in his hometown and in his own house." And He did not do many mighty works there because of their unbelief.

— MATTHEW 13:57–58

Familiarity and dishonor kill the anointing. The Jews, being the fathers and mothers of the faith, were *dishonored* and *replaced* by other church fathers that, along with Emperor Constantine, crafted a religious system that *dishonors the Jews and all things Jewish.* As a result, the anointing left, and miracles ceased. This distorted religious system affects Christians until this day as they continue to dishonor the Jewish people.

My desire is to bless those who bless you, but whoever curses you I will curse, and in you all the families of the earth will be blessed.

— GENESIS 12:3

Whenever we do not understand something we should be like Miriam (Mary), Yeshua's Jewish mother, when visited by the angel Gabriel. Instead of rejecting what is new or seems foreign to us, we need to say as Miriam, "be it unto me according to Your word."

The angel answered and said to her, "The Holy Spirit will come upon you, and the power of the Most High will overshadow you; and for that reason the holy Child shall be called the Son of God. And behold, even your relative Elizabeth has also conceived a son in her old age; and she who was called barren is now in her sixth month. For nothing will be impossible with God." And Miriam (Mary) said, "Behold, the bond slave of THE LORD; may it be done to me according to your word." And the angel departed from her.

— LUKE 1:35–38 (NASB PLUS NAME ADJUSTMENT)

The reason many are not anointed is that it demands everything from us; it requires a complete surrender to the Master. Although the Anointing is bestowed freely upon His loyal followers, it is not cheap. We must die to self and our own agenda to walk in the anointing. If we do not, we lose it like King Saul lost it because of selfish ambition, the fear of men, and jealousy of David's anointing.

Now the Ruach ADONAI (Spirit of THE LORD) had departed from Saul, and an evil spirit from ADONAI terrified him.

— 1 SAMUEL 16:14

Similarly, the fourth century church lost the Spirit of ADONAI because of selfish ambition, the fear of men (through the Roman persecution), and jealousy against the Jews who were the natural heirs of the New Covenant. Then an evil spirit of anti-Semitism possessed that church.

Constantine said, "we do not need these Jews, we know better"—by throwing away the Jews, he also threw away the anointing. But we can recover and be restored, now that God has revealed this transgression.

An Important Prayer Against Ignorance

Father in heaven, I yearn for more of You. Please forgive me for my ignorance about Your anointing and the power of Your Holy Spirit. I ask Your forgiveness for any judgmental attitude, jealousy or hatred against the Jews. Despite all theologies that I might have inherited that oppose Your glory, I ask You to fill me with Your Holy Spirit and fire so I may walk in Your anointing all the days of my life. In Yeshua's name, amen.

HOW I LOVE YOUR SPIRIT

The 3 "Don'ts"

Do not quench the Spirit, do not despise prophetic messages,
but test all things, hold fast to what is good.

—1 THESSALONIANS 5:19–21

1: Do not quench the Spirit (1 Thes. 5:19)

We quench, shrink, and diminish the Holy Spirit within us when prophetic messages are despised, mocked, dismissed, or taken lightly. Prophetic messages do not always fit within our doctrinal understanding. When that happens, people usually reject them. Sometimes a prophetic message is brought by unlikely vessels. This may offend our pride, and we may dismiss them as nothing. It is very important that we test them, before we dismiss them as ridiculous, "off the wall," or unimportant. One way to test them is by praying and asking the Father to reveal to us what truly comes from Him. Another way is by waiting to see if the prophetic word comes to pass.

For example, in 1993, I received from the Holy Spirit the Prophecy of the Rose described at the beginning of this book. I published that prophecy in my book *The Healing Power of the Roots*. Those that responded to it went into repentance and were greatly transformed. But many said it was "off the wall" and their lives dried up. 27 years later, this prophecy has come to pass, as there are many signs of apostasy and spiritual death in many churches. This generation doesn't even want to go to Church. Sin is as rampant inside of the church as outside—this includes abortion, incest, divorce, sexual abuse, pornography, adultery (even in the pulpit), drug, cigarette and alcohol addiction, and the list goes on. And most pastors do not rebuke the sheep because they themselves are immature and need to be corrected. The love of mammon and selfish ambition is ruling. It is rare to find truly anointed, surrendered, and obedient believers.

Do you remember the Prophecy of the Rose?

Before writing my first book on the subject (known worldwide as *The Healing Power of the Roots*), I asked the Almighty, "why is it so important to administer the Jewish roots to the Church?" His answer to me was loud and clear, and it has kept me running with this message for nearly three decades: "It is a matter of life and death. The Church has been like a rose that has been cut from its roots and placed in a vase with water for two days. But on the Third Day, if she is not replanted back, she will surely die." One day is like one thousand years to THE LORD. This is the Third Day, the Third Millennium—and the Rose is dying.

2: Do not grieve the Spirit (Eph. 4:30)

Do not grieve the Ruach HaKodesh (Holy Spirit) of God, by whom you were sealed for the day of redemption. Get rid of

all bitterness and rage and anger and quarreling and slander, along with all malice. Instead, be kind to one another, compassionate, forgiving each other just as God in Messiah also forgave you.

— Ephesians 4:30–32

This is deeper than quenching the Spirit. Have you ever felt like you were grieving the Spirit? I have, and it is so painful that it makes me to want to die. Nothing is more painful than grieving the Holy Spirit inside of us. In fact, many are tormented, depressed and suicidal because of grieving the Holy Spirit. Disobedience, sin, unforgiveness, unbelief, rejecting the gifts of the Spirit, the anointing, and dismissing the Word of God and His instructions causes grief to Him. This grief makes us feel like there is poison in our innermost being.

I believe that many are physically and mentally sick because of grieving the Spirit. *Teshuvah* (heartfelt repentance) would cure most of the diseases of believers.

Many have grieved the Spirit by rejecting the following things: The Jews, the Jewishness of the gospel, Davidic Worship, and the Torah (saying the Law is done away with). Often it is believed that Israel is just another country in the Middle East. Because of grieving the Spirit, many end up despising the Jews and everything Jewish.

Grieving the Holy Spirit is worse than quenching the Holy Spirit, and it can lead to serious problems—even to the closing of entire congregations. I have seen two congregations that experienced revival being completely dismantled because the pastors grieved the Holy Spirit.

In the 90s we were pastoring a congregation in Dallas, Texas. In fact, we planted it. Some friends we met in Bible School pastored another small congregation. They asked us to join them and merge the two groups. The reason for this was the fact that God had used me to bring revival to them. I came to the rescue and helped them in worship when their worship leader quit suddenly. After the pastor preached, my hands began to "tingle," and God released all heaven. The Holy Spirit fell in that place unprecedentedly—people were saved and healed miraculously. It was the first time I understood what "holy rollers" were, as people were "drunk" under the power of the Holy Spirit, and were literally rolling in the aisles. What happened was amazing!

My husband was not with me as he had separated himself to pray for seven days inside of a closet, abstaining from all food or water. He wanted the Almighty to give him guidance for "his ministry." However, the God of the universe who is no respecter of persons, fell on this Israeli woman with an anointing of revival that would accompany me for the rest of my earthly journey.

Outpourings and outbreaks of the Holy Spirit have happened in various dimensions in our 30 years of ministry traveling to over 50 nations. But back in Dallas, Texas, our pastor friends were awed and asked us to merge. They coveted what we had for their people. In hindsight, we made a mistake—we should have linked and not merged, keeping our congregation going separately. But we did not know what would happen next.

After we merged and became co-pastors, they forbade us to bring anything Jewish into the congregation, including any Israeli biblical dancing. They did not believe in Davidic worship; neither did they want what we had, except the power of the Holy Spirit to do miracles. However, we were called to bring the Church spiritually back from Rome to Jerusalem and to the original gospel made in Zion with Jewish roots. And my anointing is most particular to the message I carry. It is a matter of life and death for the Church to repent from open and hidden anti-Semitism. Believe me, both exist in most churches and in all the different denominations. God has given me the privilege to display His miracle power so people can intently listen to the message of repentance.

The moment that these pastors wanted the anointing in my life without the message, without our "Jewish dancing" and Jewish roots, the Holy Spirit was fiercely grieved. He told us to leave that relationship, as it would be *ichabod* (the glory would depart). We left, taking no one with us, and together with us, the glory departed. In a matter of months that church closed. We were very sad. How many more churches will be closed by the Father for rejecting the Jewish apostles sent from Zion?

Remember what happened with Michal (Saul's daughter who became King David's wife)? She became barren because of criticizing her dancing, worshipping husband. Well, this congregation ceased to exist because they came against the Davidic dance, which was "too Jewish" in their eyes.

The following scripture is written about us, the descendants of Abraham, Isaac and Jacob.

He allowed no one to oppress them—for their sake He rebuked kings: Touch not My anointed ones, and do My prophets no harm.

— Psalm 105:14–15

In 2006, the Spirit sent us from Israel to take part in the Azusa Street Centennial in Los Angeles. We only had two weeks to prepare a booth display and to gather our team. We had no money, but I had heard the instruction of THE LORD to go, and as those who know me can attest, I do not want to quench or grieve the Holy Spirit. We did what I call "financial acrobatics," and we showed up in the Azusa Centennial.

There were many booths in the showroom, some sponsored by Israelis. In our booth, we had all of my books and some Judaica items like shofars and tallit prayer mantles. We all had high expectations. There were many big-name preachers and thousands of attendees. Some people came by our booth to buy some of my books. One young man by the name of Doug, a Pastor's son, bought a copy of *Grafted In* (a book based on Romans 11). In this book I teach the Church how to be restored to the original gospel that came out of Israel about 2,000 years ago, with Jewish roots, the Shabbat and biblical feasts. I also expound on God's Commandments, and how to walk like the ancient Jewish apostles and disciples did, when even their shadow healed the sick.

On the following day, Doug came back to the booth and said, "I do not understand this; I have bought many books in other booths, but the Holy Spirit does not let me read anything besides your *Grafted In* book and it is life-changing!"

However, I saw the angels of revival all over that place, and they were standing idle. (Yes, YHVH-God uses angels in His revivals). I asked the Father why is it that the angels of revival are idle with so many big-name preachers and so many thousands eager for revival. The answer came on the last day when Jack Hayford was preaching about the importance of Israel.

The Holy Spirit said, "Unless the Evangelical Charismatic and Pentecostal Church repents from ignoring and taking Israel lightly and from rejecting the message of restoration to the original gospel coming from Israel 2,000 years ago, I will bypass them altogether in the coming revival."

Restoring the identity of the Messiah as Jewish is of paramount importance, and with it the restoration of the lost identity of the bride of Messiah as grafted into a Jewish olive tree. Exposing and uprooting the false Roman identity of Yeshua is the order of the hour. The Holy Spirit is being grieved in so many churches and congregations when this subject is overlooked, taken lightly, or plainly rejected.

However, grieving the Holy Spirit is not only something that happens when people reject the Jewish roots of the faith. It grieves God when people want the revival and the message, but only superficially—as they keep on sinning, or covering their sins. The original gospel as preached in Israel by Yeshua and then also by His Jewish disciples started with the word "repent." Repentance in Hebrew is *teshuva*. It means "return, repent, restore," and "the answer." The answer to all our problems is always in returning to God and His ways—leaving our ways, and our politically correct religious interpretations behind.

As what many terms "the cheap grace gospel" is now more and more popular (with many even calling it "contemporary"), they have forgotten that the Ancient of Days does not change. Whatever was sin in the Old Covenant is also sin in the New Covenant. Whatever He deemed an abomination or disgusting to Him in the Old Covenant is still an abomination in the New Covenant. In fact, in the New Covenant the standard of morality is much higher than in the Old Covenant, and so is the demand for obedience to the Master.

You have heard that it was said, 'You shall not commit adultery.' But I tell you that everyone who looks upon a woman to lust after her has already committed adultery with her in his heart. And if your right eye causes you to stumble, gouge it out and throw it away! It is better for you that one part of your body should be destroyed, than that your whole body be thrown into gehenna (hell). And if your right hand causes you to stumble, cut it off and throw it away! It is better for you that one part of your body should be destroyed, than that your whole body go into gehenna (hell).

— Matthew 5:27–30

There are consequences of accepting the Jewish roots and the manifestation of the Spirit while harboring hidden sin in the leadership and in the congregation.

During the Azusa Street Revival Centennial in Los Angeles in 2006, a local Missionary Alliance Church invited us to minister. I wish I could properly describe what happened there. These people had never seen the Holy Spirit in operation; they did not pray in tongues or understood revival. But they were hungry for a move of God. The people and the pastor were praying and believed that we were the answer to their prayers. They were obviously not expecting a woman preacher, as they seemed surprised when I went up on the stage. I told them, "We are not from the Azusa Street Revival, nor from any known denomination. We come from Israel, and we are a continuation of the Jerusalem revival that occurred 2,000 years ago."

Then I took my guitar and sang one of my songs that has become the anthem for this End time revival and move of restoration. It starts this way:

Restore, restore the glory that we lost so long ago;

Make us one in You Gentile and Jew.

Together we'll arise and reach out to all the nations;

As we are one in You, Gentile and Jew.

For the Key of Abraham has been given to mankind;

And the Key of Abraham opens all doors.

As I was singing, our youngest team member (then in her early 20s) danced under the unction of the Holy Spirit. Suddenly, the power of God fell like in the Feast's day of Shavuot (Pentecost) in Jerusalem, as mentioned in the second book of Acts. People ran to the altar in repentance, only to fall under the power of God on the carpet. One lady fell from her chair and into a trance—THE LORD took her to heaven for four hours and told her to forgive and harbor no more bitterness. The children came running to the main sanctuary from Sunday school and were falling under the power of God and weeping in repentance. They had seen on a screen what was happening in the main sanctuary, and they asked forgiveness from their peers, teachers and parents for anger, jealousy, and rebellion. The carpet was full of bodies of men, women, and children under the power of ADONAI-God—there was repenting, weeping, laughing, healing, and surrendering to the Jewish Messiah. One of the very few not on the floor was the pastor. He was watching this revival scene from the front pew with his eyes wide open, and I was watching him. He was astounded.

After four hours of this, he grabbed me and said, "You are not leaving before you explain to me what this is." We stayed and explained how the Church, divorced from its Jewish roots, has lost the power, and how anti-Semitism and fear of anything Jewish kept the Holy Spirit grieved. Further we explained how the Church divided into many denominations, forsaking the Shabbat and biblical feasts, thus bringing much division, jealousy and suspicion. Last, we shared how the God of Israel wanted the whole Church to repent and return home, to the gospel that came out of Jerusalem 2,000 years ago with Torah and Spirit.

I do not know how much he understood, but this pastor, his wife, and his congregants kept seeking us for a couple years after that, and even came on an Israel tour with us. However, the pastor was enamored with the spiritual manifestations yet refused to repent from adultery. He had been cheating on his wife for a long time. Finally, the Holy Spirit was totally grieved and closed that church.

God is very jealous about His presence, and the importance of holiness. Unfortunately, many of those who love the manifestations of the Holy Spirit take Him lightly by rejecting His written Commandments. They grieve the Holy Spirit; thus many revivals have been halted because of sin, especially in the leadership.

When we know Yeshua as the Jewish lion that He is, we realize that we cannot take Him, His Spirit, or His Word lightly. In the first Jewish congregation of Messianic believers in Jerusalem, sin could not hide. The Jewish apostles treated sin radically, like with Ananias and Saphira, who lied about an offering. It is no wonder (in such an atmosphere of holiness and the fear of YHVH) that even the shadow of the apostles healed the sick.

> But Peter said, "Ananias, why has Satan filled your heart to lie to the Ruach HaKodesh (Holy Spirit) and keep back part of the proceeds of the land? While it remained unsold, it was your own, wasn't it? And after it was sold, wasn't it at your disposal? How did this deed get into your heart? You haven't lied to men but to God." As soon as he heard these words, Ananias fell down and died. Great fear came upon all who heard about

it. The young men got up and wrapped him in a shroud, then carried him out and buried him.

— ACTS 5:3–6

Restoring the Jewishness of the Messiah does not mean forming another denomination or religious system. A true restoration to the Jewish roots of the faith and the original gospel made in Zion should lead us to a radical walk of obedience and holiness.

In the two cases above, the churches closed shortly after grieving the Holy Spirit.

Unrepentant Sin Pollutes Revivals

A few years ago, there was an outpouring of the Holy Spirit in a city of Lakeland, Florida. Like in many other meetings, people were falling under the power of God, shaking and laughing. I went there with many of my disciples, both young and old, expecting to receive a touch of His Spirit and some refreshing. I opened my heart to whatever Abba wanted to do. I always want more of His Spirit and His presence.

However, I felt nothing, and none of my people felt any anointing. Not wanting to judge, I just prayed, "Abba show me if this is from You, and why am I not feeling anything since I love your Spirit so much?"

Soon I fell to my knees, and while others were shaking and laughing and having a wonderful time, I was sobbing with deep sighs, and then I wailed asking God's forgiveness. I didn't know why I was mourning when everyone else was laughing.

A few days later everything became clear. The leader of that revival was in adultery with a woman among his followers. Later he divorced his wife and married his mistress. The Holy Spirit was grieved, and He had me wailing and repenting on his behalf without knowing why.

91

Sometimes a genuine move of the Spirit can get polluted because of sin in the leadership, or by not confronting sin among the people. That is why the Holy Spirit is called 'holy,' and if we allow sin to run unchecked, we grieve His holiness and pollute His moves!

That is why it is so important to remain close to Him - then we will have discernment, and will treat the Holy Spirit and the anointing with respect.

To him the doorkeeper opens, and the sheep hear his voice. The shepherd calls his own sheep by name and leads them out. "When he has brought out all his own, he goes ahead of them; and the sheep follow him because they know his voice. They will never follow a stranger, but will run away from him, for they do not know the voice of strangers."

— JOHN 10:3–5

When the true Jewishness of the gospel is restored and we reclaim the identity of the Lion of Judah, the healthy, holy fear of THE LORD is restored too. And with it comes the anointing of holiness, Divine authority and His glory.

If you consider yourself a Christian or Messianic, and you shun the anointing and the power of the Holy Spirit, you have been deceived by the anti-Messiah principality. You are in replacement theology, as you have replaced the Divine power for religion, church politics and professionalism. You may even do some wonderful things, but unless it is Divinely empowered, and you walk in intimate communion with Yeshua through the Holy Spirit, you may discover too late that you have been worshipping a counterfeit and not the Jewish Messiah.

3: Do not blaspheme the Spirit (Mat. 12:31)

For this reason I say to you, every sin and blasphemy will be forgiven men, but blasphemy against the Ruach (Spirit) will not be forgiven. Whoever speaks a word against the Son of Man will be forgiven, but whoever speaks against the Ruach HaKodesh (Holy Spirit) will not be forgiven, neither in this age nor in the one to come.

— MATTHEW 12:31–32

Blasphemy of the Holy Spirit is one step beyond grieving the Spirit. Rejecting the Holy Spirit is a progression that starts with quenching the Spirit and prophecies. It then moves into grieving the Spirit through pride, arrogance, unbelief, bitterness, and unrepentant sin. It culminates with the only sin that is not forgiven: blasphemy against the Holy Spirit.

To explain, whenever there is a valid manifestation of the Holy Spirit (praying in tongues, miracle healings, falling under the power of God, etc.), and you say it's of the devil, you may cross the line to the only unforgivable sin.

Only Abba knows the hearts of men. But the principle is humility and honor. Be humble enough not to judge what you do not understand. Do not be quick to put down manifestations that seem strange to you. Wait upon THE LORD, and He will show you the truth.

The manifestations of the Spirit offend the carnally minded. That is why it is so important to keep a humble heart, refrain from quenching or grieving the Spirit, and never judge anything before it's time. We have to treat the anointing with great respect and have the humility to be careful with what does not fit our doctrine. We may refrain from participating if we are uncertain, but we must also refrain from judging what we do not understand. The words are "humility and caution," until we have the revelation from the Father.

Michal, the daughter of Saul, judged David when he was dancing before the Ark of YHVH without his royal robes, arrayed only in the basic priestly garment called the ephod. He was not naked, as many have misinterpreted. God punished her with barrenness until the end of her days; she could bear no children. How many congregations are barren today, without a move of the Spirit, and no newborn babies?

> David returned to bless his own household. But Saul's daughter Michal came out to meet David and said, "How the king of Israel distinguished himself today, when he uncovered himself (from his kingly robes) today in the eyes of the slave girls of his subjects, as any vulgar fellow would shamelessly uncover himself!" "It was before Adonai," David said to Michal, "who chose me instead of your father and all his household, appointing me ruler over the people of Adonai, over Israel! So I danced before Adonai, and will dishonor myself even more than this, and will be low in my own eyes. Yet in the eyes of the slave girls whom you mentioned, I will be honored." So Saul's daughter Michal had no children to the day of her death.
>
> — 2 Samuel 6:20–23

Normally when the Most High brings in a new move, it is different, and 'out of the box' for most. We need to remain humble, pliable and teachable, and be careful not to think we have all the truth. We will never 'arrive,' we will always be on His journey to more and more light, increased truth, and abundant restoration. We must keep our hearts humble and our relationship with the Messiah Yeshua very attentive to His Holy Spirit.

Accepting the true Jewish Messiah and His kingdom will lead us to radical obedience, unreligious and unrigid holiness, and an uncompromised walk with the Holy Spirit.

One of the major marks of the New Covenant given to the people of Israel to share with the nations is *the anointing*. Without it, we are nothing except members of a dead religion. No religious system can get the people truly saved, healed and set free; only the Jewish Messiah with His anointing in us can do this.

> **The Ruach of ADONAI ELOHIM is on me, because ADONAI has anointed me to proclaim Good News to the poor. He has sent me to bind up the brokenhearted, to proclaim liberty to the captives, and the opening of the prison to those who are bound.**
>
> **— ISAIAH 61:1**

Have you rejected the Jewishness of the gospel or the manifestations of the Holy Spirit? Have you had bad experiences in charismatic circles that have made you bitter and suspicious?

Have you judged what you do not know? Has pride and rigid religion deafened your ears to the Good Shepherd? Are you afraid that surrendering to the Holy Spirit will make you "weird"? Do you feel depressed? Are you constantly sick? Do you think you have quenched or grieved the Spirit? Are you afraid that you might have blasphemed the Holy Spirit, and that there is no way back?

Teshuva—repentance is the answer.

The sacrifices of God are a broken spirit. A broken and a contrite heart, O God, You will not despise.

— PSALM 51:19 (VERSE 17 IN OTHER VERSIONS)

A Prayer of Teshuva: Repentance, Returning, and Restoration

Father, forgive me if I have quenched or grieved Your Spirit in any way. Forgive me for rejecting any part of the Jewishness of Messiah, or for any hostility, dishonor, or apathy in my heart towards the Jewish people. I renounce and resist the demon of anti-Messiah, which is against Your anointing. I surrender completely to Your Son, my Jewish Messiah Yeshua, to Your Holy Spirit, and to the fullness of Your Word. I repent of all rigidity, religiosity, and self-righteousness—and of every and any sin of heart, body, mind, or spirit that offends You and blocks me from an intimate relationship with You. Thank You for Your forgiveness and mercy and for filling me afresh with Your Holy Spirit and fire, that I may serve You and worship You wholeheartedly all of my days. In Yeshua's name and for His sake. Amen!

For further reading about head number one, I recommend reading my book, *The Healing Power of the Roots.*

* www.kad-esh.org/shop/the-healing-power-of-the-roots/

GATE 7

ISRAEL OUR MOTHER

Head Number 2: Anti-Israel

I say then, they did not stumble so as to fall, did they? May it never be! But by their false step salvation has come to the Gentiles, to provoke Israel to jealousy.

— ROMANS 11:11

———

One of the major tenets of replacement theology and THE IDENTITY THEFT of the Messiah is the lie that the church superseded or replaced Israel. In many old churches there were statues of two women placed in a prominent location of the church building. One statue was of a queenly woman, standing erect with a crown on her head, and the other statue was of a poor, broken, humiliated bowed down woman. The queenly woman represented the "Church Triumphant" over the "Vanquished Synagogue," or the Christians triumphing over the broken and humiliated Jews.

The understanding of Christianity since the divorce from the Jewish roots during the fourth century—because of the codification* of the decrees in the Council of Nicaea—was that Israel is under a curse forever. The preachers constantly declared to the masses that the Church had inherited all the blessings given by God to the people of Israel, and the Jews had inherited all the curses. Anti-Semitism was and still is a founding doctrine in many denominations and churches. "We are Israel," many Christians say arrogantly; "We are the Israel of God, the old Israel missed the time of their visitation when Jesus Christ came, so now we, the Gentile Christians, have inherited the covenant and all its blessings." And yet God is very clear in the Scriptures that He will *never* break His covenant with Israel. He may discipline her, but He will never destroy her, forsake her, or stop being the God of Israel.

> "So now, do not fear, Jacob My servant," says ADONAI, "nor be dismayed, O Israel, for behold, I will save you from afar, your seed from the land of their exile. Jacob will again be quiet and at ease, and no one will make him afraid. For I am with you," declares ADONAI, "to save you, for I will make a full end of all the nations where I scatter you. But I will not make a full end of you. For I will discipline you justly but will not leave you unpunished."
>
> — JEREMIAH 30:10–11

Nations will come and nations will go, and any nation that rises against Israel will end, but Israel will remain forever.

---

* *Codification*: "the action or process of arranging laws or rules according to a system or plan."

"Yet all who devour you will be devoured, and all your foes—
all of them—will go into captivity. Those plundering you will
be plundered, and all preying on you I give as prey. For I will
restore health to you and will heal you of your wounds." It
is a declaration of ADONAI. "For they called you an outcast:
'Zion—no one cares about her.'" Thus says ADONAI, "Indeed,
I will return Jacob's tents from exile, and have compassion
on his dwellings. The city will be rebuilt on her mound. The
citadel will stand in its rightful place. Out of them will come
thanksgiving and the sound of celebration. I will multiply
them, so they will not decrease. I will also honor them, so they
will not be insignificant. His children also will be as former-
ly—his community set up before Me—and I will punish all his
oppressors."

— JEREMIAH 30:16–20

It was an enormous shocker to most of Christendom when Israel
was reborn in its own land on May 14, 1948, after the Nazi Shoah
(Holocaust) had decimated the Jewish population by annihilating over
six million people. Yet despite the destruction of most of Europe's Jewish communities and synagogues (entire villages were wiped off the
face of the earth), this "Vanquished Synagogue" rose like a phoenix
from the ashes of Auschwitz, Birkenau, Treblinka, Sobibor and many
more death camps and concentration camps. These were true survivors:
These Jewish skeletons that had lost everything to a hate-filled regime
that was the culmination of all that Christianity had taught throughout the years since Constantine and the Council of Nicaea. Hitler said,
"I am doing the will of God," (Hitler) he also called Martin Luther a
"genius" for writing how to deal harshly with the Jews in his book "On
the Jews and their Lies." (Süss and Luther)

Both Catholic and Protestant churches have been indoctrinated throughout generations about the Jews. Replacement theology taught most of them to mock and hate us. This has continued until today in many circles. I wish I could tell you that this is over, but it is not over. There are constant posts on the internet with anti-Semitic events related to those that profess some Christianity or another.

Recently a group from New Jersey called the "Black Hebrews" murdered Jews in cold blood who were celebrating the Jewish holiday of Hanukkah in the private house of their rabbi. This group claimed that they are the true Hebrews and not these Jews, and because they supposedly murdered Christ, they deserve to die. It shocked many people that this happened in the USA within the 21st century. Still, I am not surprised, as this demonic principality is hiding in the doctrine of many churches and denominations. And yet the God of Israel said in his Holy Word many times that Israel is His chosen nation forever—and He did not mean the Church or any Christian nation.

Lately, during the coronavirus, or COVID-19 pandemic, a white Baptist pastor in Florida posted terrible accusations against Israel, saying that the Israelis caused the coronavirus. We call this a *blood libel*. This is when Jews and, in this case the whole State of Israel, is accused of crimes they did not commit, thus inciting the masses to hate them. Another anti-Semitic pastor and broadcaster in the USA, said that the coronavirus is a punishment from God to the Jews for not following Jesus. (Anti-Defamation League)

> **Thus says YHVH, who gives the sun as a light by day and the fixed order of the moon and the stars as a light by night, who stirs up the sea so its waves roar, YHVH-Tzva'ot is His Name: "Only if this fixed order departs from before Me"—it is a declaration of YHVH—"then also might Israel's (natural)**

offspring cease from being a nation before Me—for all time."
Thus says YHVH: "Only if heaven above can be measured and
the foundations of the earth searched out beneath, then also I
will cast off the (natural) offspring of Israel—for all they have
done." It is a declaration of YHVH.

— JEREMIAH 31:34–36

We must restore the Jewish identity of the Messiah to have a *holy
division* in the Church: between those that will accept Him as a Jew,
and will bless and make restitution towards natural Israel, and between
those who will continue claiming that *they* are the true Israel, and that
the Israel in the Middle East is a counterfeit country with a people that
deserve to die.

The life of many deceived Christians is hanging in the balance. The
restoration of the stolen identity of the Church—from a Romanized
usurper of Israel to a grafted in Ruth-like Church (one that joins Israel
through the blood of the Jewish Messiah Yeshua)—is the key for the
salvation of the nations and for the End time revival.

YHVH-ELOHIM, the God of Israel, promised that His covenant
with Israel is forever. He never said that He will replace Israel with the
Church. In fact, He said that the Church needs to be *grafted in or join
Israel*, not replace Israel.

But if some of the branches were broken off and you—being a
wild olive—were grafted in among them and became a partak-
er of the root of the olive tree with its richness, do not boast
against the branches. But if you do boast, it is not you who
support the root but the root supports you. You will say then,
"Branches were broken off so that I might be grafted in." True
enough. They were broken off because of unbelief, and you

stand by faith. Do not be arrogant, but fear— for if God did not spare the natural branches, neither will He spare you.

— ROMANS 11:17–21

The Jewish apostle to the Gentiles is a rabbi by the name of *Shaul*, also known by his Roman name Paul, who warned the Gentile believers to never be arrogant against the Jews, or think they can usurp their place. In fact, his warning is so serious he stated that, if Gentiles become arrogant against the Israelite-Jewish branches, their arrogance could cost them their eternal salvation. How many people has God broken off the olive tree by worshipping a Romanized Christ that hates the people of Israel? How many were broken off and are being removed from the olive tree of salvation for hating the Jews, being arrogant against them, and preaching that the Church is now Israel, replacing the nation of Israel altogether?

Paul also warned about building on any other foundation but the one he declared, which is Yeshua the Messiah, the anointed Jewish King and Savior promised to Israel alone. But replacement theology, with its five headed monster, has been intertwined in Church doctrine until this day, constantly building on a Roman-pagan foundation that breeds anti-Semitism.

For no one can lay any other foundation than what is already laid—which is Yeshua the Messiah. Now if anyone builds on the foundation with gold, silver, precious stones, wood, hay, straw, each one's work will become clear. For the Day will show it, because it is to be revealed by fire; and the fire itself will test each one's work—what sort it is. If anyone's work built on the foundation survives, he will receive a reward. If anyone's work is burned up, he will suffer loss—he himself will be saved, but as through fire.

— 1 CORINTHIANS 3:11–15

How many pastors are in danger of having all their hard labor burnt in the fire of YHVH's judgment because of replacement theology and overt or covert anti-Semitism? Espousing the deceptive theology that the Church replaced Israel is dangerous, and they root it in jealousy that breeds murder.

Then He said, "What have you done? The voice of your brother's blood is crying out to Me from the ground. So now, cursed are you from the ground which opened its mouth to receive your brother's blood from your hand. As often as you work the ground, it will not yield its crops to you again. You will be a restless wanderer on the earth."

— GENESIS 4:10–12

Cain was jealous of Abel and rose to murder him rather than repent for his jealousy. If you are looking down on Israel and the Jews, harboring spiritual arrogance and thinking to yourself that the Church is better than Israel, or has superseded Israel, think twice, lest the Almighty dismantles church after church, denomination after denomination—for He said that He has a day of vengeance to vindicate Israel. On that day, you cannot show him your denominational credentials to rescue yourself from His judgment.

For ADONAI has a day of vengeance, a year of recompense for the hostility against Zion.

— ISAIAH 34:8

Please remember that judgment always starts first in the house of God.

For the time has come for judgment to begin with the house of God. If judgment begins with us first, what will be the end for those who disobey the Good News of God?

— 1 PETER 4:17

Here is the Good News: A Jew died for you and His name is Yeshua. However, if people insist on downplaying His natural family, the known people of Israel with whom He has an eternal covenant, He might turn to become an enemy.

For thus says ADONAI-Tzva'ot (THE LORD of the Armies), He has sent me after glory to the nations that plundered you (Israel My People)—because whoever touches you touches the apple of His eye.

— ZECHARIAH 2:12

The Key of Abraham

I will bless those who bless you, but whoever curses you I will curse, and in you all the families of the earth will be blessed.

— Genesis 12:3 NASB

Israel is not "the elder brother" but the mother of the nations. Our relationship with a mother differs from our relationship with a brother. I will introduce you to the Key of Abraham: *The Divine Key that can open or close the gate of blessing and salvation for individuals, families, and entire nations.* This Key, given to Abraham, Isaac and Jacob, repeats throughout the Scriptures.

Israel is the only nation with which the God of the Universe has a covenant, and until now it is still so. All the blessings to the Gentiles come through the people of Israel, the original descendants of Abraham, Isaac, and Jacob, with whom God made the covenant. God's only covenant is with Abraham, his descendants, and all of those that:

- Join in with Israel through a Jewish Messiah
- Bless Israel

"Behold, days are coming," declares Adonai, "when I will make a new covenant with the house of Israel and with the house of Judah... "But this is the covenant which I will make with the house of Israel after those days," declares the Lord, "I will put My Law within them and on their heart I will write it; and I will be their God, and they shall be My people.

— Jeremiah 31:31,33

This scripture is referring to the New Covenant. Gentiles join into this covenant through the Blood of Yeshua the Jewish Messiah. God is not obligated to bless any nation unless that nation is grafted in with Israel and blesses Israel. Those are the only stipulations for the blessing of the nations. Are they good to Israel, or are they not? Are they walking in the ways of the God of Israel as given to Israel, or are they not?

This is *the key* for the salvation and the blessing of the nations. This key has been lost for nearly 1,700 years, but now it is being restored. When it is fully restored, the salvation of the nations will follow, and only then will we offer the Father many *Sheep Nations*!

"I will bless those that bless you, and I will curse him who curses you and in you (Abram) all the families of the earth will be blessed," (Gen. 12:3). Now let us study this verse from the Hebrew:

The word for blessing here is *bracha*. *Lebarech* from the word *bracha* means, "to decree a word of life, goodness, favor, health, success and prosperity over someone." This blessing has many wonderful and positive events and opportunities that will bring great joy, happiness, wholeness, prosperity, greatness, abundance, fruitfulness and *fulfillment* (Deut. 28:1-14)!

However, this word comes from the word *berech* which means the "knee" in Hebrew. So let me paraphrase this verse for you:

"I (the God of Israel) will bow down My royal knee to lift up and favor those who bow down their knees, and humble themselves to honor, speak well of, defend and do good to My people Israel" (Gen. 12:3a).

YHVH Tzva'ot, THE LORD of the Armies, the God of the Universe, the Creator of heaven and earth has committed Himself by His unfailing and unchanging Word to bow down His royal knee to bless, favor and exalt those who humble themselves, and bow down their knees to exalt and honor Israel! However, if they do not, He equally commits Himself to curse them.

"I will curse those who curse you,"

— GENESIS 12:3B

There are two words used in this verse in the Hebrew for the word curse, one of them is *klala,* and the other one is *meera. Klala* comes from the word *kal,* which means, "light" (opposite of heavy). This curse is referring to those that take Israel and the Jews lightly, and do not honor or respect them as His chosen ones. God uses the same word for those that curse their father or mother:

And he that curses his father or his mother shall surely be put to death.

— EXODUS 21:17

Those that disrespect their parents will die! Taking parents lightly, mocking them, not listening to their instructions, or disrespecting them brings evil occurrences to one's life. God likens Israel unto a parent, a mother, the mother of the nations. He calls the nations to honor her as a mother. God commands us to honor our parents even in their imperfection: our lives depends on it!

Honor your father and your mother just as ADONAI your God commanded you, so that your days may be long and it may go well with you in the land ADONAI your God is giving you.

— DEUTERONOMY 5:16

If we do not humble ourselves to honor our parents even in their imperfection, it will not go well with us. When we take them lightly (*kal-klala*), the curse or destruction comes to us, which is *Meera*. Israel is regarded by the Almighty as the Mother of the nations. She is the one that brought mankind the Bible, the Messiah, and the gospel. Without Israel, there would be no salvation for any nation, in the same way that without your natural birth mother, you could not have been born. This alone is enough to cause you to honor and be thankful for your mother, even in her imperfection. She gave life to you! Israel gave life to all the nations. The Messiah is Jewish, and salvation is of the Jews.

You worship what you do not know; we worship what we know, for salvation is from the Jews.

— JOHN 4:22

Meera means to "declare a word decree for the destruction of someone." It is followed by many evil occurrences that will bring anguish, distress, grief, sickness, confusion, loss, lack, bankruptcy, loneliness, strife, rejection, futility, fear, failure, terror, self-destruction and total annihilation. (Deut. 28:14-68)

Notice that in both cases (the blessing and the curse) God connects them with issuing a decree or speaking a word. From the beginning, everything is created by ELOHIM issuing a decree and speaking His Word:

In the beginning ELOHIM created the heavens and the earth. The earth was without form, and void; and darkness was on the face of the deep. And the Spirit of ELOHIM was hovering

over the face of the waters. Then ELOHIM said: "Let there be light"; and there was light.

— GENESIS 1:1–3 (FREE TRANSLATION FROM HEBREW)

Israel, beloved ones, is forever the chosen people of God, and no church can replace it or supersede the Mother of the nations. From Israel comes the Bible, the Messiah, the gospel, and the Jewish apostles to the nations. She may fall sometimes; she may be in unbelief for a while, but the God of Israel is restoring her to become the chief sheep nation that all other nations will follow.

Hear the Word of ADONAI, O nations, and declare it in the distant islands, and say: "He who scattered Israel will gather and watch over him, as a shepherd does his flock."

— JEREMIAH 31:9

"Sing for joy and be glad, O daughter of Zion; for behold I am coming and I will dwell in your midst," declares the LORD. Many nations will join themselves to the LORD in that day and will become My people. Then I will dwell in your midst, and you will know that the LORD of hosts has sent Me to you. The LORD will possess Judah as His portion in the holy land, and will again choose Jerusalem. "Be silent, all flesh, before the LORD; for He is aroused from His holy habitation."

— ZECHARIAH 2:10–13 NASB

The lie that the Church replaced Israel has prevented Christian nations from becoming Sheep Nations that will join with the God of

Israel, honoring Israel as the Mother of the nations, not replacing her. His judgment is now at the gates of every nation that has its foundation in Christianity—both personal and national repentance is mandatory if we are to see revival and global salvation.

A genuine believer in Messiah will love and honor Israel, the chosen people, and the brethren of Yeshua Himself, who is a Jew. When we restore His Jewish identity, anti-Semitism will be a thing of the past, and the bride of Messiah will arise in all her glory.

For those Christians that will not receive this urgent message, the only thing to look for is the judgment.

> **Draw near, O nations, to hear, and listen, O peoples! Let the earth hear, and all it contains, the world, and all its offspring! For ADONAI is enraged at all the nations, and furious at all their armies. He will utterly destroy them. He will give them over to slaughter. For ADONAI has a day of vengeance, a year of recompense for the hostility against Zion.**

> **— ISAIAH 34:1,2,8**

My prayer is that many will repent and become defenders of Israel in these very perilous End times.

In the next gate, we will discuss returning to the Word of God as in the first century. For further reading, I recommend my books: *Sheep Nations* and *The Key of Abraham.**

---

* *Sheep Nations*: www.kad-esh.org/shop/sheep-nations/ | *The Key of Abraham*: www. kad-esh.org/shop/the-key-of-abraham-2/

A Prayer of Repentance for Hostility Against Israel

Father in heaven, I ask Your forgiveness for harboring the lie that the Church replaced or superseded Israel. I now realize that I was wrong, and that this lie is dangerously rooted in deception and jealousy. I totally reject replacement theology and the doctrine that the Church replaces Israel. Thank You for delivering me from all the curses that fall upon those who take Israel lightly, are arrogant against her, or harm her or her reputation. Please teach me how to honor Israel as the mother of the nations, and how to make restitution for the sins committed against her by Christians because of the terrible deception of replacement theology. In Yeshua's name. Amen!

RETURNING TO GODS WORD

Head Number 3: Anti-Torah

"Behold, the days come," says Yahveh, "that I will make a new covenant with the house of Israel, and with the house of Judah: not according to the covenant that I made with their fathers... But this is the covenant that I will make with the house of Israel after those days," says Yahveh: "I will put my Torah in their inward parts, and I will write it in their heart. I will be their God, and they shall be my people."

— JEREMIAH 31:31–33 (WEB)

The anti-Torah head of the anti-MESITOJUZ demonic principality of replacement theology is keeping the Church in a "spiritual Egypt of slavery" because of its pagan mixture and Lawlessness. God gives the New Covenant to Israel and Judah, not to the Gentiles. No nation has an Old Covenant; thus, no Gentile has a New Covenant. There is no New Covenant apart from Israel and Judah, period.

The gospel came from Zion; the Messiah is Jewish, and God gives the promise of a Savior only to the nation of Israel. Gentiles join through the blood of a Jewish Messiah. They also become grafted into the commonwealth of Israel, not replacing Israel, but joining Israel as the vessel of God to bring salvation and redemption to the Gentiles. This vessel needs to be honored for eternity, regardless of all the imperfections.

Without Israel, there would be no Messiah and no Christians. The New Covenant stipulates that the same Torah (Laws of God) as given to the people of Israel would now be written in the hearts and the minds of the believers in the Messiah. It does not say anywhere that the Torah is done away with. This is one of the biggest, most dangerous lies of replacement theology, and this lie has kept the Church sick with ungodly pagan deceptions and Lawlessness.

Israel is the Mother of the nations—for 1,700 years, replacement theology has taught most of the Church to hate, reject or be suspicious to everything Jewish. This hatred of our spiritual birth origins has caused the Church to be an orphan. It leads to self-hatred because of identity confusion.

Children that hate or are ashamed of their parents suffer from personality disorders and even schizophrenia. They try their best to disassociate from their original identity and end with disassociated personalities. When Christians do not embrace the Jewish roots, the importance of the Torah, the Shabbat, the biblical feasts, and the honor of Israel, they suffer from self-hatred. There is a constant feeling of guilt and condemnation and a lack of inner *shalom*, (Hebrew for "wellbeing" and "peace")—leading all the way to what I call *spiritual schizophrenia*. It takes an enormous amount of emotional and spiritual energy to disassociate from our birth origins, which causes a host of mental, spiritual, and physical diseases.

Through Israel, the Gentiles received all their spiritual legacy: the Holy Scriptures, the Savior, and the Messianic gospel. We cannot enjoy a legacy when we hate the origins of it and those who gave it to us. When we honor the legator*, then we can also profit from the legacy they give.

> If the first fruit is holy, so is the whole batch of dough; and if the root is holy, so are the branches. But if some of the branches were broken off and you—being a wild olive—were grafted in among them and became a partaker of the root of the olive tree with its richness, do not boast against the branches. But if you do boast, it is not you who support the root but the root supports you.

> — ROMANS 11:16–18

The root of who we are, both in the natural and in the spiritual, supports and gives us a backbone. If we reject the root, we have no support and are bowed down, having no victory. That is pure misery! In this gate, we will learn to love the Jewish roots of Christianity through Israel, that received all the Father's Commandments and the tenets of faith. We will learn to embrace the roots of the faith with love and honor, so we can heal from orphanhood and spiritual schizophrenia. The Key of Abraham (as mentioned in the previous gate) leads us to *teshuva*—returning and repentance for restoration. It is *teshuva* that is the answer to all our woes.

---

* Legator: a person who has made a will or given a legacy.

When My people, over whom My Name is called, humble themselves and pray and seek My face and turn from their evil ways, then I will hear from heaven and will forgive their sin and will heal their land.

— 2 CHRONICLES 7:14

When Church doctrine is based on replacement theology, the prevalent and most deceptive teaching is based upon what the Council of Nicaea stipulated: "We have nothing in common with the Jews because the (identity thief) Savior showed us another way" (another gospel that brings a curse – Gal. 1:8). And since we have nothing in common with the Jew, then the Torah, the instructions of God and His Commandments are "done away with." Preachers proclaim this as a spiritual mantra from nearly every pulpit.

The Lie that "The Law is Done Away With."

Try to tell this to your governor or president and you will end up arrested.

God gives the New Covenant to Israel and Judah, and through them to the Gentiles. The major mark of the New Covenant is that the Torah, the Laws of YHVH, are written in the minds and hearts of the believers. But since the fourth century, Constantine replaced the Torah in the Church with the laws and traditions of Rome, and this is affecting us to this very day. When replacement theology became Church doctrine, it changed everything to include all that was Roman (like Roman pagan feasts) to the exclusion of all that was Jewish, Hebrew, or from the Old Covenant. It is time to return to the ancient paths and to find rest or *Shabbat* for our souls.

Thus says ADONAI: "Stand in the roads and look. Ask for the ancient paths—where the good way is—and walk in it. Then you will find rest for your souls. But they said, 'We won't walk in it.'

— JEREMIAH 6:16

My prayer is that you will find and walk in the ancient paths and finally gain *rest*. Another word for rest is *Shabbat*, the holy day set apart and blessed from Creation.

God completed—on the seventh day—His work that He made, and He ceased—on the seventh day—from all His work that He made. Then God blessed the seventh day and sanctified it, for on it He ceased from all His work that God created for the purpose of preparing.

— GENESIS 2:2–3

We refer to the Torah in two ways. One is the first Five Books of the Bible (which is also called the Pentateuch, or the Books of Moses). Second, it refers to all the instructions of ELOHIM—the Creator God in righteousness. The Torah is not necessarily Judaism or the Jewish Religion: the Torah is the Word of God. The Book of Leviticus often repeats:

Now ADONAI called to Moses and spoke to him out of the Tent of Meeting, saying...
ADONAI spoke to Moses, saying...
ADONAI spoke to Moses, saying...
Then ADONAI spoke to Moses saying...

ADONAI spoke to Moses, saying...

— LEVITICUS 1:1; 4:1; 5:14,20; 6:1

You get the picture; God is speaking, and the Word records what He is saying. This is found throughout the first five books of the Bible (called the Torah), beginning with the Book of Genesis when ELOHIM the Creator "speaks, and it is so," YHVH ADONAI "speaks, and it is so." Truly the God of Israel speaks, and it is so.

Then God said, "Let there be light!" and there was light.

— GENESIS 1:3

Then God said, "Let there be an expanse in the midst of the water! Let it be for separating water from water." So God made the expanse and it separated the water that was below the expanse from the water that was over the expanse. And it happened so.

— GENESIS 1:6–7

Then God said, "Let the water below the sky be gathered to one place. Let the dry ground appear." And it happened so.

— GENESIS 1:9

Then God said, "Let Us make man in Our image, after Our likeness! Let them rule over the fish of the sea, over the flying creatures of the sky, over the livestock, over the whole earth, and over every crawling creature that crawls on the land." God created humankind in His image, in the image of God He created him, male and female He created them.

— GENESIS 1:26–27

Pay attention when you read His Word and notice every time it says that He was speaking or "saying." Instead of having replacement theology interpretation in your ears, pay attention to what the Almighty said to Israel, the mother of the nations, and allow the Holy Spirit to instruct you while reading. His sayings in the Old Covenant (which is the only Holy Scriptures the early believers had until the fourth century and the Council of Nicaea) will revolutionize your faith and your walk, and you will have your spiritual identity restored. We can all become as powerful and glorious as the believers in the first century if we allow His Word, as given to Israel, to form our doctrine and not the words of Constantine and those who are wrongly called "church fathers."

The true church fathers are the 12 tribes of Israel and the 12 Jewish apostles of the Lamb. Those are the 24 elders in the book of Revelation and not Constantine, Augustine, Chrysostom, or Martin Luther.

To the 12 Jewish apostles, He said:

And Yeshua said to them, "Amen, I tell you, when the Son of Man sits on His glorious throne in the new world, you who have followed Me shall also sit on twelve thrones, judging the twelve tribes of Israel."

— MATTHEW 19:28

It is not Christian church fathers who will judge the 12 tribes of Israel as replacement theology has done: judging Israel and the Jewish people, accusing them of being murderers of Christ that deserve to die. It is the 12 Jewish apostles chosen by Yeshua, the Jewish Messiah, who will judge and rule over the 12 tribes of Israel.

> **When He had taken the book, the four living creatures and the twenty-four elders fell down before the Lamb, each one holding a harp and golden bowls full of incense, which are the prayers of the saints. And they sang a new song, saying, "Worthy are You to take the book and to break its seals; for You were slain, and purchased for God with Your blood men from every tribe and tongue and people and nation."**

> **— REVELATION 5:8–9 NASB**

In Revelation 21, in the account of the New Jerusalem, we realize fully the identity of the 24 elders. These are the biblical fathers of all the people in the New Covenant.

> **And he carried me away in the Spirit to a great and high mountain, and showed me the holy city, Jerusalem, coming down out of heaven from God, having the glory of God. Her brilliance was like a very costly stone, as a stone of crystal-clear jasper. It had a great and high wall, with twelve gates, and at the gates twelve angels; and names were written on them, which are the names of the twelve tribes of the sons of Israel. There were three gates on the east and three gates on the north and three gates on the south and three gates on the west. And the wall of the city had twelve foundation stones,**

and on them were the twelve names of the twelve apostles of the Lamb.

— REVELATION 21:10–14 NASB

Here it is, the full priestly fatherhood for the believers in Messiah, both Jews and Gentiles—they are the 12 tribes of Israel and the 12 Jewish apostles of the Lamb, headed by the Lion of Judah, the Jewish Messiah, the only One who is worthy to open the books of judgment.

Then I began to weep greatly because no one was found worthy to open the book or to look into it; and one of the elders said to me, "Stop weeping; behold, the Lion that is from the tribe of Judah, the Root of David, has overcome so as to open the book and its seven seals."

— REVELATION 5:4–5 NASB

How will a Jewish Savior, coupled with His Israelite Jewish eldership, judge a Church that is divorced from His Torah, who hates, ignores, or dishonors His Jewish people and usurps the place of Israel? What will be the fate of those who exalt Christian church fathers and theologians that were all big anti-Semites and taught the Church to hate Jews?

These same church fathers and theologians are honored and their deceptions incorporated in every church doctrine, and especially the one that says, "The Law or the Torah is done away with, we are Christians, not Jews; therefore, we keep Sunday, Easter, Christmas and Halloween—All Saints, and not Shabbat, Passover, Shavuot, Yom Kippur, and Sukkot." (See Lev. 23, He calls them "My feasts.")

How would the Lion of Judah judge a Church that has been fathered by a pagan Roman heritage that hates His Jewishness, instead of a Church that has accepted their privileged Israeli heritage (extended as great grace to the Gentile) through a Jewish Messiah and His Jewish apostles?

Torah, Teaching, and Instruction

Turn me away from the deceitful way, and be gracious to me with Your Torah.

— PSALM 119:29

Torah, in Hebrew, means "teaching or instruction." The instructions of YHVH are not "suggestions." Throughout His Word, He tells us what He loves and what He hates, and He is very clear about it. However, multitudes of Christians of all denominations are turning a deaf ear to His instructions. Most preachers are constantly sermonizing against God's Commandments, or trivializing them.

This has become such a plague that sin and Lawlessness are running rampant in many churches. So many abominations are being committed and tolerated within church buildings that He must judge. He is closing the doors of many churches. As I am writing this message, the doors of all the churches in America, and many other nations, are closed because of the coronavirus. The US government permits no gatherings above ten people. God is knocking on the door to see if there is at least ten righteous within every church family—ten, that will still praise Him and honor His Commandments, with or without church buildings.

YHVH said to Abraham that He would not destroy Sodom and Gomorra if there were at least ten righteous.

> Then he said, "Please, let not my Lord be angry, so I may speak once more. Perhaps ten will be found there?" And He said, "I will not destroy it for the sake of the ten."
>
> — GENESIS 18:32

God is giving us all an enormous opportunity to make our homes an altar of prayer and worship so we can find rest, a Shabbat for our souls. He is knocking at all our doors to return to the original foundations of faith, and to the same gospel the Jewish apostles preached—a gospel that called the believers to holiness and obedience to His Commandments, to Shabbat rest, biblical feasts and holy worship.

No Easter Celebrations

> Go, my people, enter your rooms, and shut your doors behind you. Hide for a little while, until the wrath is past. For behold, ADONAI is coming out from His place to punish inhabitants of the earth for iniquity. The earth will disclose her bloodshed, no longer covering up her slain.
>
> — ISAIAH 26:20–21

Because of the lockdown due to COVID-19, no churches could celebrate Easter; no pageantries would take place in the spring of 2020, not even in the Holy Land. For years, the shofar (trumpet) has been blowing to call the Church out of replacement theology and pagan Roman celebrations into observing the biblical feasts.

Easter is not the feast of resurrection of Messiah, but both the name and the date are from the Babylonian-Roman goddess of fertility named Ishtar. Ishtar was part of the sun worship pantheon* of Babylon, Greece, and Rome. They worshipped her through orgies, where women would have sex with the priests of the temple of Ishtar. Then they would birth babies out of these orgies. A year later, the babies would be three months old, and a tithe, or a portion of the "harvest" of babies would be sacrificed to the goddess to entreat her for more fertility and more babies.

<u>Then eggs would be dipped in the blood of the slaughtered babies, and they would display the blood painted eggs for all to see how many babies were sacrificed to the goddess.</u> Out of this worship came the Easter tradition of painted eggs—including chocolate eggs and the bunny rabbits that have nothing to do with the resurrection of the Jewish Messiah Yeshua. Bunny rabbits have been symbols of fertility and immorality ever since Babylon. Even pornographic magazines like Playboy use a bunny as their logo. Young girls dressed with bunny ears and tails serve drinks in clubs, representing Ishtar worship to the goddess of fertility and immorality.

How can we possibly refer to the Resurrection Feast of a Jewish Messiah with the name of the goddess Ishtar (Easter) and include pagan Roman traditions? This is the legacy of replacement theology that we cannot ignore any longer. Our God is knocking on the door of every heart, and every church and denomination to do *teshuva*, to repent, return and be restored to the gospel made in Zion and to a Jewish Messiah rather than a Roman Christ. Constantine instituted

---

* A pantheon (from Greek πάνθεον pantheon, literally "(a temple) is the particular set of all gods of any individual polytheistic religion, mythology, or tradition. (Oxford English Dictionary)

Easter when he forbade celebrating Passover, seen as a Jewish celebration. But Passover and First Fruits is all about the blood covenant, the death, burial, and resurrection of Yeshua.

Yeshua celebrated Passover, not "Easter" or Ishtar with His disciples when the following took place,

> For I received from THE LORD what I also passed on to you—that THE LORD Yeshua, on the night He was betrayed, took matzah;* and when He had given thanks, He broke it and said, "This is My body, which is for you. Do this in memory of Me." In the same way, He also took the cup, after supper, saying, "This cup is the new covenant in My blood. Do this, as often as you drink it, in memory of Me." For as often as you eat this bread and drink this cup, you proclaim THE LORD's death until He comes.
>
> — 1 CORINTHIANS 11:23–26

But Constantine took Easter, the pagan Roman Feast of Ishtar, and dressed her in "Christian garments." However, he kept the date and the pagan traditions intact.

The Council of Nicaea

From the letter of the Emperor (Constantine) to all those not present at the council. (Found in Eusebius, Vita Const., Lib III 18-20)

When the question relative to the sacred festival of Easter arose, it was universally thought that it would be convenient

---

* Matzah: an unleavened flatbread that is part of Jewish cuisine and forms an integral element of the Passover festival.

that all should keep the feast on one day; for what could be more beautiful and more desirable than to see this festival, through which we receive the hope of immortality, celebrated by all with one accord and in the same manner? It was declared to be particularly unworthy for this, the holiest of festivals to follow the customs (the calculation) of the Jews who had soiled their hands with the most fearful of crimes, and whose minds were blinded. In rejecting their custom we may transmit to our descendants the legitimate mode of celebrating Easter; which we have observed from the time of the Savior's passion according to the day of the week.

We ought not therefore to have anything in common with the Jew, for the Savior has shown us another way; our worship following a more legitimate and more convenient course (the order of the days of the week): And consequently in unanimously adopting this mode, we desire, dearest brethren to separate ourselves from the detestable company of the Jew. (Fordham University)

This separation has been very costly and has led to the murder of millions of Jews in the name of Jesus Christ and his followers. It has also caused the spiritual death of millions of Christians who offended the Holy Spirit by continuing the pagan legacy of the sun worshipper Emperor Constantine through Sunday, Easter, Christmas, and Halloween—All Saints worship.

Christmas or Sukkot?

The Messiah was not born on December 25th, the day of the winter witchcraft solstice. Rather, the pagan Feast of Saturnalia, the worship of the sun-god and evergreen trees occurred on that date. Yeshua was born (according to many present-day scholars) during the Feast of Sukkot, the Feast of Tabernacles, when all nations are commanded to come up to Jerusalem during His millennial reign, after God pours out His wrath on the nations that attacked Israel.

> Then all the survivors from all the nations that attacked Jerusalem will go up from year to year to worship the King, ADONAI-Tzva'ot, and to celebrate Sukkot. Furthermore, if any of the nations on earth do not go up to Jerusalem to worship the King, ADONAI-Tzva'ot, they will have no rain.
>
> — ZECHARIAH 14:16–17

The "convenient course of worship," separating Christians from everything Jewish, espoused by Constantine and the Gentile church fathers of the fourth century, has been deadly and bloody in every way. Most of the pogroms in Europe by the Church against the Jews took place either on Christmas or Easter.

Here are a few examples from the historical records:

Older Jewish religious texts instructed all Jews to stay home on Christmas Eve because Christians might attack or even kill them. Historically speaking, however, far more acts of violence were committed against Jews during Easter, when Christians mark the day Jesus died, than during Christmas when he was supposedly born.

Pogroms would also break out forty days after Easter, the day when Christians believe that Jesus ascended to heaven. Springtime generally saw more attacks against Jews than

December, as the weather was warmer and the ground wasn't covered in snow. (Gottesman)

The term pogrom came into frequent use around 1881 after anti-Semitic violence erupted following the assassination of Czar Alexander II. Anti-Jewish groups claimed the government had approved reprisals against Jews. The first violence broke out in Yelizavetgrad, Ukraine, and then spread to 30 other towns, including Kiev.

During Christmas of the same year, Russia-controlled Warsaw, Poland, exploded in violence that resulted in the death of two Jews. The stampede deaths of 29 people after a church fire was falsely blamed on Jewish pickpockets.

Murderous outbreaks against Jews continued through 1884 in Belorussia, Lithuania, Rostov and Yekaterinoslav. Nizhni Novgorod hosted the final Russian pogrom of this period, resulting in the death of nine Jews. (History.com Editors)

April 17, 1389, was the first day of a two-day assault mounted on the Jewish community of Prague by its Christian neighbors. The Prague Pogrom, as it has come to be called, led to the deaths of an estimated 900 Jews, although some of the historical chronicles that described the events give numbers far higher than that.

Like so many medieval massacres of Jews in Europe, the Prague Pogrom took place during Catholic Holy Week, around the celebration of Easter. The spark that set off the attack was, as was often the case, an accusation of "host desecration" (when supposedly "blasphemous Jews" physically abuse the Eucharist wafer which, according to Christian tradition, is transformed into the body of Christ when a churchgoer takes communion). (Haaretz.com)

Medieval Christians thus received the message on Good Friday that the Jews who lived in their midst were the enemies of Christians who killed their Savior and needed to either convert to Christianity or face divine punishment. This language about Jews in the medieval Good Friday liturgy often carried over into physical violence toward local Jewish communities.

It was common for Jewish houses to be attacked with stones. Often these attacks were led by the clergy. David Nirenberg, a scholar of medieval Jewish-Christian relations, argues that this violence reenacted the violence of Jesus' suffering and death.

Another scholar of this history, Lester Little, argues that the attack on the Jewish community was meant to be a revenge for the death of Jesus and a ritual act that reinforced the boundary between Jews and Christians. (Joslyn-Siemiatkoski)

Passover and First Fruits

But the fact is that the Messiah has been raised from the dead, the first fruits of those who have died.

— 1 CORINTHIANS 15:20 CJB

Yeshua did not die on Good Friday, but on Passover, which fell on a Wednesday. He was in the grave for three days and three nights, as He Himself prophesied when referring to the Sign of Jonah.

For just as Jonah was in the belly of the great fish for three days and three nights, so the Son of Man will be in the heart of the earth for three days and three nights.

— MATTHEW 12:40

The correct time of the resurrection of the Jewish Messiah is not during the fertility rites of Ishtar, but during the biblical Feast of First Fruits and Unleavened Bread following the Passover.

Get rid of the old hametz (leaven/sin), so you may be a new batch, just as you are unleavened—for Messiah, our Passover Lamb, has been sacrificed.

— 1 CORINTHIANS 5:7

Yeshua is not our "Easter Lamb"; He is our "Passover Lamb."

He rose from the dead during the Feast of First Fruits, and Messiah is the first fruits of the Resurrection. As YHVH gave the Passover instructions to Moses for Israel, He said to bring Him the offering of first fruits on the first day of the week after the Shabbat that falls during the Passover and Feast of Matza (Unleavened Bread).

Then the Lord spoke to Moses, saying, "Speak to the sons of Israel and say to them, 'When you enter the land which I am going to give to you and reap its harvest, then you shall bring in the sheaf of the first fruits of your harvest to the priest. He shall wave the sheaf before the Lord for you to be accepted; on the day after the sabbath the priest shall wave it.'"

— LEVITICUS 23:9–11 NASB

The biblical day starts in the evening, not in the morning with sunrise; therefore, the first day of the week starts with the sunset "after the Shabbat" or the Seventh Day of rest.

So there was evening and there was morning—one day.

— **GENESIS 1:5B**

Yeshua rises from the dead after *three* days and *three* nights in the grave.

He rises as the sun sets on the Shabbat, officially making it the first day of the week, the day of elevating the first fruits offering to YHVH. When the sun sets on the seventh day (the Shabbat), the Son of God rises from the dead. He spends three shabbats, days of rest in the grave. According to the Torah, the first day of the Feast of Passover/Unleavened Bread is a Shabbat, a day of rest and a holy convocation. According to Jewish tradition, this continues for *two* days in walled cities so that all Jews in exile in different time zones can also catch up. Then came the seventh day, which was a third Shabbat. As the weekly Shabbat ended, THE LORD of the Shabbat, Yeshua, rose from the dead.

For the Son of Man is Lord of Shabbat.

— **MATTHEW 12:8**

The "sunrise" tradition comes from Rome where the sun god is worshipped, as is Easter/Ishtar; however, the sun bowed down to the Son of Yah (God) that rises when the sun sets. That is why Miriam (Mary) came to the tomb when it was still dark on the first day, and Yeshua was not in the tomb, for He had risen on Saturday night.

> Now on the first day of the week Mary Magdalene came early to the tomb, while it was still dark, and saw the stone already taken away from the tomb.
>
> — JOHN 20:1 NASB

The Shabbat and COVID-19

> Remember Yom Shabbat (the Sabbath day), to keep it holy. You are to work six days, and do all your work, but the seventh day is a Shabbat to ADONAI your God. In it you shall not do any work—not you, nor your son, your daughter, your male servant, your female servant, your cattle, nor the outsider that is within your gates. For in six days ADONAI made heaven and earth, the sea, and all that is in them, and rested on the seventh day. Thus ADONAI blessed Yom Shabbat, and made it holy.
>
> — EXODUS 20:8–11

Most of the world works seven days a week, constantly breaking the Fourth Commandment. Since Israel is a mixture of secular with conservative and religious people, they do not keep Shabbat in many parts of Israel, like Tel Aviv for example. In Jerusalem, mostly, the shops are closed for Shabbat (the Seventh Day of rest), and there is no public transport. For the first time in modern Israel's history, the entire country had to keep Shabbat in the spring of 2020 because of the coronavirus lockdown. It was an outstanding feeling. All other nations that went into lockdown observed this. Since most businesses, schools, and churches were closed, people stayed in their houses on Shabbat. In America, Saturdays are the busiest days with shops remaining open for longer hours. But during COVID-19 nearly all of mankind was forced to *rest* and to keep Shabbat!

Most ministers have preached to their congregation that Shabbat is not for Christians, that it's acceptable to do whatever one wants on His holy day, but this is reminiscent of replacement theology. In fact, the first believers in Messiah, both Jew and Gentile, originally met on Shabbat in the synagogues. They kept Shabbat as late as AD 364, when the Council of Laodicea forbade the practice, because they said this was "Jewish."

> Canon 29: Christians shall not Judaize and be idle on Saturday, but shall work on that day; but the Lord's day they shall especially honor, and, as being Christians, shall if possible, do no work on that day. If, however, they are found Judaizing, they shall be shut out from Christ. (The Sabbath Sentinel)

"After this I will return and rebuild the fallen tabernacle of David. I will rebuild its ruins and I will restore it, so that the rest of humanity may seek THE LORD—namely all the Gentiles who are called by My name—says ADONAI, who makes these things known from of old." Therefore, I judge not to trouble those from among the Gentiles who are turning to God—but to write to them to abstain from the contamination of idols, and from sexual immorality, and from what is strangled, and from blood. <u>For Moses from ancient generations has had in</u>

every city those who proclaim him, since he is read in all the synagogues every Shabbat.

— Acts 15:16–21

The apostles expected Gentile believers to go to the synagogues to hear the Torah as given to Moses. Then the Holy Spirit would convict them of sin and write Gods Torah Commandments in their hearts. Jews and Gentiles worshipped together in the same olive tree, with the same Jewish Messiah and gospel. This was the pre-Constantine era.

I have already shared how the Eastern Roman Emperor Constantine and the Gentile church fathers of the fourth century established another gospel and another worship system with a Roman Christ, pagan Roman feasts, and traditions. However, keeping the Shabbat holy is one of the Ten Commandments, which I call the Heavenly Constitution. The people of Israel were the recipients of this Heavenly Constitution, but the purpose was to share its godly principles with all nations.

> **Also, the foreigners who join themselves to ADONAI, to minister to Him, and to love the Name of ADONAI, and to be His servants—all who keep from profaning Shabbat, and hold fast to My covenant— these I will bring to My holy mountain, and let them rejoice in My House of Prayer. Their burnt offerings and sacrifices will be acceptable on My altar. For My House will be called a House of Prayer for all nations.**

— Isaiah 56:6–7

Nowhere in the Holy Scriptures does it say that the Creator changed the Seventh Day, or that He instead blessed Sunday. He never replaced

His holy day! However, Constantine, being a sun-worshipper, established the Sun Day to worship the sun god in a Christianity that he instituted. Initially, many believers opposed this move, having known the truth for the 300 years prior to the Council of Nicaea. But Constantine, backed by the Gentile church fathers, ruled with an iron fist— so Shabbat was forbidden and Sunday worship was instituted instead. This state of affairs continues to this very day. But the God of the Bible is calling all of mankind to rest and to worship Him on his holy day, not in sun worshipper Constantine's Sun-day. In fact, true Shabbat worship will prevail throughout the millennial reign of Messiah Yeshua from Jerusalem.

> **"And it will come to pass, that from one New Moon to another, and from one Shabbat to another, all flesh will come to bow down before Me," says ADONAI.**

> — ISAIAH 66:23

I believe we can worship YHVH on *every* day of the week, and yet separate the Shabbat as the holy day of rest and worship established at Creation and lasting forever, as the first Church did. Yeshua did not say, "I am THE LORD of the Sunday," but declared, "I am THE LORD of the Shabbat" (Mat. 12:8). He is calling us back from sun worship to biblical holy worship.

For the Son of Man is Lord of Shabbat.

> — MATTHEW 12:8

Passover, Easter, and COVID-19

During the COVID-19 pandemic, people were in lockdown. All churches and most businesses were closed during March to April 2020. There was no way to hold Easter services and pageantries, since those services need a church building and many people in attendance. The government allowed gatherings of up to ten people maximum. However, Passover celebrations continued as usual as these take place within homes.

Like all the biblical feasts of Israel, Passover and Unleavened Bread are celebrated at home with family first. Jewish families could still celebrate Passover during the COVID-19 lockdown. Again, the God of Israel was emphasizing the return to the original foundations of the gospel and moving the altar of worship away from church buildings to the family homes.

God ordained the first biblical lockdown to protect His people from the plague sent against Egypt. He then commanded the people to eat the sacrificed lambs and celebrate the Passover within their families forever.

> Then Moses called for all the elders of Israel and said to them, "Go, select lambs for your families and slaughter the Passover lamb. You are to take a bundle of hyssop, dip it in the blood that is in the basin, and apply it to the crossbeam and two doorposts with the blood from the basin. <u>None of you may go out the door of his house until morning.</u> ADONAI will pass through to strike down the Egyptians, but when He sees the blood on the crossbeam and the two doorposts, ADONAI will pass over that door, and will not allow the destroyer to come

into your houses to strike you down. Also you are to observe this event as an eternal ordinance, for you and your children.

— EXODUS 12:21–24

The Romans crucified Yeshua during Passover, and He became the Passover Lamb.

> Your boasting (about sin and immorality) is no good. Don't you know that a little hametz (leaven) leavens the whole batch of dough? Get rid of the old hametz, so you may be a new batch, just as you are unleavened—for Messiah, our Passover Lamb, has been sacrificed. Therefore, let us celebrate the Feast (of Passover, not Easter) not with old hametz, the hametz of malice and wickedness, but with unleavened bread— the matzah of sincerity and truth.

— 1 CORINTHIANS 5:6–8

Time to Get Rid of the Old Leaven

> Get rid of the old hametz (leaven), so you may be a new batch, just as you are unleavened—for Messiah, our Passover Lamb, has been sacrificed.

— 1 CORINTHIANS 5:7

In Hebrew, Torah means the "instructions of God in righteousness." Though the Torah is used to describe various Jewish books such as

Talmud and Gemara,* in its original context it refers to the Five Books of Moses, the Commandments YHVH gave to the people of Israel. The Sacrificial Laws are not for us today, since Yeshua the Jewish Messiah and Passover Lamb is the ultimate sacrifice. But the moral social laws, and even worship principles are alive and well, and they need to be written in our hearts and minds. This is the mark of the New Covenant as given to the people of Israel, and what the Jewish apostles of the first century shared with the Gentiles.

> "Behold, days are coming," declares the LORD, "when I will make a new covenant with the house of Israel and with the house of Judah, not like the covenant which I made with their fathers in the day I took them by the hand to bring them out of the land of Egypt, My covenant which they broke, although I was a husband to them," declares the LORD. "But this is the covenant which I will make with the house of Israel after those days," declares the LORD, "I will put My Law within them and on their heart I will write it; and I will be their God, and they shall be My people. They will not teach again, each man his neighbor and each man his brother, saying, 'Know the LORD,' for they will all know Me, from the least of them to the greatest of them," declares the LORD, "for I will forgive their iniquity, and their sin I will remember no more."
>
> — JEREMIAH 31:31–34 NASB

---

* The Talmud is the Jewish civil and ceremonial law and legend that makes up the Mishnah and Gemara. The Mishna is the first major written collection of Jewish oral traditions, and the Gemara is a rabbinical commentary of the Mishnah.

The depth of deception is deep concerning the Laws and standards of the Almighty. A "cheap grace gospel" has been preached. People are now familiar with motivational speakers and pastors caressing their ears, turning a blind eye to the sin and Lawlessness in their churches. This has caused a situation of no glory (*ichabod* in Hebrew) as mentioned in the book of 1 Samuel, when the High Priest Eli failed to correct his sons.

> Then ADONAI said to Samuel, "Behold, I am about to do something in Israel at which both ears of everyone that hears it will tingle. In that day I will perform against Eli all that I have spoken concerning his house, from beginning to end. For I have told him <u>that I am about to judge his house forever for the iniquity that he knew about, because his sons brought a curse on themselves yet he did not rebuke them.</u> Therefore I have sworn to the house of Eli that the iniquity of Eli's house will never be atoned for by sacrifice or offering."
>
> — 1 SAMUEL 3:11–14

Pastors have not corrected their flocks; they are afraid of losing "their sheep" and with them their tithes. But our Father cannot overlook this anymore, as His sheep are being kept in a perpetual state of "spiritual Egypt" by being slaves to sin, immorality, greed, and idolatry.

The biggest deception comes from the fact that the Church is divorced from the Lion of Judah, and His ways, because it has replaced His identity with a Romanized, Gentilized Christ that winks at sin. She is far away from the gospel made in Zion, which has been replaced with a Western, humanistic, counterfeit gospel—a gospel without repentance, holiness, righteousness, and obedience.

> But even if we (or an angel from heaven) should announce any "good news" to you other than what we have proclaimed to you, let that person be cursed! As we have said before, so I now repeat: if anyone proclaims to you "good news" other than what you received, let that person be under a curse! Am I now trying to win people's approval, or God's? Or am I trying to please people? If I were still trying to please people, I would not be a servant of Messiah.

> — GALATIANS 1:8–10

Two thousand years ago, Messiah Yeshua warned us of this very thing in the Gospel of Matthew; and here we are today facing consequences that are exactly what He warned about.

> Do not think I came to abolish the Law (Torah) or the Prophets! I did not come to abolish, but to fulfill. Amen, I tell you, until heaven and earth pass away, not the smallest letter or serif shall ever pass away from the Torah until all things come to pass. Therefore, whoever breaks one of the least of these Commandments, and teaches others the same, shall be called least in the kingdom of heaven. But whoever keeps and teaches them, this one shall be called great in the kingdom of heaven. For I tell you that unless your righteousness exceeds that of the Pharisees and Torah scholars, you shall never enter the kingdom of heaven!

> — MATTHEW 5:17–20

Preachers in most churches have echoed the mantra: "The Law is done away with, and you need not keep the Laws of God; you are now under grace." They give countless deceived churchgoers a placebo every

Sunday to make them feel good about themselves with no repentance or change of lifestyle required. We are dooming an entire generation to hell if we do not change the narrative urgently!

Yeshua stated in Matthew 5, "Do not even think to yourselves that I came to abolish the Torah (My Father's Laws and Commandments) and all that the (Hebrew) prophets have instructed and prophesied. I have come to bring a full interpretation of these; without Me and My Holy Spirit you cannot walk in righteousness. But with Me and through Me, you can both keep and teach these. In fact, if you do not obey My Father's Commandments more than the religious leaders of Israel do, you who have believed in Me will not even enter the kingdom of heaven!"

This is far away from the narrative in the churches today that says: the Law is done away with. How can we expect to have victory in our walk if we do not obey the words of our Jewish Messiah? He declared that the standard of holiness and righteousness for us in the New Covenant is a much higher standard than that in the Old Covenant. He was not talking about the laws of sacrifice because He would become the ultimate sacrifice for sins. But He definitely meant that our moral, social, and worship standards should be higher than those of the Pharisees, who were the Torah observant leaders of Israel in His day.

Notice the continuation of His warning in this chapter of Matthew 5, as it states the principle of these higher standards.

You have heard it was said to those of old, "You shall not murder, and whoever commits murder shall be subject to judgment." But I tell you that everyone who is angry with his brother shall be subject to judgment. And whoever says to his brother, "*Reka*" (Aramaic for "worthless") shall be subject to

> the council; and whoever says, 'You fool!' shall be subject to fiery Gehenna (hell).
>
> — MATTHEW 5:21–22

God regards cursing or hating our brothers and sisters as murder—not only the act of killing someone, but the words and the heart of unholy anger and hatred is judged. Lord, have mercy! How many of us have unknowingly been murderers?

Yeshua continues expounding on the Torah, the Commandments of His and our Father:

> You have heard that it was said, "You shall not commit adultery." But I tell you that everyone who looks upon a woman to lust after her has already committed adultery with her in his heart.
>
> — MATTHEW 5:27–28

Under the New Covenant, the sin of adultery is not only an act of fornication with another's spouse, or with a man or woman one is not lawfully married to, but even lusting in one's heart without committing the act is judged as adultery. The millions of Christian men that delve in pornography on the internet are committing flagrant adultery, by lusting with their eyes after other women in their hearts and minds. Yeshua was very clear about what to do in these circumstances, and it has nothing to do with the self-indulgent, pale, and tolerant sermons that are preached today. This is what He said.

> And if your right eye causes you to stumble, gouge it out and throw it away! It is better for you that one part of your body

should be destroyed, than that your whole body be thrown into Gehenna (hell). And if your right hand causes you to stumble, cut it off and throw it away! It is better for you that one part of your body should be destroyed, than that your whole body go into Gehenna (hell).

— MATTHEW 5:29–30

He said we needed to be radical and thoroughly committed to uprooting sin and perversion from our lives! These wishy-washy, tolerant messages which deceive the people into Lawlessness is a great offense against the Great Shepherd of His sheep. He is about to remove those shepherds who keep their flocks in bondage to a lawless gospel rooted in replacement theology and hatred of the Torah, the Laws of God.

Therefore, shepherds, hear the Word of ADONAI: "As I live"— it is a declaration of ADONAI—"as surely as My sheep became prey and My sheep became food for all the beasts of the field, because there was no shepherd, nor did My shepherds search for My flock, but the shepherds fed themselves and did not feed My sheep," therefore, you shepherds, hear the Word of ADONAI, thus says ADONAI ELOHIM: "Behold, I am against the shepherds and I will demand My flock from their hand. I will dismiss them from tending the flock. The shepherds will no longer feed themselves. I will rescue My sheep from their mouth, so they will not be food for them."

— EZEKIEL 34:7–10

This late hour is not a time to "play church." It is time to repent and go back to the ancient ways given to the people of Israel, and as preached by the Jewish apostles two thousand years ago. I assure you that not one of these Jewish apostles would have tolerated churches full of sin, immorality, homosexuality, abortion, drunkenness, addiction, rebellion, and greed. They would be totally shocked to see today's Church, and how the true prophetic voices are silenced in favor of those who caress the ears of the flock of Yah (God).

> Or don't you know that the unrighteous will not inherit the kingdom of God? Don't be deceived! The sexually immoral, idolaters, adulterers, those who practice homosexuality, thieves, the greedy, drunkards, slanderers, swindlers—none of these will inherit the kingdom of God. That is what some of you were—but you were washed, you were made holy, you were set right in the name of THE LORD Yeshua the Messiah and by the Ruach (Spirit) of our God.
>
> — 1 CORINTHIANS 6:9–11

The Laws of God are Eternal

> What shall we say then? Are we to continue in sin so that grace may abound? May it never be! How can we who died to sin still live in it? Or do you not know that all of us who were immersed into Messiah Yeshua were immersed into His death? Therefore we were buried together with Him through immersion into death—in order that just as Messiah was

raised from the dead by the glory of the Father, so we too might walk in newness of life.

— ROMANS 6:1–4

Please notice that the New (or Renewed) Covenant is not made with the Gentiles but with Judah and Israel. The Gentiles have access to the New Covenant through the Jewish Messiah as they *join* with their Jewish brethren in the New Covenant. There is no such thing as the Gentile Church. The Church is, all of it, grafted into Israel. There is not a 'unique Gentile Church' and a 'unique Jewish Church.' There is only *one* Ecclesia Church, and it is grafted into the olive tree (read Rom. 11 and Rev. 21). The Church needs to return to its original identity!

And though each nation carries a unique identity and calling, the focal point and the foundational laws have to be the same: the same God, the same Word and Torah, the same Spirit, the same allegiance to the people of Israel.

So why is the Church celebrating different feasts than the ones written in the Bible? It is because of replacement theology that removed everything Jewish from the Church, adopting Roman pagan feasts instead, dressing them up as if they were holy. This is identity theft! Beloved ones, you can dress up a pig to look like a lamb, but it still smells like a pig. The God of Israel has been knocking at the doors of the churches for many years, urging them to forsake the Romanized feasts with its pagan traditions. However, these preachers have tried to please the flock more than please the shepherd of the flock who is Yeshua.

Even many ministers who preach about the Jewish roots of the faith and Israel have compromised the truth in order not to lose their partners and followers. Many have been careful not to offend other Christians, but have they been careful not to offend the God of Israel?

He is the one who said not to follow the ways of the Gentiles in worship. He Himself commanded not to decorate trees as a sign of worship. And yet millions of Christians bring their Christmas trees home, and pastors place them prominently in their churches and "fasten them with nails." The Christmas tree is a pagan tradition from the Feast of Saturnalia that preceded Christmas, and it is a feast of idolatry and sun worship. Why would we think this pleases a Jewish Messiah?

> Hear the Word that ADONAI speaks to you, house of Israel, Thus says ADONAI: "Do not learn the way of the nations or be frightened by signs of the heavens— though the nations are terrified by them. The customs of the peoples are useless: it is just a tree cut from the forest, the work of the hands of a craftsman with a chisel. They decorate it with silver and gold, and fasten it with hammer and nails so it won't totter.
>
> — JEREMIAH 10:1–4

There is so much "political correctness" where truth has been compromised. Preachers continue pleasing the people by teaching the traditions of men that offend the Almighty and causes the Holy Spirit to retreat from our churches. The internet is full of information about this. Many have preached and written many books about the importance of repentance from celebrating Christian feasts rooted in paganism. YHVH has been calling the Church for many, many years to embrace holy worship by rejecting Romanized Christianity with its pagan feasts—returning to the biblical feasts as He gave them to the people of Israel to share with all mankind.

As long as we dress the Church in Roman Christian feasts, its identity is still stolen, and the Jewish identity of the Messiah will remain hidden from the masses. Then, anti-Semitism will continue running rampant in many Christian circles. God is holy, and He is calling us to worship Him in Spirit and Truth (Jn. 4:24). Christmas, Easter, Halloween/All Saints and Sunday worship are an inheritance from Rome and Babylon and has nothing to do with the Jewish Messiah Yeshua. Satan established all this as part of a demonic plan through the Eastern Roman Emperor Constantine and the fourth century church fathers to separate the Church from Israel forever. By doing so, the devil wanted to separate the Church from the Jewish Messiah by bringing in a counterfeit Romanized Jesus Christ, with Roman pagan feasts and with laws contrary to the biblical Laws from the Torah.

All of this is the greatest identity theft in history! And it is costing the redemption of millions of people, causing entire nations to miss becoming Sheep Nations until the bride of Messiah is restored to her identity as the grafted-in bride of a Jewish bridegroom. Yeshua would not have dared to celebrate Roman feasts defying the Commandments of His Father, let alone put up trees or call feasts by the name of foreign gods such as Ishtar/Easter with pagan traditions.

It is high time to restore biblical holidays (holy days) to the Church worldwide, without the compromise of pagan mixtures that many are espousing, such as putting up Christmas trees next to Hanukkah menorahs, or celebrating Easter and Passover together. The God of Israel does not share worship with the gods of Rome. It is the God of Israel and His worship, or Rome. There is no compromise.

He said either to be hot or cold. He does not tolerate the mixture at all. I know that this is not politically correct, and it may ruffle many feathers, but it is biblically correct. And like my father Elijah said thousands of years ago,

> Then Elijah approached all the people and said, "How long will you waver between two opinions? If ADONAI is God, follow Him; but if Baal is, follow him."

> — 1 KINGS 18:21

All the feasts of Christianity are borrowed from Rome, from sun worship, which is Baal worship. Just like in ancient Israel, their leaders confused people. Instead of leaders teaching them the truth, they were keeping them in bondage to a mixture of worship, "A little Hebrew, a little pagan" just to satisfy the masses, but they were greatly offending the God of Israel. He sent His prophet Elijah to confront that compromise, and He is doing it again by the Spirit of Elijah. He is calling us to finally make a decision whether we will remain Roman Christians, grafted into the Christmas tree, or become a covenanted bride that is grafted into the Olive tree in our worship.

> But if some of the branches were broken off and you—being a wild olive—were grafted in among them and became a partaker of the root of the olive tree with its richness, do not boast against the branches. But if you do boast, it is not you who support the root but the root supports you.

> — ROMANS 11:17–18

How many in the Evangelical Church really know that their worship is Catholic and that they still attach to them with a spiritual umbilical cord to the Roman Catholic Church? Do they discern that

it is Roman Christianity from which Easter, Christmas, Halloween/
All Saints, and Sunday worship come? And that it was not so until the
fourth century—for 300 years believers in the Jewish Messiah celebrated Shabbat and the biblical feasts, and called the Jewish Messiah
by His name, Yeshua.

It is time to remove the Roman garments—pagan feasts—and put
on the biblical ones. Restoring holy worship will restore the identity
of the bride of Messiah and the Jewish Messiah. It will make the Jewish
people jealous to receive Him back.

"Remove the Pig Identity from My People."

> For by fire and His sword ADONAI will execute judgment on
> all flesh and those slain by ADONAI will be many. Those who
> consecrate and purify themselves to enter the groves, follow-
> ing after one in the midst, who eat swine's flesh, vermin and
> mice, will come to an end altogether.
>
> — ISAIAH 66:16–17

The COVID-19 pandemic in the spring of 2020 brought to a head the
realization that unclean animals bring terrible plagues (the coronavirus
plague reportedly started in the unclean animal market of Wuhan,
China, where they sell many unclean animals and vermin for human
consumption). Here, COVID-19 came from a bat which is a mouse
with wings. YHVH in His word says that He will bring judgment on
all of mankind for eating unclean animals. In Isaiah 66 God mentioned
swine or pigs, vermin, and mice. In Leviticus 11 He gives a longer list
and calls the unclean animals loathsome. For example, God calls shell-
fish and catfish "detestable."

But any that do not have fins and scales in the seas or the rivers, among those that swarm on the waters, or among any of the living creatures that are in the waters, they are loathsome to you. They are to be detestable to you. You shall not eat meat from them and you should detest their carcasses. Whatever has neither fins nor scales in the waters, that is a detestable thing to you.

— Leviticus 11:10–12

Jews that converted to Christianity, by force or willingly, were required to show throughout the ages they were "real Christians" and that they were "really saved" by eating pork and unclean animals. When I, being a Jew, surrendered my life to Yeshua, the first instructions some Christians gave me were:

- You are free from the Law
- You can eat all the pork you want

This was confusing: Until then I had been a sinner who had broken Yah's (God's) Commandments, and now should salvation mean that I can stay lawless? It also confuses many others when they hear these strange instructions. Until then, I had been a vegetarian and did not relish meat, let alone pork. But these well-meaning Christians wanted to see me break the Dietary Commandments of the Living God to put them at rest that I was really saved. Many Jewish believers will tell you the same story.

This is rooted in replacement theology and is anti-Semitic. The most anti-Semitic nations in Europe throughout the ages have been Christian nations where pork is the number one staple. In fact, in some of these countries, it is hard to find other meats—pork is the cheapest and the most available. This includes Spain, Portugal, Germany, Poland, and others.

Eating swine, pig, or pork and its derivatives is called "detestable," and is connected with idolatry and the worship of death. It is not surprising, therefore, that Romanized Christianity has made the pig a staple in all pagan Roman Christian feasts and church celebrations.

> **These people provoke Me continually to My face, sacrificing in gardens, burning incense on bricks, sitting among graves, spending the night in cave-tombs; eating swine's flesh, and the broth of detestable things is in their pots...**
>
> **— ISAIAH 65:3–4**

Since Yeshua did not come to abolish the Torah and the Prophets, He has not abolished the Dietary Commandments either (Mat. 5:17-21). Noah knew about the clean and unclean animals before God gave the Torah. He brought to the Ark seven by seven of the clean animals and two by two of the unclean animals.

> **Of every clean animal you shall take with you seven of each kind, male and female; and of the animals which themselves are not clean two, male and female;**
>
> **— GENESIS 7:2**

ELOHIM created the clean animals for sacrifice and food and the unclean for ecological purposes, such as garbage processors to clean the earth. Most Christians are often repeatedly ill because of unclean eating, and this also affects their spiritual lives.

It is told that a great apostle of faith named Smith Wigglesworth in the early 20th century was asked to bless a roasted pig on the table by "saying grace." People knew him well for his bluntness, and the only book he ever read was the Bible. He knew the Word of God backwards and forwards. He knew that pigs are unclean animals, and that God called them "loathsome," so he prayed:

"Dear God, if you can bless what you have cursed, bless this pig in Jesus' name. Amen." (Liardon)

Sounds funny, but it's not a joke; unclean animals bring a curse to our bodies and our spiritual walks. The God of the Universe said that He will execute judgment upon all unclean eaters. I hope God does not find you among them. The coronavirus called the world to attention.

Christendom misinterpreted many New Covenant Scriptures through replacement theology doctrines. Please understand that Yeshua is the Word made flesh; thus, He is the Torah made flesh, which is the Word of His Father. He did not come to oppose His Father's Commandments, but to bring the full interpretation of them.

Christians that break the Dietary Commandments are defiling the Temple of the Holy Spirit, which are their bodies. Just like in the holy Temple in Jerusalem, worshippers could not offer pigs or unclean animals on the altar, so eating unclean animals defiles us and makes us sick.

The vision of Peter in Acts 10 was not about sanctioning the eating of clean and unclean animals. It was about a significant change concerning the salvation of the Gentiles. Until then, Jews called Gentiles 'unclean,' because they were outside of the covenant and worshipped idols. Now Yeshua was calling His Jewish apostle to reach out to the Gentiles and not call them unclean anymore. When he came to

Cornelius, the Roman centurion in Caesarea, where all his family and friends were gathered, Peter interpreted the vision he received.

> And he said to them, "You yourselves know how unlawful it is for a man who is a Jew to associate with a foreigner or to visit him; and yet God has shown me that I should not call any man unholy or unclean."

> — ACTS 10:28 NASB

How did YHVH show him? Through a trance in a vision that has been grossly misinterpreted through the glasses of replacement theology.

> But he became hungry and was desiring to eat; but while they were making preparations, he fell into a trance; and he saw the sky opened up, and an object like a great sheet coming down, lowered by four corners to the ground, and there were in it all kinds of four-footed animals and crawling creatures of the earth and birds of the air. A voice came to him, "Get up, Peter, kill and eat!" But Peter said, "By no means, Lord, for I have never eaten anything unholy and unclean."

> — ACTS 10:10–14 NASB

Peter would not eat of it; he never saw Yeshua eating any unclean animals. Yeshua was not sanctioning breaking the Dietary Commandments of His Father, but He was causing Peter to understand that salvation was now granted to the Gentiles that used to be called unclean.

In this same way, scriptures like the following would be misinterpreted:

For everything created by God is good, and nothing is to be rejected if it is received with gratitude; for it is sanctified by means of the Word of God and prayer.

— 1 TIMOTHY 4:4–5 NASB

During Timothy's time the only Word of God available was the Tanakh, the Old Covenant or Holy Scriptures, including the Torah. The New Testament was not canonized until the fourth century after the Council of Nicaea. Until then, what we call the New Testament was made up of the recounts of the Gospels and the apostolic letters addressing issues in the churches. This was never to replace the Holy Scriptures as given to the people of Israel.

He said that our food is sanctified by two things:

- The Word of God, which is the Torah
- Prayer

Prayer alone cannot sanctify your food. It is obedience to His Word, to His Torah, coupled with prayer and gratitude that sanctifies it. The Torah never sanctifies unclean animals, and an End time judgment is already happening (through means like the COVID-19 possibly coming from a bat sold in the unclean meat market of Wuhan, China).

Here is what the end of the book says about entering into the New Jerusalem.

And nothing unclean, and no one who practices abomination and lying, shall ever come into it, but only those whose names are written in the Lamb's book of life.

— REVELATION 21:27 NASB

To find what is unclean and what is an abomination in Yah's (God's) eyes, you need to go to the Torah and have the Holy Spirit write it in your heart.

A great awakening and revival is knocking at the doors. Are you listening? And what will happen to those that refuse to listen? They will dry up, and the glory will pass them by. The Rose will die.

A Prophetic Invitation to You

"Come, let us go up to the mountain of THE LORD, to the house of the God of Jacob; He will teach us His ways, and we shall walk in His path. "For out of Zion shall go forth the Law and the Word of Yahveh from Jerusalem."

Isaiah 2:3 NASB

No Holiness, No Power, No Glory!
Are you sighing?

YHVH said to him, "Go through the midst of the city, even through the midst of Jerusalem, and put a mark on the foreheads of the men who sigh and groan over all the abominations which are being committed in its midst."

— EZEKIEL 9:4 NASB

The last time that I attended a revival meeting was in Lakeland, Florida, in 2008. The evangelist that led this revival was Todd Bentley. The revival died after August 2008, when the evangelist left the hosting place at *Ignited Church*. The reason for the sudden stop was the marital problems between Todd and his wife, which eventually led to their divorce. This divorce happened because of a wrong relationship with another woman, who he eventually married.

Charisma Magazine covered this issue; here is a quote from October 15, 2009:

> At the time, leaders of what is now known as Transform International, which is no longer affiliated with Bentley, expressed concern about the evangelist's relationship with Jessa as well as his alcohol consumption, which a senior board member said had "crossed the line." (Gaines)

Beloved ones, Todd Bentley was doing his best to be a vessel of the Holy Spirit to bring revival to the USA and to the world. People came from many nations to his meetings, about 30,000 people weekly attended. Bentley's ministry estimated that over 140,000 visited from over 40 nations, and 1.2 million people had watched via the Internet. By June 30th, over 400,000 people from over 100 nations had attended, as God TV broadcast his meetings nightly.

As a general rule, I look at the spiritual *fruit* produced at such events, and do not put my eyes on the manifestations themselves. Having been used by the Holy Spirit to start revival fires in many nations, we have seen our share of manifestations. But, after the spiritually dramatic manifestations happen, I like to taste the *fruit*. If the fruit is good, it is the proof of true revival! This is clear if there is a decrease in the area crime rate, or if the number of divorces drops. Is the move followed by more holiness, righteousness, and the fear of YHVH?

Manifestations come and go, but we should never judge them before their time. Some people pridefully oppose the manifestations of the Holy Spirit—that quenches the Spirit fire! But others worship the manifestations and give very little attention to the Word of God, and to discipleship which leads to a righteous lifestyle; therefore, excess manifestations occur that are demonic and not of God. I'd like to share about this from our personal ministry experience.

THE LORD sent us in 1990 to the USA to work as missionaries with *Youth With A Mission* (YWAM) in Kona, Hawaii, and then to attend Bible School at *Christ for the Nations* in Dallas, Texas. While attending Bible school, I wrote a series of books and I called one of them, *Satan, Let My People GO!*

This book described how the Church in America was lukewarm and filled with unrepented sin. It was a call to repentance, to radical obedience, and to righteousness. It was a Divine call to return to the original gospel as preached by all the Jewish apostles during the first century! One well-known pastor who read my book said that it was "religious" and that Christians are under grace, not Law. He strongly exhorted me to accept that we are all in a "process"—sins like immorality, idolatry, and adultery were not a big issue, as people are not perfect and that Jesus understands and forgives.

I was a relatively new believer then, having been saved at the season of Yom Kippur of 1988; I was barely two years old in Yeshua. And I had the "nerve" to write a book calling the Church to repentance, exposing the deadly compromise with sin in most of the American Church, as I experienced it.

This desire to see others walk in holiness also came to me in Israel prior to my trip to the USA, and my marriage to Rabbi Baruch Bierman in 1990. The Holy Spirit would fall on me with a word of exhortation, or rebuke to those pretending to be godly but having hidden sins. Every time I ministered, filled with the love of the Father and the fire of the Ruach (Spirit), people came to repentance. I was a born-again believer, *sighing* over the sad condition of the body of Messiah!

No one preached the gospel to me! Yeshua came to save me Himself, just like He did to the apostle Paul. (You can read my book, *YES*, that describes the very dramatic testimony of my salvation, translated into many languages). My new birth was preceded by a strong conviction of sin and a desperation for purity! When Yeshua called me at the waters of the Kinneret (Sea of Galilee), I did not need convincing that I had broken Yah's Commandments and that I deserved to die. Since no one preached the gospel to me, I understood only this: *We must hate our sins and long for **purity** and **forgiveness** from a holy God that we have offended with our rebellion against His ways and Commandments.*

I could have found plenty of excuses justifying my terrible sins because of my "extenuating circumstances." But, when the fear of YHVH comes upon our lives, there are never any justifiable excuses for immorality, idolatry, and rebellion. In that context, I experienced His amazing grace, and soon experienced the infilling of the Holy Spirit and fire that transformed me into the woman of Yah that I am today. Was I immediately "perfect"? Surely not, and I am still working out my salvation with fear and trembling. But all known sin, such as fornication, adultery, idolatry, cigarette smoking, and cussing, went out of my life in one day after I said '*yes!*' to Yeshua! His holiness did not allow those unclean things to stay in me.

Neither filthiness, nor foolish talking, nor coarse jesting, which are not fitting, but rather giving of thanks. For this you know, that no fornicator, unclean person, nor covetous man, who is an idolater, has any inheritance in the kingdom of Messiah and God. Let no one deceive you with empty words, for

because of these things the wrath of God comes upon the sons of disobedience.

— EPHESIANS 5:4–6 NKJV

Though I know fully that He reaches us wherever we are, in many and creative ways, a gospel without *repentance* from breaking Yah's Commandments, and the release of the fear of YHVH is *no gospel!* A "gospel" that leaves people in their sins, and condones them, and even excuses them in the name of "grace" is a deception!

Yeshua ministered forgiveness to a woman caught in adultery, in opposition to all her accusers who wanted to stone her to death, but His words to her were:

"Then neither do I condemn you," Yeshua said. "Go, and sin no more."

— JOHN 8:11

He had similar words for the paralytic whom he had healed near the Temple:

Afterwards, Yeshua finds him in the Temple. He said to him, "Look, you've been healed! Stop sinning, so nothing worse happens to you."

— JOHN 5:14

Pastors, leaders, saints: It is time to *sigh* and *repent* for all the abominations that are perpetrated inside of Christian churches and Messianic synagogues! We cannot be apathetic any longer! Sighing and repentance must begin, as the judgment knocks at the gates of His Temple, the body of Messiah worldwide. Soon, He will send His angels to *mark* those who *sigh* because of immorality and the idolatry, separating us from those who do not sigh, but call it "the grace gospel."

In the Word of Yah (God), I see the gospel called many things, but I do not read one scripture that refers to "a cheap grace gospel." I see the gospel of the Kingdom, the gospel of peace (or rather shalom), and the eternal gospel. But no "cheap grace gospel" is mentioned anywhere in the Holy Scriptures. The word *grace* is always with *repentance*, forsaking of sin, disobedience, and rebellion, and the ensuing *forgiveness*. Grace is *free*, but it is never cheap, and it never condones sin! His true gospel of grace leads to *repentance*.

> **Or do you have no regard for the wealth of His kindness and tolerance and patience [in withholding His wrath]? Are you [actually] unaware or ignorant [of the fact] that God's kindness leads you to repentance [that is, to change your inner self, your old way of thinking—seek His purpose for your life]? But because of your callous stubbornness and unrepentant heart you are [deliberately] storing up wrath for yourself on the day of wrath when God will reveal righteous judgment. He WILL PAY BACK TO EACH PERSON ACCORDING TO HIS DEEDS [justly, as his deeds deserve]:**
>
> **— ROMANS 2:4–6 AMP**

The purpose of *grace* is to lead us to *repentance*, which is *teshuva* in Hebrew!

> **What shall we say then? Are we to continue in sin so that grace may abound? May it never be! How can we who died to sin**

still live in it? Or do you not know that all of us who were immersed into Messiah Yeshua were immersed into His death?

— ROMANS 6:1–3

The Hebrew word, *teshuva,* means four things:

- The answer
- Returning
- Repentance
- Restoration

**For sin's payment is death, but God's gracious gift is eternal
life in Messiah Yeshua our Lord.**

— ROMANS 6:23

The gospel "made in Zion" is the gospel of the kingdom, the true
gospel of grace. It calls us to return to the Creator—to repentance from
breaking His Commandments. This leads to restoration, portrayed in
the Word as the gospel of shalom: reconciliation, healing, wellbeing,
and integrity (translated as a generic "peace" in most Bibles).

This is the eternal gospel, and there is no other! And this gospel is
followed by signs, wonders and miracles—many dramatic manifestations that culminate in *fruit*, the fruit of *teshuva* (repentance). This is
the gospel that can change and transform our societies, our schools, our
children, and generations into godly societies and into Sheep Nations!

**And I saw another angel flying in mid heaven, having an
eternal gospel to preach to those who live on the earth, and
to every nation and tribe and tongue and people; and he said
with a loud voice, "Fear God, and give Him glory, because**

the hour of His judgment has come; worship Him who made the heaven and the earth and sea and springs of waters." And another angel, a second one, followed, saying, "Fallen, fallen is Babylon the great, she who has made all the nations drink of the wine of the passion of her immorality."

— REVELATION 14:6–8 NASB

God will mark those of us who are in anguish and are sighing with the mark of YHVH, and those who condone sin will carry another mark that will lead to eternal destruction. We are sighing for YHVH to rain righteousness on our children, churches, synagogues, cities, and nations, and we beseech Him to send *revival*! A true revival is born out of *sighing* and a *desperation* for purity.

Blessed are the pure in heart, for they shall see God.

— MATTHEW 5:8

Do not quench the Spirit's Fire.

— 1 THESSALONIANS 5:19

A Life and Death Prayer for Repentance

Father in heaven, forgive me for bearing any marks on me other than Yours, and for any hatred or jealousy against Your Jewish people and Your Commandments. I ask You to mark me as holy unto You, *kadosh le YHVH* (which is Hebrew for "holy to YHVH") as I choose to repent and reject the anti-Torah head of the anti-MESITOJUZ demonic principality completely. Please come with Your Holy Spirit and fire and write Your instructions and Commandments in my heart and mind. I renounce eating all unclean animals as mentioned in Leviticus 11, any immorality and Roman pagan feasts inherited from Romanized Christianity. I hereby rededicate my life in spirit, soul, and body to be a vessel of holy fire and honor, to bring many to righteousness in Yeshua's name. Amen.

For further reading, I recommend you reading my book *Grafted In.* [*]

---

[*] www.kad-esh.org/shop/grafted-in/

ARROGANCE AND ANTI-SEMITISM

Head Number 4: Anti-Jewish

Notice then the kindness and severity of God: severity toward those who fell; but God's kindness toward you, if you continue in His kindness; otherwise you too will be cut off!

— ROMANS 11:22

Anti-Jewish is the fourth head of the monstrous demonic principality called anti-MESITOJUZ. This head results from all the other three:

- Anti-Messiah
- Anti-Israel
- Anti-Torah

The hatred of Jews is wrongly termed anti-Semitism. We coin this word from the name of Shem, the second son of Noah, from whom the Jewish people descend. However, the Arabs are also descendants of Shem, and so are the Chinese. But anti-Semitism is hatred against the Jews only. It would have been better to call it, "Hatred of Jews." Hitler was not looking to exterminate all Arabs or all the Chinese, but he surely meant to exterminate all the Jews. In fact, many prominent Arab figures, such as Haj Amin Al Husseini, the grand mufti of Jerusalem in the 1930s, was an exceptional friend of Hitler, and sought to exterminate the Jews in the land of Israel. We will expound more about this personality in gate 11.

Anti-Semitism, or the Hatred of Jews, is not unique to Christendom. In fact, it is very prevalent among Muslims and other non-religious groups, especially humanistic intellectuals nowadays. But religious persecution against the Jews has been the strict domain of Christianity from the fourth century until the present. Anti-Semitism and Hatred of Jews became Church doctrine through replacement theology. For centuries preachers ranted hatred against the Jews in many of their most passionate sermons. They accused Jews of being murderers of God, Christ killers, of being an accursed race, a brood of vipers, and the likes. Hateful religious rhetoric does not die easily.

We need to understand that the thousands and millions of sermons preached throughout the ages, that either blatantly or implied hateful and derogatory remarks against the Jews, have shaped the Christianity of today. Even if some circles have become enlightened, there are too many other Christian circles that remain in darkness.

Deep within the hearts of many Christians there is a seed of latent anti-Semitism ready to be ignited given the right circumstances. That seed is fed daily by the replacement theology espoused in most churches. Both Catholic and Protestant-Evangelical churches are in the mix. And so are Charismatic prophetic ones. Undoubtedly, there is more light in the 21st century, and today many wonderful Christians do their best to stand for Israel and the Jewish people; but, unfortunately, they are still in the minority.

My husband and I have had the privilege of ministering in over 50 nations and in many denominations. We have encountered the monster of replacement theology in churches of various denominations.

We will list some examples of this.

This Ancient Hatred is Rooted in Jealousy

We can see that the first one to hate Israel with passion is Satan himself. He knows that the very existence of Israel proves the God of the Bible to be true. If Israel disappears, so will any trace of faith in an unfailing, faithful Almighty God—then Satan could reign supremely, which has been his aim since he rebelled against YHVH.

The Fall of Lucifer/Satan

> **How you have fallen from heaven, O bright star, son of the dawn! How you are cut down to the earth, you who made the nations prostrate! You said in your heart: "I will ascend to heaven; I will exalt my throne above the stars of God. I will sit upon the mount of meeting, in the uttermost parts of the north. I will ascend above the high places of the clouds—I will make myself like Elyon." Yet you will be brought down to Sheol, to the lowest parts of the Pit.**
>
> **— ISAIAH 14:12–15**

This ancient snake, who used to be the most important angel in heaven, was thrown down to earth on his way to the pit because of *jealousy*. Jealousy is the root cause of most murders, all the way back to Cain, who murdered righteous Abel in Genesis 4. Lucifer, that means "Star of the Dawn," coveted the place held by the stars of God, and he wanted to be above the stars of God. So, who are these stars of God?

> And said, "By myself I swear—it is a declaration of ADONAI—because you have done this thing, and you did not withhold your son, your only son, I will richly bless you and bountifully multiply your seed <u>like the stars of heaven</u>, and like the sand that is on the seashore, and your seed will possess the gate of his enemies. In your seed all the nations of the earth will be blessed—because you obeyed My voice."
>
> — GENESIS 22:16–18

After Abraham obeyed the Almighty and would sacrifice his only son, Isaac, He gave Abraham the promise "... your descendants will be as the stars in heaven...": These are the stars of God, the descendants of Abraham, and Satan is jealous.

However, this promise is extended through Isaac and Jacob to all the descendants of Israel.

> Remember Abraham, Isaac and Israel, Your servants, to whom You swore by Your own self, and said to them, "I will multiply your seed as the stars of heaven, and all this land that I have spoken of I will give to your offspring, and they will inherit it forever."
>
> — EXODUS 32:13

Here we see the promise "... to be as many as the stars in heaven..." also including the Land of Canaan. We will further develop this topic in gate 11.

To make sure that the stars of God are the people of Israel, the following Scripture is very revealing. This is Moses speaking to all the people of Israel in the desert, after nearly forty years of wandering.

> **ADONAI your God has multiplied you—and here you are today, like the stars of the heavens in number.**
>
> **— DEUTERONOMY 1:10**

Lucifer wanted to be the Messiah; he wanted to exalt himself above the stars of God, above the chosen people of Israel and usurp the place of the King of kings and THE LORD of lords, the ultimate Jew—Yeshua, the Son of David.

Since ELOHIM refused him and banished him, his major plan has been to destroy Israel, the Jewish people, the natural descendants of Abraham, Isaac, and Jacob. This is his main agenda of all the demonic agendas. He is blinded and enraged with jealousy and will use any means and any system to accomplish this destruction.

He found that Gentile Christians could be perverted through jealousy. So he used the Eastern Roman sun worshipper, "pretend-Christian Constantine," together with the compromised bishops of the fourth century to craft a hideous, demonic plan. Satan would carry this plan out through a replacement Christian system that would indoctrinate all its followers to hate the Jews. The priesthood would encourage the people to humiliate and persecute Jews—their motto would be:

"Christ Killers."

The call was to separate from the detestable company of Christ killers, meaning all the Jewish nation. In the root of most Christian hearts, they still have these words resounding: "The Jews rejected Christ; the

Jews are stiff-necked and rebellious; the Jews murdered Christ; they are under a curse; they deserve to die."

The Council of Nicaea

> From the letter of the Emperor (Constantine) to all those not present at the council. (Found in Eusebius, Vita Const., Lib III 18-20)
>
> When the question relative to the sacred festival of Easter arose, it was declared to be particularly unworthy for this, the holiest of festivals to follow the customs (the calculation) of the Jews who had soiled their hands with the most fearful of crimes, and whose minds were blinded. In rejecting their custom we may transmit to our descendants the legitimate mode of celebrating Easter; which we have observed from the time of the Savior's passion according to the day of the week.
>
> We ought not therefore to have anything in common with the Jew, for the Savior has shown us another way; our worship following a more legitimate and more convenient course (the order of the days of the week): And consequently in unanimously adopting this mode, we desire, dearest brethren to separate ourselves from the detestable company of the Jew. (Fordham University)

These words of Constantine are the basis of all Christian anti-Semitism, which have caused the misery and murder of many millions of Jews throughout the centuries. They have propelled so much Jewish hatred that horrific acts, such as the kidnapping of Jewish children to raise them as Christians; the Crusades; the Spanish and other inquisitions have continued down to the end of the 19th century. These words incited devastating pogroms in Russia and Eastern Europe; the Nazi Shoah (the Holocaust) during the 20th century, and the BDS now in the 21st century—instigated by Muslim/Palestinian factors, but espoused by many "well-meaning" Christian organizations. Anti-Semitism is very blatant in the United Nations and especially in the WCC (the World Council of Churches).

I wish I could tell you that all of this is a thing of the past, and does not affect Christianity and Christians today. But I would be lying to you. The following article is very enlightening:

From the Jerusalem Post

January 14, 2019

The WCC calls itself the broadest organized group of churches and says it seeks to represent 350 member churches in 110 countries and 500 million Christians throughout the world. Its website says that the group's goal is Christian unity.

Yet one way it seems to achieve that is through anti-Israel advocacy, which at times has explicit anti-Semitic overtones, as defined by the International Holocaust Remembrance Alliance. This definition has been accepted by the EU, which along with some of its member countries, provides funding for the EAPPI,* (the Ecumenical Accompaniment Programme in Palestine and Israel).

---

* *The World Council of Churches' Ecumenical Accompaniment Program in Palestine and Israel* (WCC-EAPPI) was created in 2002 by the World Council of Churches based on a letter and an appeal from local church leaders to create an international presence in the country.

WCC leadership and EAPPI volunteers have repeatedly made comparisons of Israeli actions to those of Nazi Germany in their advocacy sessions. For example, WCC general secretary Dr. Olav Fyske Tveit said: "I heard about the occupation of my country during the five years of World War II as the story of my parents. Now I see and hear the stories of 50 years of occupation."

In 2017, an observer Rev. Gordon Timbers of the Presbyterian Church of Canada gave a presentation. When an audience member asked if "Jewish people who go in to see...the model of the gas chambers" see similarities between that and the West Bank, Timbers responded that "there are similarities," including the use of identification papers.

South African EAPPI activist Itani Rasalanavho said during an "Apartheid Week" event in his home country that "the time has come to say that the victims of the Holocaust have now become the perpetrators."

In a presentation by Rev. Joan Fisher, an EAPPI activist, she quotes a Palestinian cleric as saying: "We are sympathetic to the suffering of our Jewish brothers and sisters in the Holocaust, but you don't deal with one injustice by creating another injustice."

The IHRA* (the International Holocaust Rememberance Alliance) working definition of anti-Semitism states that

---

* *The International Holocaust Remembrance Alliance* (IHRA) until January 2013 was known as the *Task Force for International Cooperation on Holocaust Education, Remembrance, and Research* (or ITF).

"drawing comparisons of contemporary Israeli policy to that of the Nazis" is an example of anti-Semitism.

The WCC supports boycotts and divestment from settlements, but EAPPI activists have called for a boycott of all of Israel.

The EAPPI publication "Faith Under Occupation" called in 2012 for "sanctions and suspension of US aid to Israel," to "challenge Israel in local and international courts" and "economic boycotts."

EAPPI National Coordinator in South Africa Dudu Mahlangu-Masango signed a letter to then-president Jacob Zuma calling "on our government and civil society to instigate broad-based boycott, divestment and sanctions on Israel" in 2012. She repeated this call in a 2018 television interview, calling for "total sanctions" on Israel.

The organization also seeks to combat Christian Zionism. In a 2015 WCC event, Zionism was called "heresy" under Christian theology, modern Israelis were said to have no connection to ancient Israelites, and Israeli society was noted to be "full with racism and light skin privilege." Their leadership also compared Israel to apartheid South Africa.

In May 2016, EAPPI activist Hannah Griffiths made a presentation in London, in which she blamed the "Jewish lobby" for American Christian Evangelicals supporting Israel, and claimed Israel plants knives in the bodies of Palestinians who were shot after attempting to stab Israelis.

EAPPI activists have also spread falsehoods about Israel, such as one in the UK who said that Israel has a policy to reduce the Arab population by sending Arab citizens to the West Bank or Gaza. Others showed ignorance of the conflict, like an EAPPI volunteer in Canada who said that Israelis aren't allowed in Area A* not because of danger, but "to prevent Israelis from seeing what was going on."

Local Jewish communities found EAPPI volunteers have inflamed anti-Semitism.

<u>The UK Jewish Board of Deputies president in 2012 Vivian Wineman said, "members of Jewish communities across the country have suffered harassment and abuse at EAPPI meetings," and the organization said that the EAPPI "helped to create a climate of hostility towards Israel within the Church of England."</u> (The Jerusalem Post)

Satan is jealous of Israel and especially of Judah. From Judah, from the Jewish people, would come the Lion of Judah, the Jewish Messiah, Yeshua, who will rule all of mankind. Satan wanted to destroy Israel before the First Coming of Messiah, and now he is trying to do it before His Second Coming which will establish His millennial reign in the capital of Israel-Jerusalem. The evil one is still using Christianity as his central vessel for funding the enemies of Israel. We will expound on this in gate 11.

---

*The West Bank was divided into three parts: A, B, and C – and was part of the Oslo Accords that Israel and the PLO signed in 1993 and 1995. As of September 2019, Area A makes up 18% of the West Bank, and is mainly controlled by the Palestinian Authorities, which includes internal security.

Now we understand that Satan's main agenda is to murder or obliterate every Jew on the planet because of *jealousy*. His purpose is to stop the return of the Messiah, for there will be no Jewish nation to welcome Him. Yeshua said that He will return only when the Jewish people welcome Him back. If there are no Jews left, no welcome party!

> For I tell you (the Jewish people), you will never see Me again until you say, 'Baruch ha-ba b'shem ADONAI. Blessed is He who comes in the name of the Lord!'"
>
> — MATTHEW 23:39

Without the Jews on the scene, Satan will reign supreme on this earth forever. That is his plan, but below is the God of Israel's master plan:

> Why are the nations in an uproar, and the peoples mutter vanity? The kings of earth set themselves up and rulers conspire together against ADONAI and against His Anointed One: "Let's rip their chains apart, and throw their ropes off us!" He who sits in heaven laughs! ADONAI mocks them. So He will speak to them in His anger, and terrify them in His fury: "I have set up My king upon Zion, My holy mountain."
>
> — PSALM 2:1–6

How Satan has partially achieved his wicked plan to destroy the Jews over the years is through the following tactics, as recorded in the Holy Scriptures.

Murder of the Male Sons in Egypt

Joseph, the son of Jacob was sold into slavery because of the jealousy of his brothers, eventually, in a magnanimous gesture of forgiveness, saved his people from the famine in Canaan by opening the gates of Egypt before them. He had become the most important man in Egypt besides Pharaoh, the King of Egypt, because of his integrity before God and his prophetic gift. The people of Joseph, the sons of Israel, settled in a fertile area named Goshen where they pastured their flocks successfully and became numerous. However, when Joseph died, a new king arose in Egypt that did not know Joseph and did not favor Israel, his people. He began to enslave them and mistreat them, culminating in the attempted genocide of the entire nation by murdering all the Israelite male babies. In Exodus we read:

> Now there arose a new king over Egypt, who did not know Joseph. He said to his people, "Look, the people of Bnei-Yisrael (the sons of Israel) are too numerous and too powerful for us. Come, we must deal shrewdly with them, or else they will grow even more numerous, so that if war breaks out, they may join our enemies, fight against us, and then escape from the land."
> So they set slave masters over them to afflict them with forced labor, and they built Pithom and Raamses as storage cities for Pharaoh. But the more they afflicted them, the more they multiplied and the more they spread. So the Egyptians dreaded the presence of Bnei-Yisrael (the sons of Israel). They worked them harshly and made their lives bitter with hard labor with mortar and brick, doing all sorts of work in the fields. In all their labors they worked them with cruelty.

Moreover, the king of Egypt spoke to the Hebrew midwives, one of whom was named Shiphrah and the other Puah, and said, "When you help the Hebrew women during childbirth, look at the sex. <u>If it's a son, then kill him</u>, but if it's a daughter, she may live." Yet the midwives feared God, so they did not do as the king of Egypt commanded them, but let the boys live.

— Exodus 1:8–17

This is the background of the rising of Moses, Israel's deliverer, leading to the entire story of Passover. Had Pharaoh succeeded in his hideous plan, he would have murdered Moses at birth. In addition, the Torah/Law would have never been given on Mount Sinai, the tribe of Judah would not exist, neither the house of David, and Messiah Yeshua—the Jewish Savior from the house of David—would have never been born. Israel would not have been formed as the nation we know today.

However, Elohim, the God of Israel, had two women that rescued Israel from genocide, all of mankind in fact, because we already know that without Israel all the plan of salvation for the nations would have been destroyed. There would be no Messiah and no salvation, and where would you be? This is the point: If the Jews are harmed and murdered, the entire world suffers. The wellbeing of all mankind depends on the wellbeing of Israel and the Jewish people.

I will bless those who bless you and I will curse those who curse you. And in you all the nations of the earth will be blessed.

— Genesis 12:3

This was, is and will be the Key of Abraham for the wellbeing of all mankind. And Satan knows it. He knows that if he can use anyone to harm the Jews, this loss will be costly to the entire world, to all humanity that he hates.

In every story of the rescue of the people of Israel, we see that YHVH has His heroes. He uses people that stand up against the evil authorities, whether church, governmental, or both, that persecute His chosen people. Here, the midwives were simple women that feared God more than they feared the dreaded king of Egypt. They left us with an unshakable legacy and an example to follow. The God of Israel rewarded them for their courageous stand that rescued the nation, and through Israel rescued the entire world from destruction.

> **So God was good to the midwives, and the people multiplied, growing very numerous. Because the midwives feared God, He gave them families of their own.**
>
> — Exodus 1:20–21

We should all follow their example in the days to come.

Amalek in the Desert

Amalek was the grandson of Esau, the elder twin brother of Jacob. Esau was always angry and jealous of Jacob, since God continued the blessing of Abraham and Isaac through Jacob, who became firstborn by Divine election. Esau wanted to murder Jacob, but did not do so while he was alive; however, his grandson Amalek continued Esau's legacy of hatred and jealousy. Amalek made it his business to annihilate Israel altogether. His tactics were base and perverted. He would resort to attacking the weak, the feeble, the sick and the weary, the pregnant women and their babies. Hitler imitated these tactics, and most Christian and Muslim anti-Semites, who all share the tactics of Amalek.

> Joshua did as Moses said, and fought the Amalekites, while Moses, Aaron and Hur went up to the top of the hill. When Moses held up his hand, Israel prevailed. But when he let down his hand, the Amalekites prevailed. Moses' hands grew heavy, so they took a stone, put it under him, and he sat down. Aaron and Hur held up his hands, one on each side, so his hands were steady until the sun went down. So Joshua overpowered the Amalekites and his army with the edge of the sword.
> ADONAI said to Moses, "Write this for a memorial in the book, and rehearse it in the hearing of Joshua, for I will utterly blot out the memory of the Amalekites from under heaven." Then Moses built an altar, and called the name of it YHVH-Nissi. Then he said, "By the hand upon the throne of ADONAI, ADONAI will have war with Amalek from generation to generation."
>
> — EXODUS 17:10–16

The battle against Amalek is YHVH's battle; He has a battle with Amalek from generation to generation. God's private vengeance against this terrible hatred and jealousy against His chosen people is that He will blot out the memory of Amalek from under heaven. Everyone like Amalek, hating the Jewish people, is under the same judgment as Amalek. The whole world is in danger of the worst wrath ever poured out because of anti-Semitism, which the Word of God calls, "hostility against Zion."

Draw near, O nations, to hear, and listen, O peoples! Let the earth hear, and all it contains, the world, and all its offspring! For ADONAI is enraged at all the nations, and furious at all their armies. He will utterly destroy them. He will give them over to slaughter. So their slain will be thrown out, and the stench of their corpses will rise, and the hills will be drenched with their blood...

For My sword has drunk its fill in the heavens. See, it will come down upon Edom, upon the people I have devoted to judgment... For ADONAI has a day of vengeance, a year of recompense for the hostility against Zion.

— ISAIAH 34:1–3,5,8

Everyone that harbors anti-Semitism, hatred, and jealousy against the Jewish people has the seed of Amalek in them. The God of Israel Himself battles for His people against Amalek, but He needs Joshua-like warriors, Moses-like intercessors, and Aaron and Hur-like statesmen who will cooperate with Him in this life and death battle. Will you answer His call? And if you do not respond, but remain a bystander (now when anti-Semitism has escalated to a dimension not seen since Hitler was in power), what will He think of you? Being silent to a crime makes one an accomplice in that crime, and the Almighty judges the bystanders.

Rescue those being dragged off to death, hold back those stumbling to slaughter. If you say, "Look, we didn't know this." Won't He who weighs hearts perceive it? Won't He who guards your soul know it? Won't He repay each one according to his deeds?

— PROVERBS 24:11–12

Neutrality is not an option for anyone dealing with the hatred of Jews and anti-Semitism.

Remember what Amalek did to you along the way as you came out from Egypt—how he happened upon you along the way and attacked those among you in the rear, all the stragglers behind you, when you were tired and weary—he did not fear God. Now when ADONAI your God grants you rest from all the enemies surrounding you in the land ADONAI your God is giving you as an inheritance to possess, you are to blot out the memory of Amalek from under the heavens. Do not forget!

— DEUTERONOMY 25:17–19

Balaam and Balak

Balaam was a Gentile wizard "prophet," or rather a diviner as he was not walking as part of the only people of God, the people of Israel. He had powers that were well respected by the Moabites, who feared the people of Israel and sought their annihilation.

When Balak, son of Zippor, realized all that Bnei-Yisrael (sons of Israel) had done to the Amorites, Moab became terrified because there were so many people. Moab was filled with dread because of Bnei-Yisrael. Moab said to the elders of Midian, "The multitude will lick up everything around us like the ox licks up the grass of the field."

Now Balak son of Zippor was king of Moab at that time. He sent messengers to summon Balaam son of Beor, at Pethor near the River in his native land, saying to him, "Look now, a people has come out of Egypt. See now, they cover the surface of the earth and are settling beside me. Come now, curse this people for me, because they are too strong for me! Perhaps I may be able to defeat them and drive them away from the country. I know that whoever you bless will be blessed and whoever you curse will be accursed!"

The elders of Moab and Midian left with divination fees in their hand. When they came to Balaam, they told him Balak's words.

— NUMBERS 22:2–7

As the story goes, Balaam told these messengers to stay the night until he heard from God about this matter. To which the ELOHIM of Israel answered the following.

God said to Balaam, "Do not go with them! Do not curse them, for they are blessed!"

— NUMBERS 22:12

So Balaam obediently sent word to the Moabite leader, Balak Son of Zippor, "No doing—God does not let me do this." However, the king did not give up and sent yet other messengers offering more money, silver, and gold to Balaam to use his powers in cursing Israel. Balaam, who did not really know YHVH, did not know that the God of Israel does not change His mind, that He is not a man that He would break His Word. If He said, "No!" He meant *no*. So Balaam tried to convince

God to let him go, and God seemed to comply with him. However, a surprise awaited Balaam on the way. His donkey became his prophet!

> So Balaam got up in the morning, saddled his donkey, and went with the Moabite princes. But the anger of God burned because he was going. The angel of ADONAI stood in the road to oppose him. As Balaam was riding on his donkey, and two of his servants were with him, the donkey saw the angel of ADONAI standing in the road with his drawn sword in his hand. The donkey turned off the road and went into the field. So Balaam beat the donkey to get her back onto the road.
>
> Then the angel of ADONAI stood in a narrow path between two vineyards, with a wall on this side and a wall on that side. When the donkey saw the angel of ADONAI, she pressed against the wall, crushing Balaam's foot against the wall. So Balaam continued beating her.
>
> The angel again moved. He stood in a narrow place where there was no room to turn, right or left. When the donkey saw the angel of ADONAI, she lay down under Balaam. Balaam was furious and beat the donkey with his staff.
>
> Then ADONAI opened the donkey's mouth, and she said to Balaam, "What have I done to you that you have beaten me these three times?"
>
> Balaam said to the donkey, "Because you've made a fool of me! If I had a sword in my hand, I would kill you now!"
>
> The donkey said to Balaam, "Am I not your donkey, which you have ridden as always to this day? Have I ever been in the habit of doing this to you?" "No," he said.
>
> Then ADONAI opened Balaam's eyes, and he saw the angel of ADONAI standing in the road with his drawn sword in his hand. So he fell on his face.

The angel of ADONAI said to him, "Why have you beaten your donkey these three times? Behold, I came as an adversary because your way before Me is a reckless one! The donkey saw Me and turned away from Me these three times. If she had not turned away from Me, by now I would have killed you indeed, but let her live!"

— NUMBERS 22:21–33

Anyone that sets himself to curse Israel, to do evil to the Jewish people, whether out of greed or for political reasons, will find that the God of Israel Himself becomes their adversary. Eventually, Balaam learnt the lesson, and instead of cursing Israel he blessed them under the unction of the Spirit of God, with one of the most beautiful words in the Bible.

When Balaam realized that it was pleasing in the eyes of ADONAI to bless Israel, he did not resort to sorceries as at the other times, but turned his face toward the wilderness. Lifting up his eyes, Balaam saw Israel dwelling by tribes. The Ruach ELOHIM came over him. He uttered his oracle and said:
"This is the oracle of Balaam son of Beor, and the oracle of a strong man whose eye has been opened, the oracle of one hearing God's speech, one seeing Shaddai's vision, one fallen down, yet with open eyes: How lovely are your tents, O Jacob, and your dwellings, O Israel! Like valleys they are spread out like gardens beside a river, like aloes planted by ADONAI, like cedars beside the waters. Water will flow from his buckets, his seed by abundant water. His king will be greater than Agag, his kingdom will be exalted. God is bringing him out of Egypt

like the strong horns of a wild ox. He devours nations hostile
to him. He will crush their bones.
His arrows will pierce them. He crouches like a lion or a lion-
ess—who would rouse him? He who blesses you will be blessed, and he who curses you will be cursed."
Then Balak became furious at Balaam, and struck his hands
together. Balak said to Balaam, "I summoned you to curse my
enemies, but look, you have blessed them these three times!
Now, go home! I said I would reward you, but see, ADONAI has
kept you from reward!"

— NUMBERS 24:1–11

Later on the story would get stickier as Balaam did not fully learn
his lesson. He used his gifts to advise the Midianites on how to bring
Israel to destruction through sexual immorality by using attractive
women to tempt the princes of Israel. Satan keeps on trying every
devise possible to destroy the chosen people (Num. 25).

When Hitler and the Nazi regime began to annihilate all the Jews,
he said that he was following the instructions of the greatest anti-Semite and church reformer Martin Luther, who wrote the details used
for the Final Solution for the Jews that Hitler followed (MacCulloch;
Goldhagen). And yet out of the ashes of the Shoah (the Nazi Holocaust) the Jewish nation arose to be reborn in its own land after nearly
2,000 years of exile. The God of Israel turned the most terrible curse of
destruction into a blessing of restoration for all of Israel, fulfilling the
longing of all Jews throughout twenty centuries of exile to return to
their ancient homeland. And His master plan continues.

Haman in Persia

When the Jewish people were exiled to Babylon (whose kingdom was followed by the empire of the Persians and Medes), the spirit of Amalek faced them with the threat of annihilation one more time. I could call this *Amalek Chapter Two*, as the author of this hideous plan of genocide was called Haman the Agagite, a descendant of Amalek; which goes to prove that YHVH has a battle from generation to generation through the natural descendants of Amalek, or those who have the spirit of Amalek. This spirit is a demonic principality and the spirit by which the anti-Jewish head of the anti-MESITOJUZ principality operates.

Sometime later King Ahasuerus promoted Haman, son of Hammedatha the Agagite, elevating him and setting his chair above all the officials who were with him. All the king's servants who were at the king's gate bowed down and paid honor to Haman, for the king had commanded it. But Mordecai would not bow down or pay him honor.

Then the king's servants who were at the king's gate said to Mordecai, "Why are you disobeying the king's command?" Day after day, they spoke to him but he would not listen to them. Therefore they told Haman in order to see whether Mordecai's resolve would prevail, for he had told them that he was a Jew.

When Haman saw that Mordecai was not bowing down or paying him honor, Haman was filled with rage. But it was repugnant in his eyes to lay hands on Mordecai alone, for they had told him the identity of Mordecai's people. So Haman

sought to destroy all the Jews, the people of Mordecai, who
were throughout the whole kingdom of Ahasuerus.

— ESTHER 3:1–6

There were two Jews in Persia of that time who became the heroes
of this story: one of them was Mordecai the Jew, and the other one
his adopted daughter Hadassah, the daughter of Abihail. She was an
orphan from the exiles to Babylon. Actually, Hadassah was Mordecai's
cousin. This Hadassah was chosen to become the wife of Ahasuerus,
the Persian King, who did not know she was a Jewess. She was known
by her Gentile name of Esther, as she hid her Jewish identity.

When Haman got angry because Mordecai did not "bow down to
him," and knowing that he was a Jew, he was disgusted. He had inherited that jealousy and hatred against the Jews from his mother's womb,
carried over from his ancestor Amalek, the grandson of Esau. He pro-
ceeded to concoct a "Final Solution" for all the Jews in Persia, and he
convinced the king that it was for the benefit of his kingdom. The king
trusted Haman implicitly as his loyal advisor, and agreed to the plan
without knowing that his own wife, Queen Esther, was Jewish.

When Mordecai heard of the horrific plan, he mourned at the gates
of the palace, dressed in sackcloth and ashes—the tokens of traditional
Jewish mourning. He also sent couriers to ask his niece and adoptive
daughter, Esther, to plead with the king for the salvation of the Jews.
His niece, the Queen, did not want to risk her life for the sake of her
people; she was afraid the king would have her killed for approaching
him without being summoned. Mordecai then sent another letter with
words that resound through the ages until today,

Mordecai told them to reply to Esther with this answer, "Do not think in your soul that you will escape in the king's household more than all the Jews. For if you remain silent at this time, relief and deliverance will arise for the Jews from another place—but you and your father's house will perish. Who knows whether you have attained royal status for such a time as this?"

— ESTHER 4:13–14

This is the key for all to understand: ELOHIM has an infallible plan for the Jewish people to remain and become restored. He will always bring them deliverance from somewhere, but He knocks on the door of each one of us, expecting us to take action, to rescue His Jews from the age-old plan of Satan to destroy them. Anyone that says "No", it is too risky, or "I am comfortable where I am, why would I endanger my life to save some Jews?" will receive this answer from the Almighty.

For if you remain silent at this time, relief and deliverance will arise for the Jews from another place—but you and your father's house will perish.

— ESTHER 3:14A

Whatever position we have, high or low, there is something we can do to rescue the Jews. I am reminded of the story of Oscar Schindler, a Nazi businessman and entrepreneur. He rescued as many Jews as he could by using his pots and pans factory. He purchased many Jews from his Nazi peers who were charged with exterminating them in the death camp of Auschwitz. He told them he needed them for his factory, and gave the camp bosses a list of names, paying good money to the

Third Reich for each Jew. They did not have any reason to doubt his motives as he was a Nazi.

But this Nazi was different; he had a conscience—he must have feared God. He purchased about a thousand Jews, and at the end of the Nazi Shoah (the Holocaust), his Jews were still alive. But he was heartbroken when he realized that he still had an expensive car left and a diamond ring with which he could have purchased even more Jews. He had already given all his possessions to purchase those thousand Jews. Today, they honor Oscar Schindler in Israel's Yad Vashem, the Holocaust Memorial in Jerusalem, as one of the Righteous of the Nations. There is a tree dedicated to his name, and they buried him in an official Christian cemetery on Mount Zion in Jerusalem, as a sign of honor.

Queen Esther finally came to her senses and went to fast and pray. Then she approached the king, her husband, with great wisdom and favor, and had Haman exposed and hanged on the gallows together with his ten sons! Instead of there being a genocide, the Jews could now defend themselves, and it says that many became Jews from among the Gentiles, putting their trust in the God of Israel. There was a great revival followed by the historical celebration of Purim, days of rejoicing that we are mandated by Scripture to celebrate every year.

Mordecai recorded these events, and he sent letters to all the Jews throughout the provinces of King Ahasuerus, both near and far, urging them to celebrate the fourteenth and fifteenth days of Adar every year as the days when the Jews got relief from their enemies, and as the month when their sorrow was turned into joy and their mourning into celebration. These were to be days of feasting, celebration and sending presents of food to one another and giving gifts to the poor.

So the Jews agreed to continue the commemoration they had begun and do what Mordecai had written to them. For Haman, son of Hammedatha the Agagite, the enemy of all the Jews, had schemed against the Jews to destroy them and had cast the pur—that is, the lot—to ruin and destroy them. But when it came to the king's attention, he issued a written edict that the wicked scheme Haman had devised against the Jews should come back on his own head, and that he and his sons should be hanged on the gallows. (For this reason, these days were called Purim, from the word, *pur*.) Therefore because of everything in this letter and because of what they had seen and what had happened to them, the Jews established and took upon themselves, upon their descendants, and upon all who joined with them, that they would commemorate these two days in the way prescribed and at the appointed time every year. These days should be remembered and observed in every generation by every family and in every province and every city. These days of Purim should not fail from among the Jews, nor their remembrance perish from their descendants.

Then Queen Esther the daughter of Abihail, and also Mordecai the Jew, wrote with full authority to confirm this second letter of Purim. He sent letters to all the Jews in the 127 provinces of the kingdom of Ahasuerus, with words of shalom and truth, to establish these days of Purim at their designated times, just as Mordecai the Jew and Queen Esther had decreed for them and just as they had established for themselves and their descendants, matters regarding their times of fasting and lamentations. Esther's command confirmed these regulations about Purim and it was written into the records.

— ESTHER 9:20–32

Will there be a Church like Esther in these End times? This is the purpose of this book so you, the reader, whether Jew or Gentile, black or white, male or female, young or old, will join a company like Esther and Mordecai, and deliver the Jewish people one more time before the Messiah returns. By doing so, you will rescue your own self and your house.

I will bless those who bless you, curse those who curse you and in you all the families of the earth will be blessed.

— **GENESIS 12:3**

A Defining Prayer of Enlistment

Yes, heavenly Father, I join Your End time army and be part of that Esther Church to defeat all the Amalekite plans of wicked anti-Semitism to destroy the State of Israel and Your Jewish people. I renounce my comfort zone and any lukewarmness in my life, and I report for duty as Your End time soldier to fight and defeat all hatred against Your Jewish people, who are also my people because of the blood of Yeshua. Thank You for Your wisdom and empowerment for the task in Yeshua's name, amen.

GATE 10

IDENTITY CONFUSION AND ANTI-SEMITISM

Because of your violence to your brother Jacob, shame will cover you, and you will be cut off forever. On the day that you stood aloof—on the day that strangers carried away his wealth, while foreigners entered his gates and cast lots for Jerusalem—you were just like one of them. You should not look down on your brother on the day of his disaster, nor should you rejoice over the children of Judah in the day of their destruction. You should not speak proudly in the day of their distress. Do not enter the gate of My people in the day of their disaster. Yes, you. Do not gloat over their misery in the day of their disaster. Yes, you—do not loot their wealth in the day of their calamity. Do not stand at the crossroad to cut down his fugitives, and do not imprison his survivors in the day of distress. "For the day of ADONAI is near against all the nations. As you have done, it shall be done to you. Your dealing will return on your own head."

— OBADIAH 1:10–14

Though anti-Semitism is not exclusive to Christianity, it is the longest running trait in the Christian Church since the 4th

193

century. While Muslim anti-Semitism (or rather anti-Zionism) is very prevalent today, many more Jews have been persecuted and murdered in the name of Christ than in the name of Mohammed throughout history.

The Birth of Religious Anti-Semitism

The thief impersonated the Savior and Messiah by replacing the essence of who He is—a Jew that died for you!

This is the very essence of the Council of Nicaea summed up in the following statement of Constantine:

"We Should Have Nothing in Common With the Jews"

Having nothing in common with the Jews denies the importance of God's covenant with Israel that could only be fulfilled through a Jewish Messiah born of the tribe of Judah and the house of David.

> For to us a child is born, a son will be given to us, and the government will be upon His shoulder. His Name will be called Wonderful Counselor, Mighty God, My Father of Eternity, Prince of Peace. Of the increase of His government and shalom there will be no end—on the throne of David and over His kingdom—to establish it and uphold it through justice and righteousness from now until forevermore. The zeal of ADONAI-Tzva'ot will accomplish this.
>
> — ISAIAH 9:5–7

How can He be a Jew, from the family of David, and yet we have nothing in common with the Jews? This causes an immediate, terrible confusion as to the identity of the Savior. In order to somehow appease the confusion, it is mandatory that the mind readjusts its idea of the savior into a Roman Christ. Any mental or spiritual agreement with the Jewishness of Messiah, the Jewishness of the gospel, must then be replaced in order to satisfy Emperor Constantine's imperative command. This decree needed to be followed by all the consenting bishops and church leaders, and eventually by the masses of faithful Christians. This command needed to be now woven into all Christian theology throughout the ages, into every preacher's sermon and every adopted pagan Roman celebration. Since the time of Constantine, everything in Christianity needed to comply with the statement,

> We should have nothing in common with the Jews because the Savior has shown us another way. (Fordham University)

"Nothing in common because the Savior (who has nothing in common with the Jews) has showed us another way" (a way that has nothing in common with the Jews, the Jewish identity of Messiah, the gospel as given to the Jewish apostles, the Torah and the holy feasts as given to the people of Israel). Nothing in common.

The Christian Roman Savior is now the real Messiah; he is now the real Savior, His name is Jesus Christ and we will now forget the original birth name given to the Jewish Messiah by the Father in heaven. And worse than that, His eternal covenant name, His birth name of Yeshua will be *forbidden*, since His true identity is in His holy name!

The following Scriptures are references that establish the fact that it is impossible for a genuine believer in the Messiah that gets salvation to have "nothing" in common with the Jews.

- Yeshua is the Jewish Savior—Salvation is of the Jews (Jn. 4:22)
- Yeshua is the Lion of Judah—He is Jewish Lion that will judge the world (Rev. 5:5)

- Yeshua is the Word made flesh—He is the Torah incarnate (Jn. 1:14)
- Yeshua is the King of the Jews—He is the Jewish Messiah (Mat. 27:37)

Identity Confusion and it's Ripple Effects

The danger of replacing the identity of Yeshua with a savior of our own making, is that it leads people that profess to be Christians into terrible confusion. This opens the door to dangerously harmful deceptions, including the acceptance of concepts that *seem to be unrelated*, such as the possibility of sex change and the LGBTQ agenda. Prominent denominations have lesbian and homosexual priests, including the Lutheran, Methodist, Presbyterian, and some Baptist churches. Once the identity confusion of the Savior took root in Christianity, it led to an untold amount of sin, crimes, murder, and other woes.

> **Or don't you know that the unrighteous will not inherit the kingdom of God? Don't be deceived! The sexually immoral, idolaters, adulterers, those who practice homosexuality, thieves, the greedy, drunkards, slanderers, swindlers—none of these will inherit the kingdom of God.**
>
> **— 1 Corinthians 6:9–10**

Yeshua died for all sinners but once we surrender to Him, we must forsake that which He calls unrighteous and sinful, and He gives us the power to do so by His Holy Spirit.

Another dangerous result coming from this identity theft is the prevalent trend to mix Freemasonry with Christianity. Such practice follows naturally from the syncretism*, or all-inclusiveness, of replacement theology from the fourth century which adopted pagan feasts to satisfy the masses. Saturnalia became Christmas; the feast to the goddess of fertility, Ishtar, (or the goddess of bounty), Easter was adopted (to replace the Passover and the Feast of First Fruits) at the time of the resurrection of Messiah; and Sunday (Constantine's day of sun worship) replaced the holy Shabbat on the seventh day. This attitude makes other religious trends such as Freemasonry an acceptable form of worldview for many Christians and prominent leaders. If all paganism can be "made holy," then technically they can dress Freemasonry in acceptable "Christian garments"—and this is the case.

Freemasonry has become a sacred cow that almost no one is willing to touch. However, this is a secret society that worships Lucifer hiding behind good works and charity. Those in the higher degrees know this, while those of lower degrees go through the "slow frog boiling treatment,"** immunizing them to deception, as the temperature gradually increases.

> What harmony does Messiah have with Belial? Or what part does a believer have in common with an unbeliever? What agreement does God's Temple have with idols? For we are the Temple of the living God—just as God said...
>
> — 2 CORINTHIANS 6:15–16

---

* Syncretism: the mixture or attempted mixture of different religions, cultures, or schools of thought.

** It is said that if you put a frog in a pot with warm water and gradually heat it, the frog will remain in the water until it boils to death.

Replacement theology keeps on having many ripple effects until this day.

Changing the identity of the Messiah causes terrible confusion in the believer. The Hebrew word for confusion is *babel*. This confusion leads to a modern Tower of Babel with the multiplicity of denominations that exist, and each one claims to own the truth.

> **This is why it is named Babel, because ADONAI confused the languages of the entire world there, and from there ADONAI scattered them over the face of the entire world.**
>
> **— GENESIS 11:9**

This spirit of confusion affects believers, especially young ones, who see the inconsistency and the hypocrisy, but are taught to comply. Confusion can cause terrible anxiety and even serious mental problems.

The Jewish Lion

> **Then one of the elders tells me, "Stop weeping! Behold, the Lion of the tribe of Judah, the Root of David, has triumphed— He is worthy to open the scroll and its seven seals."**
>
> **— REVELATION 5:5**

When we seek truly to know Him, we will discover Him as a Jew. The word for knowledge in Hebrew is *yada*, which is the same word for "matrimonial intimacy." *Yada* (intimacy) will lead people to discover Yeshua's circumcision. That is a profound discovery, albeit an alarming one. Imagine a woman, engaged to a man, discovering that he is someone else after marriage? She says, "I thought you were a Gentile Christian, and now I have to cope with the fact that my husband is a Jew? Now the whole Jewish and Israel narrative has become my predicament, as I am one with you, including the all-prevalent discrimination and hatred against the Jews called anti-Semitism." This is exactly what happens when a Gentile realizes that Jesus is a Jew, and His name is Yeshua.

This woman, who stood aloof from Israel's problems, and even put up with cruel and demeaning jokes against the Jews, now realizes that people in her own family (other Christians that professed to love her husband as a Roman Christian), now hate Him when they discover He is a Jew. They hate His roots, His family, His customs, His Torah, His Shabbat, His feasts and traditions, and yes, even His name. They totally reject His actual name, and by rejecting His name, Yeshua, they also reject His identity as a Jew.

Then the great divide begins, a chasm opens up between those who will truly know Him and will be ready to marry Him as a Jew, and between those who will persist in worshipping the fiction of *their own imagination*—the Roman Christ with a pagan name, pagan feasts and pagan customs.

Seeking an intimate, personal relationship will lead to discover the Jewishness of the Messiah. The fact is that His circumcision, alongside the crucifixion nail prints, were not erased will be made known. The response to this undeniable truth will determine eternity for millions.

A Jew died for you, and the only one worthy to open the books of judgment is a Jew. And if so, how will He judge those Christians that hate, despise or dishonor the Jews? Is it not Him they are despising then?

Why is it Urgent to Restore His Jewish Name?

Here are some important facts to consider.

- Millions of Jews and other peoples that Christianity conquered, such as the American Indians of First Nations, were killed in the name of Jesus Christ.
- The true covenant birth name of the Messiah *Yeshua* has never been used to murder anyone. In Hebrew, *yeshua* means, "salvation," "healing," and "deliverance."
- Jesus Christ is not a translation of His name—it is a transliteration to satisfy the Roman masses that identified with a name that sounded like their sun god, Zeus (Ie-sous).

> **That at the name of Yeshua every knee should bow, in heaven and on the earth and under the earth, and every tongue profess that Yeshua the Messiah is Lord—to the glory of God the Father.**
>
> — **PHILIPPIANS 2:10–11**

A person's name is his calling card. When identity theft happens, the name of the person is stolen and misused. Someone else poses as that person and wreaks havoc. When the name of Yeshua was changed to the Roman *Jesus Christus*, it hid His identity as a Jew. This was an anti-Jewish act, and through this, it was easier to persecute and kill Jews in this Romanized name without having to deal with His Jewish identity. The following true story will illustrate this point.

On one of our trips to Poland and the death camps, we visited the Jewish memorial in the city of Cracow, about one hour away from the death camps of Auschwitz-Birkenau. The Nazi regime had murdered all the Jews of Cracow in Poland. However, contrary to what the 21st century Polish government wants us to believe, there was much cooperation between the Nazis and the Polish Christian population by choice and not only because of fear. Many Poles were blaring anti-Semites. Most of Poland was and is Catholic, and it ingrains hatred of the Jews within the entire organized Christian system (see quotes from the church fathers at the beginning of this book). Some also helped the Jews and even some nuns in convents* hid them. There are always some righteous people who refuse to be deceived by evil doctrines.

We were visiting the memorial to all the Jews from Cracow who had been exterminated in Auschwitz. To my dismay (though not surprisingly) I saw swastikas and fresh anti-Jewish graffiti drawn over this sacred and painful memorial. I pointed this out to my group, and we prayed. Leaning on the side of the memorial fence were three young Polish girls, 14 to 16 years old on bicycles. One of them was smoking, and she sneered and pointed her fingers towards us mockingly and disrespectfully crying *jid*, which is a derogatory term for 'Jew' in Polish.

I stopped praying and talking to our group and suddenly went near the girl that was mocking. I spoke boldly to her, "Do you know that the Jesus Christ that you worship is a Jew? If you hate the Jews, it is Him you are hating!" Startled, she threw away her cigarette and straightened up into attention. Then I asked her, "Have you ever seen a Jew? Do you know any Jews?" She said, "No, never." So I challenged her, "So, how come you hate the Jews whom you do not even know?"

Then, I asked her to accompany me and the group to one of the last remaining synagogues in the Jewish quarter of Cracow, and she

---

* Convent: a community of priests or religious peoples; or the building used by the community, particularly in the Catholic, Lutheran, and Anglican denominations.

followed me. Inside of the synagogue, I introduced her to Yeshua, the Jewish Messiah. As she wept in repentance, I covered her with the tallit prayer shawl and cut off the spirit of replacement theology, the anti-MESITOJUZ, and all hatred against the Jews. She was gloriously born again and Spirit-filled, and I would bet she will never hate the Jews again.

These anti-Jewish deceptions and deceptive doctrines hiding within Christianity are not only murdering Jews but also killing many Christians that harbor them.

Had replacement theology not changed the name of Yeshua, it would be impossible to ignore His Jewishness. That is the reason Christendom has killed so many Jews in the name of Jesus Christ, but no one has ever been killed in the name of Yeshua! Restoring His name will be one important factor in decreasing anti-Semitism in the world.

The Deception that the "Jews Killed Christ"

This one deception has led to the murder of more Jews than any other. The following is an authentic story from my family.

My mother had twin cousins whom she loved very much. When the twins were about three years old, they all went on a summer vacation to the coast of Chile. The twins had been visiting with the neighbor girls and playing together for many hours. When their mom came to pick them up, to her dismay she found them in tears and distraught and she took them home. The three-year-old twins screamed, "Mom, we did not kill anybody, we did not kill anybody," and they wept and wept. When they calmed down enough to respond more reasonably, one twin confided, "Our friend, the daughter of the neighbors told us we killed God because we are Jews and the Jews killed God."

This story is by no means an exception. Countless Jews have been bullied and murdered under the accusation that "you Jews killed Jesus Christ, so you deserve to die."

Jewish deicide is a belief held by some Christians which states that the Jewish people as a whole were responsible for the death of Jesus. Mobs used the anti-Semitic slur "Christ-killer" to incite violence against Jews and contributed to many centuries of pogroms, the murder of Jews during the Crusades, the Spanish Inquisition and the Holocaust.

In the catechism produced by the Council of Trent, the Catholic Church affirmed that the collectivity of sinful humanity was responsible for the death of Jesus, not only the Jews. In the deliberations of the Second Vatican Council (1962–1965), the Roman Catholic Church under Pope Paul VI repudiated belief in collective Jewish guilt for the crucifixion of Jesus. It declared that the accusation could not be made "against all the Jews, without distinction, then alive, nor against the Jews of today." (Wikipedia Contributors)

Though this view has been amended by the Vatican, one can imagine that until 1962 or 1965, nearly every child indoctrinated in the tenets of Christianity would have learned that the Jews killed Christ and that they need to be collectively punished.

The following is my personal story.

I was six years old, and I was studying at a British School in Santiago, Chile. We were a few Jews in the class among many Christians. Every time there was a lesson on religion, they allowed us Jews to leave and play in the yard at the request of our parents, who paid a hefty sum to keep us in this high-class private school. Since I was a very curious girl,

I stayed in the religion classes where I learned about Jesus Christ and about how we Jews are guilty of murder.

I loved to draw, so while the teacher was speaking, I used to draw some illustrations of her lessons. One of my pictures was of a bonfire with big flames and all the Jews burning in it. One day my mom found my religion notebooks and discovered my shocking drawing. In utter disgust, and with good reason, she complained to the school and then took me out and placed me in a Hebrew school to receive a Jewish education instead. This occurred in 1965—now in the 21st century we continue reaping the effect of this destructive lie. It takes many years to re-educate the world when it has been wrongly educated. Hitler stated: "Tell a lie that is big enough, repeat it continuously and everyone will believe it" (Wikipedia Contributors). This indeed has been the case.

To make it clear, the ones that killed the Messiah were not "the Jews," but the Romans instigated by a mob hired by the apostate high priest of the time. The Jews did not have the jurisdiction under Rome to execute the death penalty. Many thousands of Jews followed Yeshua across Israel, and there was a great revival even among the priesthood. This following and revival happened before and after His crucifixion.

All the first apostles, the true church fathers, are Jewish. Not one of them "became a Christian," or changed his or her Jewishness or religion. They only surrendered to their Jewish Messiah, not by becoming Christians nor to serve a Romanized Christ.

Only the Jews were waiting for a Messiah, an anointed king, to save them. Those Jews that recognized Yeshua followed the Jewish king who said, "My Kingdom is not of this world" (John 18:26). They kept the Shabbat, celebrated the biblical feasts, and kept the Torah. They had nothing to do with Roman pagan feasts or traditions. That's the reason why after Constantine, together with the Gentile bishops of the fourth century, signed the divorce from the Jews called the Council of Nicaea, no one could find any Jews in the Church anymore. Jewish believers left that apostate church and went underground, as their lives were in danger continuously from the hatred of the Christian Church authorities, and from the common folk that had been indoctrinated. Persecution against the Jews for being "Christ killers" continues in various degrees and in many countries to the present day.

Yeshua, the Jewish Messiah, was not murdered. He was a willing sacrifice, and only a willing sacrifice can atone for the sin of both Jews and Gentiles alike.

> **For this reason the Father loves Me, because I lay down My life, so that I may take it up again. No one takes it away from Me, but I lay it down on My own. I have the authority to lay it down, and I have the authority to take it up again. This command I received from My Father.**
>
> **— JOHN 10:17–18**

And, to make it even more clear, the ones who mocked, tortured and crucified Him with gusto were Romans, not Jews—and yet no one has persecuted the Romans or the Italians for it. Only the Romans had the authority to torture, kill, and crucify. Can you imagine someone come to the Vatican with a sign: "You, the Romans, killed the Christ"?

So, why have they done this to the Jews?

> **Then Pilate took Yeshua and had Him scourged. The (Roman) soldiers twisted together a crown of thorns and put it on His head, and dressed Him in a purple robe. They kept coming up**

to Him, saying, "Hail, King of the Jews!" and slapping Him over and over.

— JOHN 19:1–3

This hatred against the King of the Jews, the Jewish Messiah (and against His people the Jews) is still communicated to the entire world through a Romanized Christianity and a Romanized Jesus Christ.

Christian Anti-Semitism in the 21st Century

As Episcopal minister William Nicholls describes the following.

"The very presence of the Jewish people in the world... puts a great question against Christian belief... cause[s] profound and gnawing anxiety."

From its earliest beginnings Christianity described itself "inheritor" of God's Covenant, the "New Israel." Augustine, possibly most "moderate" of church fathers reasoned, based on scriptural representation of "the Jews" as Christ-killers, that the murder of Jesus is the reason for God having transferred his favor from Jew to gentile. This reasoning continues today. The same 1965 Vatican Council II which produced Nostre Aetate* "absolving" present-day Jews of guilt for the death of Jesus also made sure to reaffirm "the Church "is the new people of God." And thirty-five years later, in its closing summary of the Vatican's 2010 Special Synod of Bishops for the Middle East,

---

* Nostra Aetate is the declaration of the relation of the Church with non-Christian religions of the second Vatican council.

"We Christians cannot speak of the 'Promised Land' as an exclusive right for a privileged Jewish people. This promise was nullified by Christ... In the kingdom of God... there is no longer a chosen people." (The Jerusalem Post)

While writing this book, Pope Francis has contacted all world leaders to unite under a global banner of re-education. He chose the State of Israel's historical birth date (May 14, 2020) for this alarming but not surprising, deceptive event. However, because of the coronavirus pandemic of 2020, the Pope had to change the date. Is this a coincidence? Or is there an anti-Israel message hidden in the date's choice, usurping the place of Israel again by the Catholic Church, with the Pope as the head of the Church. Could it be that God sent COVID-19 to disrupt this ungodly meeting on Israel's anniversary date?

Most alarming is the number of Evangelical leaders who have consented and are *aligning* with the Pope to advance his agenda of a New World Order. How can they do it unless replacement theology, including anti-Semitism, is still alive and well in many Evangelical ranks? The same church fathers that wrote the most horrendous things against the Jews are still revered and their beliefs are being taught in most Evangelical seminaries.

In fact, I remember attending Bible school in Dallas 1990, where the genuine Church history about Christian hatred and anti-Semitism was never taught—even though it is the most prevalent part of Christian history since AD 325, to the present. However, we were taught supposedly wonderful things about Emperor Constantine, and how he established Christianity as the religion of the Roman Empire and what a hero he was for doing so. Since then, these lies have been and are being repeated in Evangelical, Pentecostal, Charismatic and other circles, Bible schools, High schools, and theological seminaries. Anti-Semitic theologies remain part of the Christianity of the 21st century.

Here is a recent blog from Jerusalem Post.

How does Judeophobia pass from generation to generation? Most obviously transmission is directly by contact with the source documents, Christian scriptural references to "the Jews" as "murderers of Jesus." Since eighty percent of residents of the United States are Christian according to the 2011 census it is safe to assume that most have had at least some contact with scriptural anti-Judaism. Anti-Semitism as prejudice represents common beliefs fed by historical stereotypes by which Jews represent a threat justifying exclusion. Recall that 1939 Roper poll of American Christians which found that,

"Fifty-three percent believed that 'Jews are different and should be restricted' and <u>ten percent believed that Jews should be deported</u>."

That survey, taken soon after Kristallnacht is significant in representing both "moderate" and "extremist" anti-Semitism as fairly constant over intervening years to 2011! Whether by "restricted" (moderate) was meant "concentration camps." How restrict Jews (the "moderate" position)? The model provided by Germany, and soon also by America regarding Japanese Americans was concentrations camps. As to the "extremist" demand for "deportation," what destination might they have had in mind?

In 2012 in a speech before the House of Representatives, Republican Don Manzullo attacked fellow Virginian and Jewish House

Majority Leader Eric Cantor: "Mr. Cantor, an observant Jew, would not be "saved." Cantor avoided a direct response but, in an April, 2012 interview, referred instead to "the darker side" of America that has "not always gotten it right in terms of racial matters, religious matters, whatever." In fact Manzullo's views regarding Jews and salvation is fairly common among many Americans who proudly refer to the United States a "Christian country."

In 2007 Jerry Falwell, regarded a leading American Evangelical leader stated that, "God Almighty does not hear the prayer of a Jew." (The Jerusalem Post)

Notice how Secular Anti-Semitism feeds on religious anti-Semitism.

But anti-Jewish prejudice is not limited to religious expression. It is also present as secular expression. There are abundant examples of anti-Semitic epithets (labels) appearing in the media by American politicians and culture icons. "FDR," pressed by Henry Morgenthau to agree to even a token bombing of Auschwitz reminded his Jewish Treasury secretary, "You know, this is a Protestant country," that the Jews are here "under sufferance."

In July, 2013 the chairwoman of the board of a small Florida town, Cheryl Sanders, announced at a board meeting that they were "not to be up here jewing over somebody's pay." "Jewing" refers to the medieval stereotype of Jews as usurers. Unfortunately for the chairwoman her words were picked up by the media. Surprised and offended by the national attention Sanders insisted, "I am not anti-Semitic and there was no malice toward anyone." She described "jewing" as commonly used in everyday speech and that nobody should take her use of it as anti-Semitism.

Such "expressions" in pop-culture are examples of how deeply embedded anti-Semitism is in the psyche of Western society. So "common and accepted" that even some Jews are comfortable in its presence, accept it as innocent and normal part of American life. (The Jerusalem Post)

The Link Between Hitler and Luther

In 1923 Hitler praised Luther and called him the greatest German genius, who "saw the Jew as we today are starting to see him." In the days after the Kristallnacht, the Bishop of Thüringen wrote happily that Luther, who was born on November 10th 1483, couldn't wish a more beautiful birthday gift. (VU University Press)

Here, Adolf Hitler states that he is "fighting for THE LORD's work."

"I believe today that I am acting in the sense of the Almighty Creator. By warding off the Jews, I am fighting for THE LORD's work."—Adolf Hitler, Speech, Reichstag, 1936 (Cline; Burleigh and Wippermann)

The following are excerpts from the infamous book of Martin Luther that Hitler used in his equally wicked book *Mein Kampf*:

But this attitude did not last. Frustrated by Jewish steadfastness, and misinformed regarding Jewish practices, Luther in his later years undid his early openness toward the Jewish people and penned anti-Jewish rants. "On the Jews and Their Lies" (1543) is a patently anti-Semitic document. He writes:

And so, dear Christian, beware of the Jews . . . you can see how God's wrath has consigned them to the devil, who has robbed them not only of a proper understanding of the Scriptures, but also of common human reason, modesty and sense. . . . Thus, when you see a real Jew you may with a good conscience cross yourself, and boldly say, "There goes the devil incarnate." (Luther, On The Jews and Their Lies, Luthers Works)

Never was that hatred more painfully clear than with the rise of Nazism. Those who appropriated and influenced Hitler re-energized Luther's anti-Jewish discourses. Chillingly, in November 1938, just two weeks after Kristallnacht, Martin Sasse, bishop of the Evangelical Church of Thuringia, published a pamphlet titled *Martin Luther and the Jews: Away with Them!* Sasse wrote the following.

On the 10th of November, Luther's birthday, the synagogues are burning... At this moment, we must hear the voice of the prophet of the Germans from the sixteenth century, who out of ignorance began as a friend of the Jews but who, guided by his conscience, experience and reality became the greatest anti-Semite of his age, the one who warned his nation against the Jews. (Marans; Sasse)

Hitler continued selling to all of Germany what their beloved German Christian reformer had said. And with gusto, most of the Protestant and Catholic Christians belonging to the Nazi party exterminated six million Jews, or stood by passively as they committed the crime.

If you wish to find a scapegoat on whose shoulders we may lay the miseries which Germany has brought upon the world–I am more and more convinced that the worst evil genius of that country is not Hitler or Bismarckor Frederick the Great, but Martin Luther. (TIME.com)

Here is the Final Solution according to Martin Luther.

After ranting and raving about the Jews, he gave his advice to his fellow Christians. This advice is in the form of an eight-point plan to deal with the Jews. This plan is most often referred to when scholars attempt to connect Luther with Hitler.

First, Luther told Christians to "set fire to their synagogues or schools and to bury and cover with dirt whatever will not burn." This advice was implemented by the Nazis during the anti-Semitic pogrom known as Kristallnacht...

Second, he recommended that "their houses also be razed and destroyed."

Third, he advised that "all their prayer books and Talmudic writings, in which such idolatry, lies, cursing, and blasphemy are taught, be taken from them."

Fourth, he declared that "rabbis be forbidden to teach henceforth on pain of loss of life and limb."

Fifth, he urged that "safe-conduct on the highways be abolished completely for the Jews."

Sixth, he wrote that "usury (moneylending) should be prohibited to them, and that all cash and treasure of silver and gold be taken from them and put aside for safekeeping." Acting on this advice during the Third Reich, the Nazis often stole money and valuables from the Jews, especially after they were sent to concentration camps.

Seventh, he recommended "putting a flail, an ax, a hoe, a spade, a distaff, or a spindle into the hands... letting them earn their bread in the sweat of their brow." The Nazis also took this advice when they implemented concentration camps, where Jews were forced into hard manual labor.

Finally, he wrote that "if we wish to wash our hands of the Jews' blasphemy and not share in their guilt, we have to part company with them. They must be driven from our country...like mad dogs." This also directly contradicted Luther's earlier statement criticizing the Catholics treatment of the Jews. This advice was taken by the Nazis as well, but they took it a step farther when they implemented their "final solution."

Is it "true" that Luther was anti-Semitic? I have to answer with a resounding yes. However, I think the term "anti-Judaic" better describes Luther, considering the fact that "anti-Semitic" is a modern word, first used in the mid-19th century. Anti-Semitism also concerns the issue of race, whereas Luther's objection to the Jews had nothing to do with their race, but their religious beliefs. (**The Darker Side of Martin Luther**)

Note: The "better solution" that Luther advised became the *Final Solution* that Hitler implemented.

In brief, dear princes and lords, those of you who have Jews under your rule—if my counsel does not please you, *find better advice,* so that you and we all can be rid of the unbearable, devilish burden of the Jews, lest we become guilty sharers before God in the lies, blasphemy, the defamation, and the curses which the mad Jews indulge in so freely and wantonly against the person of our Lord Jesus Christ, this dear mother, all Christians, all authority, and ourselves. Do not grant them protection, safe-conduct, or communion with us. . . . With this faithful counsel and warning I wish to cleanse and exonerate my conscience. (Luther, On The Jews and Their Lies, Luthers Works)

The following is an important insight from the translator of Luther's book *On the Jews and Their Lies* from German to English by Martin H. Bertram.

Although Luther's comments seem to be proto-Nazi, they are better seen as part of tradition of Medieval Christian anti-Semitism. While there is little doubt that Christian anti-Semitism laid the social and cultural basis for modern anti-Semitism, modern anti-Semitism does differ in being based on pseudoscientific notions of race. *The Nazis imprisoned and killed Jews who had converted to Christianity: Luther would have welcomed them.*

I find this to be a very important remark in favor of Martin Luther being a real Christian. Some people, in their attempts to escape Christian collective responsibility for the sin of anti-Semitism, tend to say things like "well, Martin Luther was not a real Christian." He was a real Christian, beloved, as were all the former anti-Semitic church fathers. We must tackle this fact with humility and responsibility and take all the measures possible to rid the Church of the monster of anti-Semitism and of the replacement theology that established it. (Luther, On The Jews and Their Lies; Bertram)

I believe that Martin Luther meant well at first, but then his anger and bitterness led him to a blind hatred—after which he wrote the basis for *the Final Solution* that Hitler followed. However, Hitler took it one step further, but not further from the original doctrines of the Catholic Church in Spain. They considered the blood of a Jew so impure that even after their forceful or willing conversion to Christianity, their blood remained "impure" in the eyes of the Spanish Inquisition; thus, they called Jewish converts by the name of *Marranos* that means "pigs." Adolf Hitler was a professing Catholic turned pagan, who followed the advice of the father of all Protestants and Evangelicals, Martin Luther.

We will see again and again that the combination of Catholic and Protestant Christianity has brought the biggest and most encompassing misery, devastation, and genocide to the Jewish nation.

That Satan has tried so many powerful tactics to annihilate Israel, and yet the Jewish nation survives is a sign and a wonder. Benjamin Disraeli, the Prime Minister of Great Britain during the reign of Queen Victoria in the 19th century, is said to have had a conversation with the Queen when she asked him, "What evidence is there that God is real?" To which Prime Minister Disraeli answered, "The Jews, my lady, the Jews."

That the Jews still exist is enough proof that the God of Israel is real. Satan has tried to exterminate His chosen people in every way possible and has failed, though repeatedly inflicting much pain on the Jews. Benjamin Disraeli belonged to a Jewish family that had converted to Anglican Christianity. Because of this conversion, Disraeli could pursue a political career and eventually became the prime minister of England. The only way to hold public office was to swear allegiance on a Bible to the tenets of Christianity—thus practicing Jews could not hold public office in England or other European Christian nations. This measure was part of the discrimination against Jews in Europe. The following story about Disraeli is very enlightening concerning this political issue.

In 1847 a small political crisis occurred, which removed Bentinck* from the leadership and highlighted Disraeli's differences with his own party. In that year's general election, Lionel de Rothschild had been returned for the City of London. As a practicing Jew, he could not take the oath of allegiance in the prescribed Christian form and therefore could not take his seat. Lord John Russell, the Whig leader who had succeeded Peel as Prime Minister and, like Rothschild, was a member for the City of London, proposed in the Commons that the oath should be amended to permit Jews to enter Parliament. <u>Disraeli spoke in favor of the measure, arguing that Christianity was "completed Judaism", and asking the House of Commons, "Where is your Christianity if you do not believe in their Judaism?"</u> (Wikipedia Contributors)

This powerful statement by Disraeli sums up the whole subject of this book: unveiling identity theft. Where is your belief in the Savior if you reject the fact that He is a Jew and that His Jewish people are still the chosen people? What kind of Savior do you worship if you reject the Jews and everything Jewish?

* Lord George Bentinck was an English Conservative politician

Disraeli's statement was rejected and so was the bill; the Jews were not allowed to serve in public office. Christianity continued its course of anti-Semitism.

A Prayer of Repentance Against Anti-Semitism

Father in heaven, I thank You for letting me know the truth about Christian anti-Semitism. I am appalled, and I repent in dust and ashes for harboring any hatred for Your Jewish people in my heart. I also ask Your forgiveness for the sins of anti-Semitism in my Christian ancestors, pastors and leaders I have had throughout the years. I ask You to cleanse my heart and mind from these deadly theologies of hatred that have caused the humiliation, torment, and death to millions of Jews. I reject and renounce all hatred of the Jews, and I declare the anti-Jewish demon be gone from my life, and from all generations in Yeshua's name! I accept You, Yeshua, as a Jew, as my Jewish Messiah. I honor Your Jewish people and You as the Lion of Judah. I ask You to make my life count as a life of restitution, so that many others will come to the knowledge of the truth and be set free. Thank You for Your amazing grace and compassion for me and all those I represent in Yeshua's name, amen.

For further reading, I recommend my books *Yeshua is the Name,* and *The Bible Cure for Africa and the Nations.**

THE RESTORATION OF ISRAEL

Head Number 5: Anti-Zionist

ADONAI will inherit Judah as His portion in the holy land and will once again choose Jerusalem. Be silent before ADONAI, all flesh, for He has aroused Himself from His holy dwelling.

— ZECHARIAH 2:16–17

This is the fifth and last head of the monster and it is also the final battle front before the return of the Messiah. I would call this head "Political anti-Semitism," which is opposition to YHVH's master plan to restore the Jewish people back to their Promised Land, the land which He gave to Abraham, Isaac, and Jacob for one thousand generations.

He remembers His covenant forever—the Word He commanded for a thousand generations—which He made with Abraham, and swore to Isaac, and confirmed to Jacob as a decree, to Israel as an everlasting covenant, saying, "To you I give the land of Canaan, the portion of your inheritance."

— Psalm 105:8–11

On 26 May 2016, the Plenary in Bucharest adopted the following non-legally binding working definition of anti-Semitism:

"Antisemitism is a certain perception of Jews, which may be expressed as hatred toward Jews. Rhetorical and physical manifestations of anti-Semitism are directed toward Jewish or non-Jewish individuals and/or their property, toward Jewish community institutions and religious facilities."

To guide IHRA* in its work, the following examples may serve as illustrations:

<u>Manifestations might include the targeting of the State of Israel, conceived as a Jewish collectivity.</u> However, criticism of Israel similar to that leveled against any other country cannot be regarded as anti-Semitic. Anti-Semitism frequently charges Jews with conspiring to harm humanity, and it is often used to blame Jews for "why things go wrong." It is expressed in speech, writing, visual forms and action, and employs sinister stereotypes and negative character traits. (United States Department of State)

The United Nations has consistently targeted the State of Israel above all other countries in the world, exposing extreme, international anti-Semitism comparable or greater than during World War II.

---

* IHRA: International Holocaust Remembrance Alliance

In the current 74th session of the UN General Assembly (2019-2020), all EU member states voted for one resolution each to criticize (1) Iran, (2) Syria, (3) North Korea, (4) Myanmar, and (5) the US, for its embargo on Cuba, and two resolutions on Crimea.

By contrast, **EU states voted for 13 out of 18 resolutions singling out Israel.** Yet these same EU states failed to introduce a single United Nations General Assembly resolution on the human rights situation in China, Venezuela, Saudi Arabia, Belarus, Cuba, Turkey, Pakistan, Vietnam, Algeria, or on 175 other countries. (UN Watch)

This state of affairs is not unique to the year of writing this book. It has been the norm for many, many years. And this flagrant anti-Semitism (with a new name "anti-Zionism") has gone majorly uncontested by the member nations of the UN, with the exception of the USA, and occasionally other American partners.

As of 2013, Israel had been condemned in 45 resolutions by the United Nations Human Rights Council. Since the creation of the Council in 2006, it has tabled more resolutions condemning Israel than nearly all the rest of the world combined (45 resolutions against Israel comprised 45.9% of all country-specific resolutions passed by the Council) (Wikipedia Contributors)

Countries that consistently violate human rights to the point of plundering and even murdering their populations (such as Syria, China, North Korea, Venezuela, and others) have barely been condemned, if at all, by the UN. But "little Israel"—that since 1948 has become a beacon of light, agriculture, technology, medicine, and disaster relief for other nations (their enemies included)—has been condemned non-stop.

This is anti-Semitism at its worst, and from now on, we will equate anti-Zionism with anti-Semitism.

Christian, Political Anti-Semitism

However, we cannot disconnect political anti-Semitism from the deeply rooted anti-Semitism in Christian circles. A Church steeped in replacement theology is in grave danger of rewriting the Bible in order to conform it to their political anti-Semitism. The following excerpt is alarming, to say the least, but by no means surprising.

A recent official translation of the Bible into Danish arouses wonder among religious people. The Danish "Bible Society", which is responsible for the translation, has obliterated and removed the word "Israel" from the New Testament (which in the new edition is now called "The New Agreement").

According to Jan Frost, who has read the new edition, it applies both when the *land* of Israel and when the *people* of Israel are mentioned. Israel is otherwise mentioned in this way in the New Testament more than 60 times.

Mr. Frost states in a video posted on YouTube that the word "Israel" is only used once in the "Bible 2020", which is the name of the new edition.

The translators of the new edition, according to Frost, offer the explanation that the land of Israel in biblical times was not identical to present Israel.

But the same logic is not applied by the translators when the land of Egypt is mentioned: Egypt is still Egypt, even in this new 2020 edition.

On social media, several users are furious at the radical change of such a central element of the New Testament, and a widespread criticism suggests a suspicion that they have removed Israel for political reasons. (24NYT)

O God, do not remain quiet; Do not be silent and, O God, do not be still. For behold, Your enemies make an uproar, and those who hate You have exalted themselves. They make shrewd plans against Your people, and conspire together against Your treasured ones. They have said, "Come, and let us wipe them out as a nation, that the name of Israel be remembered no more." For they have conspired together with one mind; against You they make a covenant...

— Psalm 83:1–5 NASB

What is anti-Zionism?

Anti-Zionism is the complete political and religious opposition to the ultimate plan of redemption for the Jewish people, which includes the return of all the descendants of Abraham, Isaac, and Jacob to their ancestral Promised Land of Zion/Israel. Many prophecies speak about it within the Holy Scriptures. There are also many warnings in the Scriptures of great judgment against all nations that dare to oppose YHVH's master plan for His chosen people and their land. More about this judgment will be discussed in Gate 12.

He has remembered His covenant forever, the word which He commanded to a thousand generations, the covenant which He made with Abraham, and His oath to Isaac. Then He confirmed it to Jacob for a statute, to Israel as an everlasting covenant, saying, "To you I will give the land of Canaan as the portion of your inheritance"

— PSALM 105:8–11 NASB

To understand anti-Zionism, we need to know what Zionism is. Zionism is a religious and political effort that brought millions of Jews from around the world back to their ancient homeland in the Middle East and re-established Israel as the central location of Jewish identity. While some critics call Zionism "an aggressive and discriminatory ideology," the Zionist movement has successfully established a Jewish homeland in the land of Israel.

In 1890, Nathan Birnboim coined the term Zionism, while studying at the University in Vienna. Zionism is the Jewish movement that started at the end of the 19th century for the purpose of establishing a Jewish national home for all the Jews scattered in the diaspora. The uncontested father of Zionism was Theodor Benjamin Herzl, his Hebrew name is Benjamin Zeev Herzl. He was a Hungarian Jew, a journalist that was very impacted by the unjust Dreyfuss Trial in France.

In the Dreyfuss Trial in 1894, a Jewish officer in the French Army was arrested and convicted of treason. As he was being taken away to be exiled, crowds of Frenchmen shouted, "Death to the Jews!" It shocked the young, Jewish journalist covering the story.

Herzl had been an "emancipated" Jew until then, thinking that it was possible for the Jews to be equal to all others in the nations and to have equal rights.

He decided that the only way to prevent anti-Semitism from happening again was to create a Jewish state. From that conclusion, he began working with the Zionist movement propelling it to a level that the world could not ignore.

In 1897, the First Zionist Congress was held in Basel, Switzerland. It lasted three days, in order for the leaders of Zionism to thoroughly discuss Herzl's and others' plans. They laid out a plan, including Herzl's idea of bringing international leaders on board.

After the meeting, Herzl went home and wrote in his journal, "Today I established a Jewish state. If I were to say this out loud, everyone would laugh at me. But if not in five years, in fifty years, there will be a Jewish state."

Herzl was right; fifty years later, in 1948, the Jewish state was born in the land of Israel, the biblical Promised Land of the Jewish people.

After traveling through Europe, meeting both Zionist communities and political leaders, Herzl wrote a pamphlet called *The Jewish State* in 1898. (Avraham)

Herzl did not insist on the land of Israel being the place for the Jewish state, and was willing to explore other possible land purchases or grants like in Uganda, for example. He also envisioned the language of this Jewish state as German. However, soon after a visit to Palestine, and seeing what the first Jewish pioneers were achieving there, he was convinced that the only viable option for the Jewish people was what he called in his book, *Altneuland* or *Old-New Land*, the area then called Palestine—which is none other than the ancient, biblical land of Israel.

Many from the Eastern European Jewish community realized that it was time to return to Zion, fulfilling the ancient proclamation that Jews have made at Passover during two thousand years of painful exile,

Le Shana Habaa Byerushalayim Habnuya

"Next year in rebuilt Jerusalem!"

From Palestine to Rebuilt Israel

The Spirit of God stirred many young Jews and Jewesses, especially Eastern European university students and intellectuals, to go and possess the land of Israel employing agriculture. When these idealistic and visionary youngsters arrived, the land was called Palestine, and under Turkish rule, it had become a wasteland.

400 years of the Ottoman Empire, and numerous previous empires that had coveted this land, had left it ravaged and desolate, a land good for nothing—full of malaria infested swamps, as well as rock and sand deserts.

Zionism was Fueled by the Kishinev Pogrom

As we have seen in previous gates, vicious Christian anti-Semitism and its endless persecutions, pogroms, and genocides had left the Jewish people constantly displaced. So many Jews all over Europe were expelled from one village or city to another, or even one country to another until there was no corner on earth that could be called their own. The Kishinev Pogrom was "the straw that broke the camel's back." As many other brutal pogroms and expulsions before it, this one happened on the Christian Easter Sunday festivities declaring "death to the Jews that murdered Christ."

On April 8, 1903—Easter Sunday—a "mild disturbance" against local Jews rattled Kishinev, a sleepy city on the southwestern border of imperial Russia.

"Little property was destroyed," said Jewish cultural historian Steven J. Zipperstein, who is a Radcliffe Fellow this year, "and the outbreak seemed little more than a bacchanal (drunken riot) of rowdy teenagers."

But the next day, and for half the next, violence escalated. Gangs of 10 or 20 armed with hatchets and knives stormed through the town's narrow streets and into its courtyards, where Jewish families defended themselves with garden implements and other meager weapons.

In the end, 49 Jews were killed, an untold number of Jewish women were raped, and 1,500 Jewish homes were damaged. This sudden rush of hoodlum violence—prompted by accusatory rumors of Jewish ritual murder—quickly became a talisman of "imperial Russian brutality against its Jews," said Zipperstein.

"The Protocols of the Elders of Zion," a long-lived anti-Semitic slanderous concoction that outlines a plan for world Jewish domination, appeared in its first sustained form just months after the Kishinev massacre.

Chayim Nachman Bialik, the man who one day would be known as the national poet of the Jewish people was dispatched in 1903 to interview survivors of the Kishinev pogrom by the Jewish Historical Commission in Odessa. Going house to house, he filled five notebooks with fresh testimonies of violence. (Ireland)

The Development of Zionism

We must address three groups of proto-Zionists: Zionists calling for a Jewish state before the formally established Zionist movement.

Harbingers of Zionism: from the 1840s to the 1860s the Harbingers of Zionism was a group of highly educated Englishmen. They believed that if the world's Jews moved to Israel to convert to Christianity, then the Messiah, or the Second Coming of Jesus would happen. As part of their work, the Palestine Exploration Fund (PEF) was established to do archeological and geological work in the Holy Land.

Rabbis al Kalai and Kalischer: These two Rabbis were living in an area of Europe with a lot of national movements buzzing around them. And yet, like so many other Jews, they didn't feel like they fit in any of them. They believed that Jews should settle in Israel to bring the Messiah. This was exceptional for two Rabbis at the time, for most religious Jews believed one could not move to Israel until the Messiah came.

Moses Hess and the publication of his book *Rome and Jerusalem* in 1862

Moses Hess was an important Jewish and socialist thinker in Central Europe. In his book, he writes that Jews also have a right to be a nation with the same definition as other nations.

With nationalism on the rise, Proto-Zionists catching on, Eastern European Jews fearing physical danger, and Western European

Jews fearing total assimilation, Zionism became a very serious answer.

The land of Israel, called Palestine at the time, was controlled by the Ottoman Empire (originating from modern day Turkey). In 1800, 275,000 Arabs and 5,500 Jews were living there. Most of the Arab residents were living in rural areas, while most of the Jewish residents were living in urban areas, like Jerusalem, Tzfat, Tiberius, and Hebron.

Fifty years later, in 1850, there were 400,000 Arabs, and 10,000 Jews living in Palestine. When the Ottoman powers saw the changes beginning to unfold, they made two very important land reforms:

In 1858, non-Muslim, Ottoman subjects could buy land and build on it. In 1867, non-Ottoman subjects could buy land and build on it.

This would prove essential for the success of the Zionist movement. Before the Zionists moved there, two groups of Jews were living in the land. The first group was Spanish (or Sephardic) Jews and the Arabic Jews, also called the Mustaf Aravim. The second group was made up of elderly and single people coming to study Torah and to die in the Holy Land.

In 1870, the *Mikve Israel* agricultural school was established to teach young students agriculture. It is part of the Alliance Isra-elite Universelle schools established across the Middle East and North Africa. (Avraham)

Mark Twain's Report of the Holy Land

After the invention of the steamboat in the nineteenth century, hundreds of American pilgrims flooded into the Holy Land, in boatload after boatload. In an era when the typical American Protestant was required to master the Bible, many Americans knew the basic geography and the names of the historical sites of the ancient land of Israel before even arriving in the Holy Land. The first American pilgrims reached Palestine in 1819. With the normalization of diplomatic relations between the United States and the Ottoman Empire in 1832, the final bureaucratic barrier to the already arduous journey was removed.

In 1866, the young author Samuel Clemens, who was just beginning to become known under the pen name Mark Twain, set out to examine the attractions for himself. The rapidly developing religious tourism industry contributed to Twain's natural tendency toward ridicule and satire. He latched on to a group of pilgrims, whom he deridingly dubbed "the innocents," and boarded the "Quaker City" en route to the land of Israel.

Prior to his departure, Twain had signed a contract to write fifty-one short articles during the journey. The letters he penned while in Palestine were combined with articles he wrote later on, the result being *The Innocents Abroad*, a book which detailed his impressions of the strange country he encountered.

Twain was fed up with the primitiveness of the settlements and roads he encountered: *"The further we went the hotter the sun got, and the more rocky and bare, repulsive and dreary the landscape became... There was hardly a tree or a shrub anywhere. Even the olive and the cactus, those fast friends of a worthless soil, had almost deserted the country."* The statement reflects his general attitude to the ancient land throughout his journey.

One exception to the rule was the city of Jerusalem, which Twain described in glowing terms, "Perched on its eternal hills, white and domed and solid, massed together and hooped with high gray walls, the venerable city gleamed in the sun. So small! Why, it was no larger than an American village of four thousand inhabitants... Tears would have been out of place. The thoughts Jerusalem suggests are full of poetry, sublimity (truly wonderful), and more than all, dignity. Such thoughts do not find their appropriate expression in the emotions of the nursery."

A central motif that weaves through Twain's writings is the polarization between American progress and the enslavement of the Holy Land to its own past. In his opinion, it was precisely the reverence of the three religions towards the land of Israel that was responsible for the miserable state he perceived it to be in. In one of the sharpest and most beautiful passages in the book, Twain states that, *"Palestine is desolate and unlovely. And why should it be otherwise? Can the curse of the Deity beautify a land? Palestine is no more of this work-day world. It is sacred to poetry and tradition – it is dream-land."* (The Librarians)

Despite the terrible condition of the land of Israel, the first Jewish pioneers from Eastern Europe arrived to redeem it, even at the cost of their lives and all worldly possessions. Someone much greater than themselves was propelling them out of their academic studies into the trade of farming and agriculture, which they did not master at first. Though most of them were not religious but socialists, their spirits arose within them unbeknown to them to apprehend the promise described below:

> See, I will gather them out of all the countries, where I have driven them in My anger, My fury, and great wrath, and I will bring them back to this place and cause them to dwell securely. They will be My people, and I will be their God. I will give them one heart and one way, so they may fear Me forever; for their good and for their children after them.
> I will make an everlasting covenant with them: I will never turn away from doing good for them. I will put My fear in their hearts, so that they will not depart from Me.
> Yes, I will delight in doing good for them, and with all My heart and all My soul I will in truth plant them in this land.
> For thus says ADONAI: "Just as I have brought all this great evil on this people, so I will bring on them all the good that I have promised them. So fields will be bought in this land, about which you are saying: 'It will be a desolation, without man or beast; it is handed over to the Chaldeans.' Men will buy fields for money and sign and seal the deeds and call witnesses in the land of Benjamin and in the areas around Jerusalem, and in the towns of Judah, in the towns of the hill-country, in the towns of the foothills, and in the cities of the South— because I will bring them back from exile." It is a declaration of ADONAI.
>
> — JEREMIAH 32:37–44

Through the establishment of a fund called the Jewish National Fund (JNF), lands were purchased and trees planted. They purchased portions of swampland infested by malaria mosquitoes at exorbitant prices from the Turks. The Jewish pioneers paid any price to obtain legal rights over the land no one else wanted, nor invested in its wellbeing. It is said that about 80% of the young Jewish men and women that went into the swamps to drain them died of malaria. The land was not only obtained according to God's many promises in the Bible, but by purchase (at high prices from the Turks), and by blood, as many paid with their lives to redeem it.

Jewish National Fund, a non-profit organization, was founded in 1901 to buy and develop land in Ottoman Palestine (later the British Mandate for Palestine, and subsequently Israel and the Palestinian territories) for Jewish settlement. By 2007, it owned 13% of the total land in Israel. Since its inception, the JNF says it has planted over 240 million trees in Israel. It has also built 180 dams and reservoirs, developed 250,000 acres (1,000 km²) of land and established more than 1,000 parks.

In 2002, the JNF was awarded the Israel Prize for lifetime achievement and special contribution to society and the State of Israel. (Wikipedia Contributors)

The Biggest Miracle of the 20th Century

Just like Theodore Herzl prophesied, exactly fifty years after the First Zionist Congress in Basel, Switzerland, "Israel will become a country among the nations." The prophet Isaiah also prophesied that the nation of Israel will be reborn in one day.

> **Who has heard such a thing? Who has seen such things? Can a land be born in one day? Can a nation be brought forth at once? For as soon as Zion was in labor, she gave birth to her children.**
>
> — ISAIAH 66:8

By far the biggest miracle of the 20th century was the establishment of the reborn State of Israel after 2,000 years of devastating exile. This miracle state is like a phoenix rising from the ashes of the Nazi Shoah (Holocaust) that left over six million Jews dead, and many more scarred for life. Entire family lines were wiped out, and Jewish villages and communities in Nazi Europe were totally erased. The devastation of Jewish life caused by the Nazi regime was so deep and so cruel that it looked impossible to restore the Jewish people again. It looked like this horrendous satanic regime, led by Adolf Hitler, had finally fulfilled Satan's dream of eliminating the Jews forever.

However, the promises from the ELOHIM of Israel were manifest at the Jews' darkest and the most impossible moment. Israel rose from the dead, out of the ashes of the Shoah (Holocaust) to become the State of Israel that we know today, the only democracy in the Middle East. Israel is a country that, though small, is the first one to send disaster relief to nations in distress, and to find cures for plagues, viruses, and diseases. It is one of the leading, high-tech groundbreaking nations of the world, a country of innovations that helps better the world.

Arise, shine, for your light has come! The glory of ADONAI has risen on you. For behold, darkness covers the earth, and deep darkness the peoples. But ADONAI will arise upon you, and His glory will appear over you. Nations will come to your light, kings to the brilliance of your rising. Lift up your eyes and look all around: they all gather—they come to you—your sons will come from far away, your daughters carried on the hip.

— ISAIAH 60:1–4

Those who rebuilt Israel were mostly Shoah (Holocaust) survivors that lost everything; Nazi Germany annihilated most of their family members in the horrible gas chambers of death camps in Poland. Some pioneers of this newborn state looked like skeletons when they arrived as refugees in the land of Israel, ready to work hard to assure that the Jews would reconstitute their national homeland.

The same UN that now condemns Israel most of the time is the one that voted to partition Palestine into two countries, one Arab and one Jewish. However, the Arabs refused the offer, but the Jews accepted it. On May 14, 1948, the first prime minister of Israel, Mr. David Ben Gurion, read the Declaration of Independence from a hall in the city of Tel Aviv. Two years later, once the besieged west Jerusalem was secured from the attacking Jordanian and pan-Arab armies, the capital of Israel was moved to the western side of its historical location: Jerusalem, the capital of King David, the king of Israel, and Judah 3,000 years ago.

Finally, every Jew in the world had a home; the time of the "wandering Jew" or rather the "expelled and persecuted Jew" was over. Jews from all the nations of the world flocked back home, just like the prophet Isaiah foresaw over 2,500 years ago.

The ransomed of ADONAI will return and come to Zion with singing, with everlasting joy upon their heads. They will obtain gladness and joy, and sorrow and sighing will flee away.

— Isaiah 35:10

The State of Israel in the land of Israel is the only historical and biblically promised home of the Jewish people. There is no other. And the Jewish people are the only people who have returned to their own ancient land after 2,000 years of exile, and have revived their ancient language, Hebrew, which is also the language in which they wrote most of the Bible.

The Revival of the Hebrew Language

The following biography explains the process of this amazing revival of the Hebrew language.

Eliezer Ben-Yehuda (1858-December 16, 1922) is known as the father of modern Hebrew. He was one of the earliest supporters of Zionism, and it due primarily to his initiative that Hebrew was revived as a modern spoken language.

Ben-Yehuda was born in Luzki, Lithuania, in 1858 as Eliezer Perelman. His father, a 'Chabad orthodox Jew, died when he was 5. At age 13 his uncle sent him to a Yeshiva in Polotsk. The head of the Yeshiva was a secret follower of the Haskalah (enlightenment) movement* and turned Ben-Yehuda into a free thinker.

---

* Haskala, also spelled Haskalah (from Hebrew sekhel, "reason," or "intellect"), also called *Jewish Enlightenment*, a late 18th and 19th century intellectual movement among the Jews of central and eastern Europe that attempted to acquaint Jews with the European and Hebrew languages and with secular education and culture as supplements to traditional Talmudic studies. (The Editors of Encyclopaedia Britannica)

His uncle tried to save him from heresy by sending him to study in Glubokoye. There, Ben-Yehuda met Samuel Naphtali Hertz Jonas, and was taught Russian by his eldest daughter, Deborah, who later became his wife. His Russian studies enabled Ben-Yehuda to enter the gymnasia (high school) which he graduated in 1877. He soon became a convinced Zionist. The Russo-Turkish War of 1877-1878 and the struggle of Balkan nations for liberation inspired Ben-Yehuda to form the idea of revival of the Jewish people in its ancestral soil. He held that the Jews, like all other peoples, had a historic land and language.

He wrote in the preface to his dictionary: "it was as if the heavens had suddenly opened, and a clear incandescent light flashed before my eyes, and a mighty inner voice sounded in my ears: the renascence of Israel on its ancestral soil.... the more the nationalist concept grew in me, the more I realized what a common language is to a nation..." He decided to settle in the land of Israel and in 1878 went to study medicine in Paris so as to have a means of support.

Ben-Yehuda's plan for a national home did not interest Hebrew writers for the most part. His first essay, "The burning question" (She'elat Hasha'ah) was published by the Hebrew periodical, "The Dawn" (Hasha'har), in 1879, edited by Peretz Smolenskin, after it was rejected by others. It called for emigration to the land of Israel and creation of a national spiritual center of the Jews there. Thus, Ben-Yehuda was also the real father of Cultural Zionism, later popularized by Achad Haam. (Zionism-Israel)

In Paris, Ben-Yehuda contracted tuberculosis. He discontinued his medical studies and decided that the climate of Jerusalem would be better for his illness. While in Paris, he learned from travelers that Hebrew was not a dead language among Asian Jews. He also enrolled in the teachers' seminary of the Alliance Israelite Universelle where he was to be trained as an instructor in the Mikveh Yisrael agricultural school. He attended lectures of Joseph Halevy, who had been an early advocate of coining new Hebrew words.

Ben-Yehuda moved to Jerusalem in 1881, with his new wife, Deborah Jonas. Eliezer and Deborah established the first Hebrew-speaking home in Eretz Yisrael*, and their son, Ben-Zion (who became known by his penname, Itamar Ben-Avi) was the first child in modern times to be nurtured with Hebrew as his native language. He attempted to disguise himself as an orthodox Jew in order to maintain contact with them and learn Hebrew and propagate it. However, the latter soon rejected him, and Ben-Yehuda became actively anti-religious.

Ben-Yehuda gathered friends and allies in Jerusalem. In 1881, together with Y.M. Pines, D. Yellin, Y. Meyu'has and A. Mazie, he founded the "Te'hiyat Yisrael" – the Rebirth of Israel society based on five principles: work on the land, expansion of the productive population, creation of modern Hebrew literature and science reflecting both a national and universalistic spirit, and opposition to the halukah (charity) system that maintained the Yeshiva** students of Jerusalem.'

Soon after his arrival in Jerusalem, Ben-Yehuda became a teacher at the Alliance School, on condition that his courses would be

* Hebrew, meaning "land of Israel"

** Yeshiva: an Orthodox Jewish college or seminary

taught in Hebrew. Thus, this became the first school where some courses were taught in Hebrew. Ben-Yehuda wrote for "Ha'havatzelet" (The Lily), a Hebrew literary periodical, and launched "Hatzvi" (The Deer), a weekly newspaper. "Hatzvi" was the first Hebrew paper to report on news and issues in Turkish Palestine. This was a considerable achievement, given the limitations of Hebrew, the Turkish censorship and draconic financial limitations. Ben-Yehuda had to coin new Hebrew nouns and verbs for modern concepts.

Debora Ben-Yehuda, his first wife, died of tuberculosis in 1891. Her younger sister soon offered to marry Ben-Yehuda and care for his two small children. An emancipated woman of great drive and conviction, she made it her life's work to support Eliezer and his enterprise. She took the Hebrew name Hemdah, quickly learned Hebrew, became a reporter for his paper, and later became its editor, allowing her husband to focus on his research of the lost Hebrew words that the reborn tongue required and coinage of new ones.

Orthodox fanatics were angered at the depictions in Hatzvi of corruption in the distribution of Halukah, their charity dole (benefits paid by the government to the unemployed). They deliberately mistranslated a line in a Hanukkah story in Hatzvi, "Let us gather strength and go forward" to mean: "Let us gather an army and proceed against the East." They informed the Ottoman government that Ben-Yehuda was calling on his followers to revolt. He was arrested, charged with conspiracy to revolt and sentenced to a year's imprisonment. Jews throughout the world were outraged; his sentence was appealed and he was eventually released.

In 1904, Ben-Yehuda together with Yellin, Mazie and others, founded and presided over "Va'ad HaLashon", the forerunner of the Hebrew Language Academy which he later advocated in 1920. He worked 18 hours a day on his "Complete Dictionary of Ancient and Modern Hebrew." In 1910 he published the first of six volumes to appear before his death in 1922. After his death his widow Hemdah and son Ehud continued publishing his manuscript until all 17 volumes had been published by 1959. The dictionary lists all the words used in Hebrew literature from the time of Abraham to modern times, meticulously avoiding Aramaic words and other foreign influences that had entered biblical and Mishnaic Hebrew.

Ben-Yehuda was forced to leave Palestine during World War I, when the Turks deported "enemy nationals." Along with other Zionist leaders he spent the war in the United States, returning to Palestine in 1919.

In November of 1920 he succeeded in prevailing on Herbert Samuel, British High Commissioner of Palestine, to make Hebrew one of the three official languages of the Palestine Mandate.

It is difficult to exaggerate the contribution and achievement of Ben-Yehuda. His lexicographical achievement itself – to innovate a modern language on the remains of an ancient and fossilized one, was monumental in itself, but it was only an instrument in a successful one-man campaign, to make Hebrew the spoken language of the Jewish people. Thanks to his almost single-handed initiative, this was accomplished in the space of less than 40 years. (Zionism-Israel)

The Balfour Declaration

On the road to the national rebirth and restoration of Israel, we cannot overlook the most important document called the Balfour Declaration.

On November 2, 1917, Foreign Secretary Arthur James Balfour writes an important letter to Britain's most illustrious Jewish citizen, Baron Lionel Walter Rothschild, expressing the British government's support for a Jewish homeland in **Palestine**. The letter would eventually become known as the **Balfour Declaration**.

Britain's support for the Zionist movement came from its concerns regarding the direction of World War I. Aside from a genuine belief in the righteousness of Zionism, held by Lloyd George among others, Britain's leaders hoped that a statement supporting Zionism would help gain Jewish support for the Allies.

On November 2nd, Balfour sent his letter to Lord Rothschild, a prominent Zionist and a friend of Chaim Weizmann, stating that, "His Majesty's Government view with favor the establishment in Palestine of a national home for the Jewish people."

The influence of the Balfour Declaration on the course of postwar events was immediate: According to the "mandate" system created by the Versailles Treaty of 1919, Britain was entrusted with the administration of Palestine, with the understanding that it would work on behalf of both its Jewish and Arab inhabitants. (History.com Editors)

This issuance of this historic document was duly attained, at least in part, through the intervention of Dr. Chayim Weizmann, a brilliant Jewish scientist who eventually became the first president of the State of Israel. Dr. Weizmann "bartered" science that helped the allies win World War I, for a promise from the British crown to be favorable to the idea of a homeland for the Jewish people in the land then called Palestine. After the war, Great Britain received a mandate over all of Palestine based on this promise, which came to be known as the British Mandate.

However, later during World War II, and its aftermath, when many Jewish refugees escaping Nazi Europe tried to get to the land, the British Mandate closed its doors to tens of thousands of these half-dead Jews, and deported them to detention camps in Cyprus, the Indian Ocean, and even some back to Nazi Europe where most of them perished. The British declared the attempt by Jewish refugees to enter the land of Israel during the Nazi Holocaust, and its aftermath, "Illegal Immigration" (in Hebrew *Haapala or Aliyah Bet*). This unfortunate closure caused the unnecessary death of many Holocaust victims and survivors.

Over 100,000 people attempted to illegally enter Mandatory Palestine. There were 142 voyages by 120 ships. Over half were stopped by the British patrols. The Royal Navy had eight ships on station in Palestine, and additional ships were tasked with tracking suspicious vessels heading for Palestine. Most of the intercepted immigrants were sent to internment camps in Cyprus. Some were sent to the Atlit detention camp in Palestine, and some to Mauritius. The British held as many as 50,000 people in these camps (see Jews in British camps on Cyprus). Over 1,600 drowned at sea. Only a few thousand actually entered Palestine.

The pivotal event in the *Ha'apala* program was the incident of the SS Exodus in 1947. The *Exodus* was intercepted and boarded by a British patrol. Despite significant resistance from its passengers, *Exodus* was forcibly returned to Europe. Its passengers were eventually sent back to Germany. This was publicized, to the great embarrassment of the British government.

One account of Aliyah Bet is given by journalist I. F. Stone in his 1946 book *Underground to Palestine,* a first-person account of traveling from Europe with displaced persons attempting to reach the Jewish homeland.

Some 250 American veterans from World War II, including Murray Greenfield (of the ship *Hatikvah*), volunteered to sail ten ships ("The Jews' Secret Fleet") from the United States to Europe to load 35,000 survivors of the Holocaust (half of the illegal immigrants to Palestine), only to be deported to detention camps on Cyprus. (Wikipedia Contributors)

The British Mandate mainly favored the Arabs over the Jews. Another unfortunate decision by the British was to place Haj Amin Al Husseini as the grand mufti of Jerusalem, the highest Muslim leader in the land. He had a tremendous influence on the Arab population that had been under Turkish rule for 400 years and now under the British Mandate. As leader of the Muslims, Al Husseini incited horrendous massacres of entire Jewish communities in the cities of Yafo, Hebron, and Motsa in 1920 and 1929. This man eventually sided with Hitler for the annihilation of all the Jews in Palestine. He is the father of what we call today "The Palestinian Cause." I call it "Hitler's Child" since it was born of a private meeting between Haj Amin Al Husseini and Adolf Hitler in Berlin in 1941. And though he had been removed from his post as grand mufti after the riots of 1936, Haj Amin Al Husseini's legacy of fifteen years in leadership under the British authorities, positioned him to gather momentum and influence that have harmed Israel to this day.

The British Mandate officially ended when Israel was proclaimed a State on May 14, 1948. The British handed the keys of most guard, police, and army posts and fortresses to the newly formed Jordanian Army that opposed the establishment of the State of Israel. They attacked the newborn state less than 24 hours after its inception. The ensuing conflict is called "The War of Independence." The Arab armies besieged Jerusalem from December 1947 until July 1948. The Jews in the city were starving without food or ammunition. Israel did not yet have an army like today, but they had something similar to militias. Many of those youngsters who gave their lives on the bloody road to open the way to Jerusalem, to bring food to the starving population and weapons to defend themselves, were Shoah (Holocaust) survivors. The British had armed the Jordanian Army well, and young emerging Israel did not stand a chance against her enemies—except the God of Israel was with them.

> **Behold, anyone fiercely attacking is not from Me. Whoever stirs up strife with you will fall because of you. Behold, I created the smith who blows the fire of coals and produces a weapon for its work, and I created the destroyer to ruin. No weapon formed against you will prosper and you will condemn every tongue that rises against you in judgment. This is the heritage**

of ADONAI's servants—their vindication is from Me." It is a declaration of ADONAI.

— ISAIAH 54:15–17

This trend of Israel winning impossible wars after being attacked by the Arab nations against her has repeated itself again and again throughout every one of the major wars. Arab nations usually attack Israel first, and Israel does not stand a chance as the armies of her enemies are ten times bigger and well-armed, as in 1948, and yet, somehow, Israel wins every war. This should have been enough to make the UN understand that the God of the Universe, also called the God of Israel, is fighting for His people, and that whoever tries to hinder His plan for their restoration to their ancient homeland will fight against a Formidable Enemy.

Within fifteen years of the end of the British Mandate, the vast Empire of which it was said, "The sun never sets on the British Empire" was no more. Today the country is called the United Kingdom, and there is no British Empire. In what way did the measures taken by the British Mandate against the Jews affect the ending of the great British Empire? We can only quote what the Holy Scriptures say about those that either harm or do not help Israel. Here is what ADONAI Tzva'ot, THE LORD of the Armies says, the One who battles the wars of Israel.

"For thus says ADONAI-Tzva'ot, He has sent me after glory to the nations that plundered you—because whoever touches you touches the apple of His eye— 'For behold, I will shake My hand against them and they will be plunder to their servants.' Then you will know that ADONAI-Tzva'ot has sent me."

"'Sing and rejoice, O daughter of Zion! For behold, I am coming and I will live among you'—it is a declaration of ADONAI. 'In that day many nations will join themselves to ADONAI and they will be My people and I will dwell among you.' Then you will know that ADONAI-Tzva'ot has sent me to you. ADONAI will inherit Judah as His portion in the holy land and will once again choose Jerusalem. Be silent before ADONAI, all flesh, for He has aroused Himself from His holy dwelling."

— ZECHARIAH 2:12–17

Here is the same passage from another easier translation.

The LORD rules over all. His angel says to Israel, "The Glorious One has sent me to punish the nations that have robbed you of everything. That's because anyone who hurts you hurts those the LORD loves and guards. So I will raise my powerful hand to strike down your enemies. Their own slaves will rob them of everything. Then you will know that the LORD who rules over all has sent me. "'People of Zion, shout and be glad! I am coming to live among you,' announces the LORD. 'At that time many nations will join themselves to me. And they will become my people. I will live among you,' says the LORD. Then you will know that the LORD who rules over all has sent me to you. He will receive Judah as his share in the holy land. And he will choose Jerusalem again. All you people of the world, be still because the LORD is coming. He is getting ready to come down from his holy Temple in heaven."

— ZECHARIAH 2:8–13 NIRV

As you can see, the God of Israel is not "politically correct"; He espouses His own "politics." I call this "biblical politics."

The Truth Behind the Palestinian Cause

Adolf Hitler once said: "Tell a *lie*, make it big enough, repeat it over and over, and everyone will believe it." (Wikipedia Contributors)

This statement also applies to the political concoction of the Palestinian cause, one of the biggest deceptions ever perpetrated. I call the Palestinian Cause "Hitler's Child." You will soon understand why.

What politicians call today the Palestinian cause, is a "child" born of the historical meeting between one of the greatest terrorists and butchers who ever existed, the grand mufti of Jerusalem, Haj Amin Al Husseini, and the cruelest and wickedest man who ever lived named Adolf Hitler. The meeting took place in Berlin, Germany in 1941. The mufti asked Hitler to build him an army in Palestine to apply Hitler's Final Solution to the Jews inside the land. Hitler complied with this hideous idea, and the forerunner of the Palestinian Liberation Organization (PLO) was born. Every other organization, including Fattah, Al Qaeda, Hezbollah, Hamas, the Muslim Brotherhood, and all other terror organizations, are derivatives of Hitler's Child, the PLO.

The Palestinian Liberation Organization's (PLO) only aim is the annihilation of all the Jews in the land of Israel. That is why they have accepted no "peace plan," no matter how much land and money is offered to them. They want all the land and no Jews alive on it. In the maps of the so-called Palestinian Authorities, Israel does not exist. The entire land has reverted to being called Palestine. Jerusalem exists neither in their maps; it is called Al Kuds.

When the Romans conquered the land of Israel they changed the name to Palestine. They gave it the name of Israel's archenemies, the Philistines. In most Christian Bibles, Israel is still called Palestine, and the map supplements at the back of the volumes use the term, "Maps of Palestine." It plays into the great deception, and is an insult to the God of Israel, who calls His land by the name of Israel. It is the eternal covenant name. God has restored His Jewish people to His land and restored the name. He is referring to "My enemies" as those who refuse to call Israel 'Israel.' How many Christians have become His enemies on this one subject alone?

> **God, do not keep silent. Do not hold Your peace, O God. Do not be still. For look, Your enemies make an uproar. Those who hate You lift up their head. They make a shrewd plot against Your people, conspiring against Your treasured ones. "Come," they say, "let's wipe them out as a nation! Let Israel's name be remembered no more!" For with one mind they plot together. Against You do they make a covenant.**
>
> **— Psalm 83:2–6**

The Palestinian people do not exist as a historical nation. They are a "created" people by the politicians of the nations who use the Palestinian cause as a Trojan horse to destroy Israel. Let me explain.

From the 16th to the 20th centuries, the Ottoman Empire ruled the area then called Palestine. The area comprised all of Israel and Jordan of today. During the time of Turkish Ottoman rule, there were many migrations of people from areas within the empire, which included the area known as the Levant. These migrations brought into Palestine Arab people of different nationalities and made Palestine their home.

It was not their historical homeland, but as Ottoman citizens, they could settle there.

The History of Migration to Palestine

Ottoman Period of 1800 to 1918

Some Egyptian migration to Palestine happened at the end of the 18th century due to a severe famine in Egypt, and several waves of Egyptian immigrants came even earlier due to escape natural disasters such as droughts and plagues, government oppression, taxes, and military conscription. Although many Palestinian Arabs also moved to Egypt, Egyptian immigration to Palestine was more dominant. In the 19th century, large numbers of Egyptians fled to Palestine to escape the military conscription and forced labor projects in the Nile Delta under Muhammad Ali. Following the First Egyptian-Ottoman War, which saw the Egyptian conquest of Palestine, more Egyptians were brought to Palestine as forced laborers. Following the Second Egyptian-Ottoman War, which saw Egyptian rule in Palestine terminated, massive numbers of soldiers deserted during the Egyptian army's retreat from Palestine to permanently settle there. Egyptians settled mainly in Jaffa, the Coastal plain, Samaria and in Wadi Ara. In the southern plain there were 19 villages with Egyptian populations, while in Jaffa there were some 500 Egyptian families with a population of over 2,000 people. The largest rural concentration of Egyptian immigrants was in the Sharon region. According to David Grossman, statistics show the number of Egyptian immigrants to Palestine between 1829 and 1841 exceeded 15,000, and he estimated that it was at least 23,000 and possibly up to 30,000. In 1860, there was significant immigration to **Safed** by **Moorish** (i.e. **Arab-Berber**) tribes from **Algeria** and a small number of **Kurds**, while some 6,000 Arabs from the **Beni Sakhr** tribe immigrated to Palestine from what is now **Jordan** to settle in **Tiberias**. In addition, considerable numbers of **Turks** stationed in Palestine to garrison the land settled there.

In 1878, following **Austro-Hungarian occupation of Bosnia and Herzegovina**, many Bosnian Muslims, apprehensive of living under Christian rule, emigrated to the Ottoman Empire, and significant numbers went to Palestine, where most adopted the surname **Bushnak**. Bosnian Muslim immigration continued throughout the following decades and increased after Austria-Hungary formally annexed Bosnia in 1908. To this day, Bushnak remains a common surname among Palestinians of Bosnian origin.

The number of Bedouins who started settling the Negev region from the 7th century considerably increased during Ottoman rule as a result of immigration of both Bedouin tribes from south and east and peasant farmers (fellahins) from Egypt. The Egyptian fellahins settled mostly in the region around Gaza and received protection from Bedouins, in return for goods. Bedouins brought African slaves (abid) from Sudan who worked for them. To reduce frictions and to stabilize the boundaries between Bedouin tribes, the Ottomans established an administrative center in Beersheba around 1900, as the first planned settlement in Negev since the Nabatean and Byzantine times. In the beginning of the 20th century, most of the population of

Hebron were descendants of Bedouins who migrated to Palestine from Transjordan in the 15th and 16th century.

British Mandate Period of 1919 to 1948

According to Roberto Bachi, head of the Israeli Institute of Statistics from 1949 onwards, between 1922-1945 there was a net Arab migration into Palestine of between 40,000-42,000, excluding 9,700 people who were incorporated after territorial adjustments were made to the borders in the 1920s. Basing himself on these figures, and including those netted by the border alterations, Joseph Melzer calculates an upper boundary of 8.5% for Arab growth in the two decades, and interprets it to mean the local Palestinian community's growth was generated primarily by natural increase.

Martin Gilbert estimated that 50,000 Arabs immigrated to Mandatory Palestine from neighboring lands between 1919 and 1939 "attracted by the improving agricultural conditions and growing job opportunities, most of them created by the Jews." According to Itzhak Galnoor, although most of the local Arab community's growth was the result of natural increase, Arab immigration to Palestine was significant. Based on his estimates, approximately 100,000 Arabs immigrated to Palestine between 1922 and 1948.

Based on Jewish Agency statistics from 1947, Deborah Bernstein estimated that 77% of Arab population growth in Palestine between 1914 and 1945, during which the Arab population doubled, was due to natural increase, while 23% was due to immigration. Bernstein wrote that Arab immigration was primarily from Lebanon, Syria, Transjordan, and Egypt (all countries that bordered Palestine). (Wikipedia Contributors; Büssow; Bernstein; Merry; Cohen)

During the time of the Turkish rule and all the way to the British Mandate, the land of Israel, then called Palestine, was populated by different nationalities and religions, including Jews, Christians and Muslims. Under the British rule they were all called Palestinians. There was no *nationhood* like in the USA, for example. Being a Palestinian was not a nationality; it only meant that one lived in Palestine under British rule or Turkish rule during the Ottoman Empire. Jews were called "Palestinians" and Arabs were called "Palestinians"; British men born in Palestine were called "Palestinian." It really did not matter, as Palestine was not a nation, neither was there a Palestinian people living in it, but there was a mixture of people living in the land regardless of the ruling power. There was not a common culture, not even a common history or language, and not a central authority of a "Palestinian" nation. Jews were Palestinians and Arabs were also Palestinians.

In my own Sephardic Jewish family that lived in Jerusalem during the British Mandate, I had relatives who carried ID cards that said "Palestinian." There has always been a Jewish community in the land of Israel dating back to the time of Joshua and the conquest of the Canaan by the twelve tribes of Israel about 3,500 years ago.

Nationhood only started with the establishment of the State of Israel in 1948; they formed the Nation of Israel with a central government and with a common purpose, to be a national home to the Jewish people, yet regarding the different non-Jewish inhabitants of the land, they would have to submit to Israel's national authority.

The Jewish people, or rather the nation of Israel, have been the only inhabitants of the land that, despite all exiles and conquests by various empires, have remained in the land of Canaan (renamed 'Israel' by the God of Israel) since the conquest 3,500 years ago! No Arab or politically so-called "Palestinian" has roots in this covenant land. They are all migrants from other Muslim countries and empires of various ages, and particularly from the Ottoman Turkish period dating from the 16th to the 20th centuries.

When the God of Israel stirred up many Jews from the nations where they were scattered to return to the land of Israel, this land was desolate and devastated—a true waste. No one cared for it. In fact, the Turks had implemented a tree tax, forcing people to pay taxes on every tree they owned. Most people chopped down their trees, especially trees that bore no edible fruit, to avoid taxes, turning the land into a desolate terrain. This is how the Jewish pioneers at the end of the 19th century and early 20th century found it: full of malaria-infested swamps, barren rocks, and sand dunes. There was no "Palestinian people" that cared for the land. The so-called "Palestinian Nation" did not exist. The Arab villagers did not care for it, and they were not a "nation;" they were a motley collection of different nationalities under Turkish and then British rule. The Jewish population was very religious, ultra-Orthodox and poor, living mainly in the Old City of Jerusalem, and a few other towns, who depended on charity from the Jewish communities outside Palestine.

When the secular Jewish pioneers came, they drained the swamps at the cost of their lives, many dying from malaria. They established agricultural farms called *moshavim* and *kibbutzim*.* They reconquered the ancient land of their ancestors with hard work, sacrifice and agriculture.

---

* *Moshavim* is a type of Israeli town or settlement, in particular a type of cooperative agricultural community of individual farms pioneered by the Labour

The Miracle of the Gladiola Flowers

The Negev Desert in the south makes up over half of the present-day territory to the State of Israel. An international commission was considering how to implement a partition plan for the land, whether to grant the Negev to the Arabs or the Jews. The commission visited *Kibbutz Revivim*, a communal farm, established with sweat and tears by young Jewish pioneers in a dry land with little rain or freshwater. There was a source of brackish (slightly salty) groundwater, and they adapted to drinking that brackish water, and to work in inhumane conditions to conquer the dry, forsaken desert of Israel with agriculture. There was no "Palestinian nation" then to covet that wasteland, or compete in the attempt to make it bloom.

When the international delegation (which later worked with the United Nations) neared the *kibbutz* (a communal settlement in Israel, typically a farm) along the dirt road in the scorching desert sun, they saw a "mirage." From a distance, an amazing field covered with white gladiola flowers glistened in the sun and "smiled" at the astonished delegation, welcoming them to a miracle. The delegation could not believe their eyes! Gladiola flowers in this scorched wasteland? Impossible! They thought the young Jews from *Kibbutz Revivim* were playing tricks on them and had "pretend planted" the flowers to impress them. But Alas! No! This was for real; the flowering plants had roots; this was a Gladiola flower plantation in an impossible desert.

The delegation was so amazed that they decided, "If the Jews can make flowers grow in this forsaken wasteland, let them have the Negev Desert!"

Zionists during the second wave of aliyah. *Kibbutzim* is a socialist version *Moshavim*, where the area is controlled by a governing entity.

This is how the State of Israel was allocated 50% of its present-day land area! The *kibbutzniks* (the young Jewish pioneers), tell that this was the only time that Gladiola flowers bloomed in their field. Today they grow prize-winning olive trees and produce olive oil and other desert agriculture. The God of Israel made the Gladiolas flower bloom so that it would grant His people their ancient homeland, the place where Abraham and Isaac lived thousands of years ago.

The Accursed Sands of Gaza

When the first Jewish settlers established the villages of Gush Katif near the city of Khan Yunis, in the Gaza Strip, the local Arab *sheik* (an Arab leader) received them with bread and salt, making a covenant with them, and saying, "If you Jews can make these accursed sands bloom with agriculture, we welcome you!"

The people of Gush Katif developed the most beautiful organic agriculture in that place. They conquered the "accursed sands" of the Gaza Strip with much love, sweat, tears, blood, sacrifice, and hard work. The best organic vegetables in Israel, and maybe the world, were grown by them. This beautiful growth lasted until they were uprooted mercilessly to satisfy the aspirations for a false peace treaty, promoted through the demonically inspired Oslo Accords. Prime Minister Ariel Sharon surrendered this land, under pressure from the international community of nations, and especially US President George W. Bush. Sharon suffered a stroke right after the Jewish disengagement from Gaza; he remained unconscious in a coma for eight years and never recovered.

God judges all that try to uproot His Jewish people from their land. At the same time as the heroes buried in the Gush Katif cemetery were being moved to the Mount of Olives, caskets floated in the waters of New Orleans dislodged by the horrendous devastation of Hurricane

Katrina. In gate 12, we will see how YHVH judges the nations because of the cause of Zion.

Today, instead of greenhouses with organic vegetables, the Gazan Arabs, through their ruling party and terror organization called Hamas, have used the former land of Jewish communities for launching hundreds of missiles, incendiary balloons and kites to harm and destroy Israel. Hamas has dug hellish tunnels towards Jewish kindergartens and community farms to murder children and innocent civilians. Thousands of Jewish children have been raised in bomb shelters, and thousands of Jewish civilians have suffered shell shock repeatedly.

The year 2015 saw the 10-year anniversary of two major events that occurred near one another: the Israeli disengagement from the Gaza Strip and Hurricane Katrina. On the surface, the two events seem to have no relation to one another. However, further examination reveals a startling divine connection.

The following article is from *Israel Breaking News*, written in 2015.

Beginning on August 15, 2005, the Israeli government, led by then prime minister Ariel Sharon, launched a plan to dismantle all Jewish communities in Gaza and hand over the territory to the Palestinians. Over 10,000 Israelis were displaced due to political pressure from the US government. The unilateral disengagement was unaccompanied by any peace agreement. Since then, the Gaza Strip has turned into a **hotbed of terrorist activity**, with thousands of rockets threatening the Jewish state over the last 10 years.

Hurricane Katrina was undoubtedly one of the worst **natural disasters** that has ever struck the US. Eight days after the beginning of the Gush Katif pull-out, the category 5 hurricane hit the

Gulf Coast on August 23, 2005, causing over $108 billion in damage and the deaths of 1,833 people. Approximately 1.3 million people were displaced by flooding and many areas, including parts of New Orleans, have still not been restored to their pre-Katrina days.

Like those affected by the hurricane, most of the **Gush Katif families** that were expelled have not recovered emotionally or financially from the man-made catastrophe. Many still remain without permanent housing promised by the government and high rates of unemployment have left Gush Katif families living in poverty. (Berkowitz)

"At the time of those events," says the LORD, "when I restore the prosperity of Judah and Jerusalem, I will gather the armies of the world into the valley of Jehoshaphat. There I will judge them for harming my people, my special possession, for scattering my people among the nations, and for dividing up my land. They threw dice to decide which of my people would be their slaves. They traded boys to obtain prostitutes and sold girls for enough wine to get drunk.

— JOEL 3:1–3 NLT

Any "peace plan" that attempted to divide the covenant land and to uproot its Jewish citizens from that land has failed in the face of judgment. This judgement is the reason why the infamous Oslo Accords are gone.

November 2nd, 1917

Dear Lord Rothschild,

I have much pleasure in conveying to you. on behalf of His Majesty's Government, the following declaration of sympathy with Jewish Zionist aspirations which has been submitted to, and approved by, the Cabinet.

His Majesty's Government view with favour the establishment in Palestine of a national home for the Jewish people, and will use their best endeavors to facilitate the achievement of this object, it being clearly understood that nothing shall be done which may prejudice the civil and religious rights of existing non-Jewish communities in Palestine or the rights and political status enjoyed by Jews in any other country.

I should be grateful if you would bring this declaration to the knowledge of the Zionist Federation.

Yours,

Arthur James Balfour (Text of the Balfour Declaration)

The Broken Promise and the Creation of Jordan

The State of Jordan never existed prior to the British Mandate over Palestine. Great Britain created this artificial state in over 70% of the land that was then called Palestine and that, according to the Balfour Declaration (see above), was deeded as a "Jewish National Home." Britain broke its promise, and established a country in the Middle East which they armed, and which they could control for their own purposes. Most of Jordan is situated on the biblical land allotted to the tribes of Reuben, Gad, and half-tribe of Menashe (Jos. 13 and 14).

British rule replaced Turkish rule in Transjordan. The mandate, confirmed by the League of Nations in July 1922, gave the British virtually a free hand in administering the territory. However, in September, the establishment of "a Jewish national home" was explicitly excluded from the mandate's clauses, and they made it clear that the area would also be closed to Jewish immigration. On May 25, 1923, the British recognized Transjordan's independence under the rule of Emir Abdullah, but, as outlined in a treaty and the constitution in 1928, matters of finance, military, and foreign affairs would remain in the hands of a British "resident." They finally achieved full independence after World War II by a treaty concluded in London on March 22, 1946, and Abdullah subsequently proclaimed himself king. A new constitution was promulgated (declared), and in 1949 the name of the state was changed to the Hashemite Kingdom of Jordan.

Throughout the interwar years, Abdullah had depended on British financial support. The British also assisted him in forming an elite force called the Arab Legion, comprising Bedouin troops under the command of and trained by British officers, which was used to maintain and secure the allegiance of Abdullah's Bedouin subjects. On May 15th, 1948, the day after the Jewish Agency proclaimed the independent State of Israel and immediately following the British withdrawal from Palestine, Transjordan joined its Arab neighbors in the first Arab-Israeli war. (Encyclopaedia Britannica; Bickerton and Irvine)

Not only did the British create Jordan illegitimately, but they helped fund and train its military, known as the Arab Legion, that subsequently viciously attacked the emerging new State of Israel in 1948.

The Abandonment of Lands

After the Arab nations rejected the November 29, 1947 United Nations plan to partition Palestine into an Arab and Jewish state, they called on the Arab inhabitants of Palestine to abandon their lands.

The Arab leaders said, "The Jews will now establish their state, and they will kill you all, so *flee*! You will return in victory when our armies defeat the Zionistic state."

They thought the feeble Jews, Holocaust survivors, penniless with no organized army, would not stand a chance against all the Arab nations surrounding them. How wrong they were! Israel has won all its wars ever since when attacked by their Arab neighbors' armies. Had the God of Israel not been with them, they could have never survived!

> A Song of Ascents. Of David. "Had ADONAI not been on our side"—let Israel now say—"Had ADONAI not been on our side, when men rose up against us, then they would have swallowed us alive, when their wrath burned against us. Then the waters would have engulfed us, the torrent would have swept over our soul, then the raging waters would have swept over our soul." Blessed be ADONAI, who has not given us as prey for their teeth. Our soul has escaped like a bird out of the snare of the trappers—the snare is broken, and we escaped! Our help is in the Name of ADONAI, Maker of heaven and earth.
>
> — PSALM 124:1–8

Of course, wars always bring casualties, and atrocities can sometimes be committed by both sides. However, in fact Israel did not purposely intend to expel the 700,000 Arabs that fled, abandoning their lands out of fear, driven by rumors and propaganda promises made by their own leaders.

Here is a quote from an article in The Guardian.

A far greater proportion of the 700,000 Arab refugees were ordered or advised by their fellow Arabs to abandon their homes than I had previously registered. It is clear from the new documentation that the Palestinian leadership in principle opposed the Arab flight from December 1947 to April 1948, while at the same time encouraging or ordering a great many villages to send away their women, children and old folk, to be out of harm>s way. Whole villages, especially in the Jewish-dominated coastal plain, were also ordered to evacuate. There is no doubt that, throughout, the departure of dependents lowered the morale of the remaining males and paved the way for their eventual departure as well.

Looking at the big picture, there can be no avoiding the simple Arab argument, "No Zionism - no Palestinian refugee problem." But adopting such a slogan means accepting the view that a Jewish state should not have been established in Palestine (or, presumably, anywhere else). Neither can one avoid the standard Zionist rebuttal: "No war - no Palestinian refugee problem," meaning that the problem wasn't created by the Zionists but by the Arabs themselves, and stemmed directly from their violent assault on Israel. Had the Palestinians and the Arab states refrained from launching a war to destroy the emergent Jewish state, there would have been no refugees, and none would exist today. (Morris)

Jordan/Palestine

The Arab villagers fled to Jordan, including what they termed the "West Bank," Gaza, and other Arab territories as ordered by their own leaders. A Palestinian nation never existed! These were Arabs with different nationalities, such as Iraqi, Turkish, Egyptian, Lebanese, and the likes. They lived in Palestine from the times of Turkish and British rule, but their loyalties were to the Arab clans and nationalities whence they originated. Hence, they obeyed their leaders and *fled* the newly emerging State of Israel. They *abandoned* their lands and houses in panic and believed the promise of their leaders that they would return in victory. Albeit, that promise could never be kept as the Arab nations lost the War of Independence, which they started to destroy the emergent State of Israel in 1948.

When you sign a rental agreement in the USA, it says that if the tenant abandons the premises for over one week, the landlord can remove all his possessions, and they can end the rental agreement. Israel became the landlord of its own land after 2,000 years of exile, suffering, and persecution. Most Arab villagers abandoned their land and villages in 1948.

The Responsibility of the Arab Nations

Since the start of the Israeli-Palestinian peace process in the early 1990s, the Palestinian leadership has demanded that Israel both accept responsibility for the creation of the refugee problem and accept the refugees' "right of return", as embodied in UN general assembly resolution 194 of December 1948. From June to August 1948, the Israeli cabinet endorsed a policy of barring a return, arguing that a mass return of those who had fought and tried to destroy the Jewish state would mortally threaten the state's existence.

This argument is as valid today as it was in 1948. Israel today has five million Jews and more than a million Arabs. There were 3.5 to 4 million Palestinian refugees—the number listed in the UN census—roused to return immediately to Israeli territory. The outcome of this return would be widespread anarchy and violence. Even if the return were spread over a number of years or even decades, the ultimate result, given the Arabs' far higher birth rates, would be the same: gradually, it would lead to the conversion of the country into an Arab-majority state, from which the (remaining) Jews would steadily emigrate. Would Jews wish to live as second-class citizens in an authoritarian Muslim-dominated, Arab-ruled state? This also applies to the idea of replacing Israel and the occupied territories with one unitary binational state, a solution that some blind or hypocritical western intellectuals have been trumpeting. (Morris)

These refugees and their descendants do not have the right of return. They abandoned their villages; mostly, with a few exceptions, Israel did not expel them. It is their Arab governments that have maintained them as refugees, playing their own people as a "political card." On top of it, over 70% of the land promised by the Balfour Declaration to the Jewish people as a homeland—called Palestine during the British Mandate—is called Jordan today. If the "Palestinians" insist on "having Palestine back" or returning to "Palestine," Jordan is their place. The Arab nations are responsible for all the woes of their people, and they have played this political game for long enough. They have sided with "Hitler's Child," and now YHVH, the God of Israel, is judging. He is judging Syria, Lebanon, Egypt, and Jordan. What they termed "the Arab Spring," has become an Arab nightmare of death, poverty, and refugees.

Israel is the First to Help Even Her Enemies

You have heard the Law that says, "Love your neighbor" and hate your enemy. But I say, love your enemies! Pray for those who persecute you! In that way, you will be acting as true children of your Father in heaven. For he gives his sunlight to both the evil and the good, and he sends rain on the just and the unjust alike...

— MATTHEW 5:43–45 NLT

Despite all the hatred of enemies against her, Israel continues to treat the wounded from all countries along her borders, including Lebanon, Syria, Gaza, and Jordan.

Go tell this to the United Nations, which has condemned Israel unceasingly, instead of condemning the Arab countries that are abusing, killing, and spoiling their own people.

Seven wounded—two children, four women and a man—waited in pain for darkness to fall so that they could cross into enemy territory. Under the faint moonlight, Israeli military medical corps quickly whisked the patients across the hostile frontier into armored ambulances headed to hospitals for intensive care.

It was a scene that has recurred since 2013, when the Israeli military began treating Syrian civilians wounded in fighting just a few miles away. Israel says it has quietly treated 3,000 patients—a number that it expects to quickly grow as fighting heats up in neighboring Syria in the wake of a chemical attack and, in response, an unprecedented US missile strike.

While the numbers are a tiny fraction of the hundreds of thousands of dead and wounded in the six-year Syrian war, both doctors and patients say the program has changed perceptions and helped ease tensions across the hostile border. (McNeil)

Israel is the first nation to respond and give relief to countries that oppose her and vote against her in the United Nations.

A first response team after the devastating Haiti earthquake; decades of humanitarian assistance and capacity building in Africa; emergency medical aid and transfers into Gaza: the Israeli government and its people show exemplary levels of humanitarian aid, both internationally and locally.

Even after years of provocation, rocket attacks, and bombings, Israel defies terror organizations and works to uphold the highest standards of help and support to civilians everywhere, whether it's in Asia, Africa, Europe, Iraq, or the West Bank and Gaza.

Israel has a heightened sense of humanitarian awareness and responsibility. With aid teams poised to respond in the wake of natural or man-made disasters anywhere in the world, Israel's 200-strong relief team was the first on the scene in January 2010 after the earthquake hit Haiti. Israel helped save thousands of lives. In March 2011, following the devastating earthquakes in Japan, Israel was one of the first countries to send aid according to the needs and request of the Japanese government, and one of the first states to send a medical team and set up a field clinic.

By tragic circumstance, Israel is a world leader in handling mass casualties. No other country can dispatch search and rescue teams and field hospitals as fast and effectively.

Israeli efforts also include relief to New Orleans after Hurricane Katrina, and first response aid in the wake of the 2004 tsunami with 60 tons of international aid to Indonesia, and 82 tons of relief to Sri Lanka alone. (Israel Ministry of Foreign Affairs)

Israel is a Blessing to the Nations

The American Israel Public Affairs Committee (AIPAC) writes the following.

Israeli Technology Advances Key Agricultural Techniques

Because Israel is 60 percent desert, its farmers and agricultural scientists have long focused on expanding both the yield and quality of crops, as well as making agriculture more efficient overall.

Drip irrigation has become popular with fruit and vegetable growers in dry weather areas, from Southern California to the Middle East. The world's first surface drip irrigation system was developed in the 1960s at Kibbutz Hatzerim near Beersheba.

Israeli Doctors Have Developed Life-Saving Treatments and Drugs

Throughout Israel's history, Israeli doctors, scientists and researchers have produced countless medical advances. Whether achieved through independent research or joint projects with the United States, the medical discoveries made by the Jewish state are improving the lives of millions of Americans and others around the globe.

Israeli High-Tech Developments Are Used Around the World

Israel's high-tech civil innovations have left an important mark on homes, offices and businesses around the world.

Many offices now have computerized phones that plug into the Internet, taking advantage of Voice over Internet Protocol, or VoIP. VocalTec Communications of Herzliya, Israel, developed the first practical Internet phone software. Similarly, those who enjoy chatting with friends over the Internet might be interested to know that this online phenomenon originated in Israel. Although the technology now belongs to AOL, Israel's Mirabilis developed the first popular Internet chat program, ICQ.

Every day, millions of Americans watch online streaming video for entertainment or educational purposes. Metacafe, the world's third-most-popular video sharing website, was founded in Israel. Likewise, tech-savvy Americans over age 30 remember the original IBM Personal Computer of the early 1980s. What they may not know is that its brain, the Intel 8088 processor, was developed by Intel's Israel division. More recently, the Pentium M series of processors for laptop computers using the Intel Centrino platform, as well as some of Intel's latest processors (Yonah, Merom, Woodcrest), were also designed by Intel Israel. In addition, Amazon.com's Kindle e-reader owes much of its success to technology developed in Israel.

Israel Contributes to a Cleaner World

In an era of booming populations, shrinking resources and environmental degradation, Israel leads the world in such critical fields as solar power generation and seawater desalination. As nations struggle to make the best use of their resources, Israel's cutting-edge technologies promise to improve the health and living standards of hundreds of millions across the globe, while making industry more efficient and minimizing the environmental impact of human activities.

Israel's plan to break from gasoline dependence is providing structure and predictability to the marketplace, combining long-term public sector commitment with regulatory stability to send a clear message that innovation will have a home in Israel. Through investments in basic science and industrial R&D, and the launching of pilot programs and full scale-ups for promising technology, Israel is taking the lead in confronting one of the most pressing security issues of our time. A country of under 8 million people, Israel alone cannot end gasoline's global monopoly nor end the West's dependence on hostile petro-regimes. But together with international partners, Israel can serve as a generator of intellectual property and a testbed for innovative solutions, challenging the economic and security vulnerability that the United States and Israel both face through gasoline dependence.

Israel has also set a national goal consistent with the Copenhagen Accord to increase its share of renewable energy in electricity generation to 10 percent by 2020. In the same period of time, Israel plans to reduce its electricity consumption by 20 percent. (Aipac.org Editors)

It would be impossible for me to list all the Israeli innovations and medical discoveries that have improved the lives of every person on planet earth. And yet, despite this, the United Nations condemns Israel more than any other country, ignoring the fact that Israel helps the nations more than any other country, notwithstanding its small size.

Hatikva—Israel's National Anthem

As long as in the heart within,

The Jewish soul yearns,

And toward the eastern edges, onward

An eye gazes toward Zion—

Our hope is not yet lost,

The hope that is two thousand years old,

To be a free nation in our land,

The land of Zion, Jerusalem.

A Prayer of Repentance for Hostility to Israel

Dear Father in heaven, I come before You today in solemn repentance for myself, my ancestors, and the people I represent and stand in the gap for. I ask You to forgive us of resentment against Zion, either through taking Israel lightly or cursing her. I repent from a stubborn mouth, heart, and mind, and I ask You to make Israel my chief joy (Ps. 137:6). I commit to blessing her, as those who bless her become blessed, and those who curse her become cursed. In Yeshua's name, amen!

For further reading, I recommend my book *Stormy Weather.*

* www.kad-esh.org/shop/stormy-weather/

THE JUDGMENT OF THE NATIONS

I will bless those that bless you, and I will curse him who curses you, and in you (Abram) all the families of the earth will be blessed.

— GENESIS 12:3 NASB

There is one key that "makes the world go around," and I call it *the Key of Abraham*. It determines the curse or the blessing for every country, regime, empire, and nation. The God of Israel has made the truth of this key the basis for His relationship with entire nations, peoples, and individuals.

I have explained this key previously, but will repeat it in this chapter to refresh our memories.

Now let us study this verse above from the Hebrew:

The word for blessing here is *bracha*. *Lebarech* from the word *bracha* means "to decree a word of life, goodness, favor, health, success and prosperity over someone." This blessing is followed by many wonderfully positive promises, events and opportunities that bring great joy, happiness, wholeness, prosperity, greatness, abundance, fruitfulness and *fulfillment!* (Deut. 28:1-14).

However, this word comes from the word *berech* which means "the knee" in Hebrew. So, let me paraphrase this verse for you: I (the God of Israel) will bow down My royal knee to lift and favor those who bow down *their* knees and humble themselves to honor, speak well of, defend, and do good to My people Israel (Gen. 12:3a).

YHVH Tzva'ot, THE LORD of the Armies, the God of the Universe, the Creator of heaven and earth, has committed Himself by His unfailing and unchanging Word to bow down His royal knee to bless, favor and exalt those who humble themselves and bow down *their* knees to exalt and honor Israel! However, if they do not, He equally commits Himself to curse them.

I will curse those who curse you...

— GENESIS 12:3B

There are two words used in the Hebrew verse for the word *curse.* One of them is *klala,* and the other is *meera. Klala* comes from the word *kal,* which means "light," (opposite of heavy). *Meera* is the Hebrew word for a "declaration and decree for destruction." So, this verse refers to those who take Israel lightly and do not honor or respect her as His chosen one. The Scriptures use the same word for those who curse their father or mother.

And he that curses his father or his mother shall surely be put to death.

— EXODUS 21:17

Those who disrespect their parents will die! Taking parents lightly, mocking them, not listening to their instructions, or disrespecting them brings evil occurrences to one's life. God likens Israel to a parent, a mother, the mother of the nations. God calls the nations to honor her as a mother. He commands us to honor our parents—even in their imperfection—and our lives depends on it.

> **Honor your father and your mother just as ADONAI your God commanded you, so that your days may be long and it may go well with you in the land ADONAI your God is giving you.**
>
> **— DEUTERONOMY 5:16**

If we do not humble ourselves to honor our parents even in their imperfection, it will not go well with us, as when we take them lightly, (*kal-klala*), the curse comes, which is *meera*.

The Almighty regards Israel as the mother of the nations. She is the one that brought the world the Bible, the Messiah, and the gospel. Without Israel, there would be no salvation for any nation, in the same way that without your natural birth mother you could not have been born. This alone is enough to cause you to honor and be thankful for your mother, even in her imperfection. She gave life to you! Israel gave life to all the nations. The Messiah is Jewish, and salvation is of the Jews.

> **You worship what you do not know; we worship what we know, for salvation is from the Jews.**
>
> **— JOHN 4:22**

Remember, *meera* means "declaring a decree of utter destruction," followed by many evil occurrences that will bring anguish, distress, grief, sickness, confusion, loss, lack, bankruptcy, loneliness, strife, rejection, futility, fear, failure, terror, self-destruction, and total annihilation. (See Deuteronomy 28:14-68)

Judgment is knocking at the door of every nation that sides with the Palestinian cause to annihilate Israel, seeking to erase the name of Israel so it's remembered no more. All unbiblical political correctness has been, is, and will be punished by the Almighty. He is in a hurry to keep His Word after 2,000 years of exile, to restore all the land promised by the covenant to Abraham, Isaac, and Jacob. And this land comprises the entire area from the River Nile in Egypt to the River Euphrates in Iraq.

Every plan calling for a two-state solution has ended in failure. The Oslo Accords are now dead, which endeavored for nearly twenty years to divide God's land. The United Nations already submitted the concept of dividing the land into two states on the 29th of November 1947. It was a very unfavorable plan to the Jews, who were allotted a mere sliver of land, and yet the Jews accepted the plan while the Arabs rejected it, despite the plan favoring the Arabs. The Arabs are not interested in any peace. They were not interested in 1948, and they are not interested today—they have embraced Satan's plan to annihilate Israel.

Here is a serious warning of judgment about this wicked scheme in Scripture.

> Here is what the LORD says. "All my evil neighbors have taken over the land I gave my people Israel. So I will pull them up by their roots from the lands they live in. And I will pull up the roots of the people of Judah from among them."
>
> — JEREMIAH 12:14 NIRV

And to the United Nations and all those who agree with condemning Israel day and night, He says this.

> God, don't remain silent. Don't refuse to listen. Do something, God. See how your enemies are growling like dogs. See how they are rising up against you. They make clever plans against your people. They make evil plans against those you love. "Come," they say. "Let's destroy that whole nation. Then the name of Israel won't be remembered anymore."
>
> — PSALM 83:1–4 NIRV

He does not, and will not remain silent. White House correspondent William Koenig summarizes this in his enlightening book *Eye to Eye*, expanded edition of 2017.

> Over one hundred billion-dollar, record-setting catastrophes and/or events occurred while US presidents George H. W. Bush, Bill Clinton, George W. Bush, Barack Obama and Donald Trump were pressuring or calling on Israel to divide their covenant land.

The costliest insurance events, the costliest hurricanes, the largest tornado outbreaks, the "Perfect Storm," the 9/11 terror events, and Hurricane Katrina corresponded to White House pressure on Israel to divide their land.

- The US, the UN, and the EU do not have the authority to divide God's covenant land.
- Calling the Israeli-Palestinian talks "Middle East peace talks" is a false narrative.

- Jews have a three-thousand-year history with Jerusalem, and Christians have a two-thousand-year history.

- The biblical heartland of Israel—Judea, Samaria, and East Jerusalem—is not to be part of an Arab State.

- The Bible declares that Jerusalem will become a burdensome stone, and efforts to divide the city and land will lead to Armageddon, the ultimate battle for Jerusalem.

- The God of Israel will continue to rebuke those leaders and their nations for attempting to divide His land! (William)

One of the main defining events for the USA was the moving of its embassy from Tel Aviv to the capital of Israel, Jerusalem. Many presidents before Donald Trump promised the move since it passed as a resolution in the House of Representatives in the 1960s. However, every president regularly postponed the move and kept the US Embassy in Tel Aviv. Can you imagine the contempt and disrespect Americans would feel, if all the nations of the world had their embassies in New York rather than Washington DC? It would represent total disrespect of the USA as a sovereign nation! This was the case until May 14, 2018, when all the nations of the world had their embassies in Tel Aviv, though Jerusalem had been the official capital of Israel since 1950—actually since King David's reign 3,000 years ago. Israelis and Americans celebrated this significant move, and Israelis acclaimed President Trump as a hero on banners on the streets and walls of Jerusalem. The US did the right thing; finally, Donald Trump was the first president to do so. A few other countries followed Trump's leading, while others have shown they will follow.

However, the most revealing thing happened prior to Donald Trump deciding to make good on his campaign promise to move the Embassy. Trump, like all presidents before him, appeared to stall and delay the move. The American people elected him in November 2016, and it took him nearly two years to fulfill his word.

Hurricane Irma, September 2017

We were in St. Augustine, Florida during that time and stayed put in prayer and broadcasting via internet until the last minute. As a Jewish Israeli apostle to this nation, I stood in the gap, seeking from the God of Israel forgiveness on behalf of President Trump, for stalling the US Embassy move to Jerusalem as his predecessors had done. I knew that this move was the most significant factor concerning the wellbeing of America, according to the Key of Abraham (Gen. 12:3). Governor Rick Scott ordered everyone to evacuate. I will not forget his words:

"Irma can destroy the entire state of Florida. The government can't help you; you must flee."

Irma should have destroyed the entire state of Florida, but I asked the Father for one more chance for President Trump to do what is right, and to move the embassy. During our prayer meeting, broadcasted online, the hurricane decreased to a tropical storm. On September 11th, marking the anniversary of 9\11, God downgraded it to a category one storm.

I will never forget the meteorologists as they exclaimed things like, "This is unbelievable, Tampa should have disappeared under the flooding, but the water is receding..." (we have our son and grandsons in Tampa) or, "This is unbelievable, Irma has gone from category 4 to

3, and now it's a tropical storm," ... "We do not understand how this happened!"

It baffled people; weather professionals were confused and shocked. I was not. <u>The God of Israel has answered our prayers once more and had given President Trump a window of time to do what is right and to move the embassy to Jerusalem.</u>

The day after the hurricane, I went out to our condo balcony, and I saw a spider that had survived the hurricane. Immediately, the Holy Spirit gave me a book to write to warn President Trump called *The Spider that Survived Hurricane Irma*. It was a warning to move the US Embassy to Jerusalem ASAP.

I called my husband and asked him to remove the spider and the web, and in less than half a minute he had sprayed it, and it killed the spider. Florida was like that spider: we survived Hurricane Irma, but if the USA did not do what is right concerning Israel, we could be gone just as quickly.

Hurricane Irma was the most powerful Atlantic hurricane in recorded history. It was a Category 5 storm when it made landfall on Barbuda on September 6, 2017. Its winds were 185 miles per hour for 37 hours. An unofficial wind gust was clocked at 199 miles per hour. These winds extended 50 miles from the center.

Tropical storm-force winds extended 185 miles from the center. Its coastal storm surges were 20 feet above normal tide levels. Above-average ocean temperatures of 86 degrees Fahrenheit sustained the storm. These temperatures are worsening due to global warming.

Irma held 7 trillion watts of energy. That's twice as much as all bombs used in World War II. Its force was so powerful that earthquake seismometers recorded it. It generated the most accumulated cyclone energy in a 24-hour period.

Irma's attack was the first time in 100 years that two storms Category 4 or larger hit the US mainland in the same year. Hurricane Harvey devastated Houston on August 25, 2017.

Timeline

President Trump declared emergencies in Florida, Puerto Rico, and the US Virgin Islands. On September 6, Florida's governor ordered residents of the Keys to evacuate.

- **September 6, 2017:** Irma hit the Leeward Islands with winds over 180 mph. The Prime Minister of Antigua and Barbuda described Barbuda as "barely habitable."

- **September 7:** Irma left hundreds in Puerto Rico without power. It hit the northern part of Haiti and the Dominican Republic with 15 inches of rain.

- **September 8:** Irma remained a Category 5 hurricane with winds of 175 mph. It affected the Turks and Caicos Islands and the eastern Bahamas. The storm passed over waters warmer than 86 degrees Fahrenheit. Barbuda's government issued a watch for Hurricane Jose.

- **September 9:** Irma affected the north coast of Cuba flooding Havana. Winds at approximately 150 mph and waves of up to 36 feet. Wind gusts of 55 mph hit southeast Florida. The storm was downgraded to a Category 3 but was projected to regain strength before hitting Florida.

- **September 10:** Irma was upgraded to a Category 4. It hit Cudjoe Key, 20 miles north of Key West, and then Naples. Miami didn't get the core of Irma but still received life-threatening conditions. The Florida Keys received approximately 12 inches of rain and a 10-foot storm surge. Rainfall averaged 10 to 15 inches.

- **September 11:** Irma downgraded to a Category 1 hurricane as it headed to Tampa. Twelve million people were without power. Irma was downgraded to a tropical storm as it hit Georgia. There were 1.5 million people who lost power. The state had ordered people to begin evacuating on September 9th.

- Irma's death toll was 129 people. Florida officials ordered 6.5 million people to evacuate. There were 77,000 people in 450 shelters. (Amadeo)

In the aftermath of Irma that threatened to wipe Florida off the map, the US moved the embassy to Jerusalem. Three months later, on December 6, 2017, what had been an indefinite stalling and delay ever since the 1960s, finally ended.

On December 6, 2017, US President Donald Trump announced the **United States recognition of Jerusalem as the capital of Israel** and ordered the planning of the relocation of the US

Embassy in Israel from Tel Aviv to Jerusalem. Benjamin Net-anyahu, the Prime Minister of Israel, welcomed the decision and praised the announcement. On December 8th, Secretary of State Rex Tillerson clarified that the President's statement "did not show any final status for Jerusalem" and "was very clear that the final status, including the borders, would be left to the two parties to negotiate and decide."

A majority of world leaders rejected Trump's decision to recognize Jerusalem as Israel's capital. The United Nations Security Council held an emergency meeting on December 7th, where 14 out of 15 members condemned Trump's decision, but the United States vetoed the motion. (Fassihi)

Britain, France, Sweden, Italy and Japan were among the countries that criticized Trump's decision at the emergency meeting. Other countries supported the move: Guatemala said that they will follow up and also move their embassy; Paraguay, the Czech Republic, Romania, and Honduras said that they were considering relocation. The European Union's foreign policy chief Federica Mogherini said that all governments of EU member states were united on the issue of Jerusalem and reaffirmed their commitment to a Palestinian State with East Jerusalem as its capital. Representatives from 32 countries were present at the opening of the embassy, including EU members Austria, Czech Republic, and Romania. (Sandhu)

To all those who come against YHVH's plan to restore his chosen Jewish people to His land, look at what He says in Scripture.

My God, make them like straw that the wind blows away. Make them like tumbleweed. Destroy them as fire burns up a forest. Destroy them as a flame sets mountains on fire. <u>Chase them with your mighty winds. Terrify them with your storm. LORD, put them to shame so that they will seek you.</u> May they always be filled with terror and shame. May they die in dishonor. May you, the LORD, let your enemies know who you are. You alone are the Most High God over the whole earth.

— PSALM 83:13–18 NIRV

COVID-19 and the Division of Israel

Though President Donald Trump has been the most supportive American president ever concerning Israel, he is treading on very dangerous grounds when he tries to implement any peace plan that divides the covenant land—handing any part of it, in any way, shape or form to Israel's enemies. The God of Israel does not endure compromise on this subject. He will allow no one, great or small, to define the borders He has already defined for the Land of Promise as He declared to Abraham, Isaac, and Jacob, as He swore to one thousand generations.

I will set your **border from** the Sea of Reeds to the sea of the Philistines, and **from** the wilderness to the Euphrates River. For I will deliver the inhabitants of the land into your hand, and you are to drive them out before you.

— EXODUS 23:31

He is Adonai our God. His judgments are in all the earth. He remembers His covenant forever—the word He commanded for a thousand generations—which He made with Abraham, and swore to Isaac, and confirmed to Jacob as a decree, to Israel as an everlasting covenant, saying, "To you I give the land of Canaan, the portion of your inheritance."

— Psalm 105:7–11

The coronavirus pandemic follows the same pattern described by White House correspondent William Koenig in his book *Eye to Eye*, where he shows 127 events of anti-biblical politics against Israel by espousing the division of the land, the two-state solution, and the defining of borders by US presidents. In each case, within 24 hours a terrible catastrophe or storm struck that caused billions of dollars in damage and much loss of life. Some of these are well-known events, such as 9\11, and Hurricane Katrina, which hit the US after it supported the Palestinian cause by dividing or uprooting Israeli settlements (in the case of Gush Katif in Gaza). Within 24 hours, disasters pounded the USA.

At that time I will bless Judah and Jerusalem with great success again. I will gather together all the nations. I will bring them down to the Valley of Jehoshaphat. There I will put them on trial. I will judge them for what they have done to my people Israel. They scattered them among the nations. They divided up my land among themselves. They cast lots for my people. They sold boys into slavery to get prostitutes. They sold girls to buy some wine to drink.

— Joel 3:1–4 NIRV

In a talk show hosted by Pastor Sam Rohrer from *Stand in the Gap Today*, Bill Koenig was the guest speaker on Passover Eve, April 8, 2020. He mentioned:

On January 28, 2020, President Donald Trump presented the Middle East Plan that he called the "Deal of the Century." He also presented a *map*, defining the borders of Israel under his plan. In this map, 70% of the biblical Land of Judea and Samaria would be under a Palestinian State.

Within hours of him presenting his peace plan to divide Israel, Miami was hit with a 7.7 earthquake on the Richter scale.

A powerful magnitude-7.7 earthquake struck south of Cuba and northwest of Jamaica on Tuesday, the US Geological Survey said. The quake was felt in Miami, and police said some buildings were being evacuated in the city. (NBC News; Rohrer)

Within 24 hours, the US administration was discussing what to do concerning the coronavirus pandemic that spread since discovered in Wuhan on December 31, 2019. On January 30, they declared the outbreak a public health emergency of international concern by the World Health Organization; this was only two days after the peace plan to divide Israel was submitted on January 28, 2020, and was accepted by Prime Minister Benjamin Netanyahu.

Meanwhile, the EU and the international community reiterated their allegiance to the division of the land of Israel. They insisted on Israel returning to the pre-1967 borders prior to the Six Day War. The international community insisted on defining the borders of the Promised Land that the God of Israel already defined thousands of years ago.

The COVID-19 pandemic became a judgment on the entire world, quarantining most of the world population and affecting the economies of all—especially of the USA and Israel, as Prime Minister Benjamin Netanyahu agreed to a plan that is not God's plan for Israel. On top of this, Prime Minister Netanyahu was unsuccessful in forming a government after the March elections, until the coalition agreement signed with Ganz on April 20, 2020.

Bill Koenig believes (and so do I) that the coronavirus is a judgment on the entire world, for two reasons:

- For attempting to divide the land of Israel into two states by defining anti-biblical borders and drawing maps that are an affront to the Living God.
- By disobeying God's moral Laws and Commandments

It is likely that further attempts to implement any peace plan, dividing Israel and establishing a Palestinian state contrary to the covenant, will catapult the world into what the Bible calls the wrath of God. COVID-19 will look like child's play then. He will punish the entire world for opposing His land covenant with Israel, and for all the immorality, rebellion, homosexuality, murder, abortions, and greed (Rom. 1:18-32).

For the wrath of God is revealed from heaven against all ungodliness and unrighteousness of men. In unrighteousness they suppress the truth.

— ROMANS 1:18

Today is a crossroads of a time when nations and individuals must make a choice whether to obey God or be swept away by His anger.

My people, go into your houses. Shut the doors behind you. Hide yourselves for a little while. Do it until the Lord's anger is over. He is coming from the place where he lives. He will punish the people of the earth for their sins. The blood spilled on the earth will be brought out into the open. The ground will no longer hide those who have been killed.

— ISAIAH 26:20–21 NIRV

Because of the anti-Zionist head of the five headed monster of anti-Semitism, the entire world is ripe for judgment

As I write these lines all of Israel and most of the USA is in quarantine because of the plague of the coronavirus. Nations that do not repent for being anti-Zion, and who espouse dividing the land given by YHVH to His people Israel, will be destroyed. Most member countries of the United Nations are right now hanging in the balance.

Draw near, O nations, to hear, and listen, O peoples! Let the earth hear, and all it contains, the world, and all its offspring! For ADONAI is enraged at all the nations, and furious at all their armies. He will utterly destroy them. He will give them over to slaughter. So their slain will be thrown out, and the stench of their corpses will rise, and the hills will be drenched with their blood. Then all the host of heaven will dissolve, and the skies will be rolled up like a scroll—so all their array will wither away, like a leaf drooping from a vine, like a fig shriveling from a fig tree.

For My sword has drunk its fill in the heavens. See, it will come down upon Edom, upon the people I have devoted to judgment. The sword of ADONAI is filled with blood, gorged with fat—the blood of lambs and goats, the fat of kidneys of rams. For ADONAI has a sacrifice in Bozrah, a great slaughter in the land of Edom. Wild oxen will go down with them, bull calves with mighty steers. So their land will be soaked with blood and their dust greasy with fat.

For ADONAI has a day of vengeance, a year of recompense for the hostility against Zion.

— ISAIAH 34:1–8

Yeshua, the Jewish Messiah, will Himself fight against all the nations that come against His people, Israel, His land, and the city of Jerusalem. He Himself will judge all the nations on how they have treated Israel. Prior to His return, we will see this battle become ferocious. He will not sit on His throne on the Temple Mount in Jerusalem until He subdues all the nations that have opposed His plan to restore his Jewish people to all the land promised to Abraham, Isaac, and Jacob. He will not accept the re-drawing of borders by anyone; no politician will change His mind or make Him go back on His Word.

Then the Lord will go out to fight against those nations, as he has fought in times past. On that day his feet will stand on the Mount of Olives, east of Jerusalem. And the Mount of Olives will split apart, making a wide valley running from east to west. Half the mountain will move toward the north and half toward the south. You will flee through this valley, for it will reach across to Azal. Yes, you will flee as you did from the earthquake in the days of King Uzziah of Judah. Then the Lord my God will come, and all his holy ones with him.

— ZECHARIAH 14:3–5 NLT

Where will you be on that day when He returns? Will you be among the company of nations that fought against His plan? Will you be one to defy His plan to restore His Jewish people to their Promised Land, and be considered an enemy of the Jewish Messiah, the Lion of Judah? Or, will you be His friend and among the holy ones that come with Him to rule and reign from Jerusalem?

Your relationship with Him and His plan to restore Israel in full—the people and the land—will determine whether you will be Yeshua's friend or enemy.

A Life Changing Prayer

Heavenly Father, forgive me for any ignorance, apathy or opposition of Your divine plan to establish the Jewish people in the land You promised and gave to them forever. I commit myself to support Your plan—to restore Israel to the entire land given to Abraham, Isaac, and Jacob. I will not be "politically correct," siding with anti-Zionists, but "biblically" correct to defend Your covenant with Israel in any way possible. I renounce the anti-Zionist head of the anti-MESITOJUZ principality and command all thoughts and demons of anti-Zionism to leave me and never return in Yeshua's name, amen!

For further reading about the effects of anti-Zionism, I recommend you read my book, *Stormy Weather.**

END WORD

*... for God is not a God of confusion but of peace,
as in all the churches of the saints.*

—1 CORINTHIANS 14:33 NASB

Writing this book was very difficult for me. I knew that the Father was challenging me to expose this horrendous blood-thirsty monster of replacement theology, the anti-MESITOJUZ principality. This meant that I had to revisit Christian anti-Semitism through the ages and into our modern era. This is painful for a Jew and especially for this Jew, that is both a believer in the Messiah, a minister in His body and a Jew that has suffered at the hands of Christian anti-Semitism both personally and in my family. I would have preferred that YHVH had given this work to someone else. I would have liked to minister about something "prettier" and "easier to digest." But the Holy Spirit has been "sitting on me" for years to expose and defeat this blood-thirsty monster. I can feel His heart burdened with deep anguish—desiring to free His bride from it altogether, to rescue her from the coming judgment because of the hostility against Zion (Isa.

34:8), and to be revealed through His bride as a victorious Jewish Messiah longing to bring redemption to His beloved Israel.

My prayer and hope as I finish this manual is that you will now share all that is presented here, so that we will rescue many from this terrible age-old deception. Judgment is already at the gates of many churches and upon Christians globally because of the unrepentant sin of anti-Semitism and anti-Zionism—rooted in replacement theology, pagan feasts, and immorality birthed from Torahlessness or Lawlessness (Mat. 5:17-19, 7:23-24).

> **On judgment day many will say to me, "Lord! Lord! We prophesied in your name and cast out demons in your name and performed many miracles in your name." But I will reply, "I never knew you. Get away from me, you who break God's Laws."**
>
> **— MATTHEW 7:23 NLT**

He is yearning for His bride to call Him by His covenant name of Yeshua, thus restoring His Jewishness. This will bring "life from the dead" to the freshly replanted Rose, to His newly grafted in bride (Romans 11:15) as the final *Third Day Revival* will break out, bringing in the last and greatest harvest of the fullness of the Gentiles. Then "all Israel will be saved," just as it is written! (Rom. 11:25-27)

True repentance from the deceptive religious theologies and making restitution towards Israel, His Jewish people, is urgently needed to overturn judgment and to ensure the victory of the true gospel made in Zion. It will unveil the Jewish Messiah, in all His splendor as a Jew, through His glorified bride, who will have her identity restored like Queen Esther had hers restored. Then, Yeshua will be ready to return, landing on the Mount of Olives to the sound of Israel's welcoming cheers, ready to establish His Millennial Reign—and we will reign with Him.

> **For I tell you, you will not see me again until you say, "Blessed is he who comes in the name of THE LORD."**
>
> **— MATTHEW 23:39 NIV**

Baruch HaBah Beshem ADONAI, which in Hebrew means, "Blessed is He who comes in the name of YHVH."

> **In Jerusalem, the Lord of Heaven's Armies will spread a wonderful feast for all the people of the world. It will be a delicious banquet with clear, well-aged wine and choice meat. There he will remove the cloud of gloom, the shadow of death that hangs over the earth. He will swallow up death forever! The Sovereign Lord will wipe away all tears. He will remove forever all insults and mockery against his land and people. The Lord has spoken!**
>
> **— ISAIAH 25:6–8 NLT**

I am very grateful that you have read up this point, and desire to stay in touch with you.

If you would like to contact us, send us an email at hello@zions-gospel.com, or write to 52 Tuscan Way, Ste 202-412 St. Augustine, FL 32092, USA. You can visit our website for the Global Re-Education Initiative at www.against-antisemitism.org to continue your studies. With the purchase of this book, you will receive free access to the course.

Go and tell: The long-awaited revival depends on repentance from this age old identity theft of the Jewish Messiah.

For the Lion of Judah —Archbishop Dr. Dominiquae Bierman, president of *Kad-Esh MAP Ministries and the United Nations for Israel.*

LIVING A LIFE OF RESTITUTION

He will remove forever all insults
and mockery against his land and people.

— ISAIAH 25:8 NLT

Your actions to take part with His plan to remove forever *all insults and mockery against his land and people* will make a sizeable difference in a world that has been growing more and more anti-Semitic. It is this very fact that will remove plagues, restore joy and assure Divine favor.

Every Christian in the world is being called to make restitution for the sins of many generations of Christians *and all nations* throughout the ages against the Jewish people. Restitution has the power to overturn judgments. It turns the Key of Abraham, opening the door of Divine favor. Making restitution lands the final blow that assures the demonic five headed principality, whose poison had infected the whole earth, will never rise again!

Restitution is the Right Thing to Do
For Every Christian in the World

We invite you to "pay it forward" with your donations so we may continue our mission of making this Global Re-Education Initiative (GRI) platform free for all. You can go to www.against-antisemitism.org to pay this mission forward with your generous support.

The following is a letter written by Pastor Cesar Silva in Tamaulipas, Mexico.

Restoring Honor to Israel

May my testimony of His goodness and faithfulness to His holy Word be a blessing to all. It begins when suddenly I realized that restoring Israel's honor was as *urgent* as it was *necessary* for the healing of my city, nation, life, and family. I realized that it was no longer time to remain bankrupt spiritually, physically, financially, and emotionally, because it all leads to the same thing: emptiness and destruction.

This process to restore honor all begins with the wonderful teachings we have received from the ministry of the Apostle Dominique Bierman, who, through the revelation of the powerful Key of Abraham (which opens the doors), sowed within my heart that seed which is now bearing fruit in and around my life.

A day came when the Ruach (Spirit of ELOHIM) gave me a dream. In the dream, I saw that I had left my vehicle at a primary entrance of the city of Rio Bravo (where I live) and along that avenue came a river of blood (because of deaths caused by the drug trade). I saw the river was almost reaching us. I quickly went out to my vehicle because I knew that inside it was the offering that the church had given to be sent to Israel—and I knew that this offering was bringing restitution—the only thing that would cause the decrease of that river of blood and also its disappearance. So I tried to open the truck and quickly check that these offerings were there. The Ruach HaKodesh was also telling me that this was truly what would stop this river of blood. Thanks be to THE LORD, they were there!

In northern Mexico, there is a constant war between drug cartels and the armed forces. There is a constant danger of finding yourself in the middle of a firearms confrontation. That is why the Ruach told me through this dream that we must restore honor to Israel through offerings, along with prayer and humbling ourselves for the hatred of Israel by the nations of the earth. This strategy brings freedom from death and the river of blood. This will make a difference because the powerful Key of Abraham is put into action—it is the key to answered prayers and mercy to be poured out instead of anger.

Just about the time I dreamed this, we spoke, prayed, and blessed Israel with genuine actions and offerings. Then we saw our prayers of protection for our city answered, and I felt an atmosphere of peace. It diminished the criminal activity of the cartels.

Restore Honor—It's a Commandment of the Torah!

Then the Lord spoke to Moses, saying, "When a person sins and acts unfaithfully against the Lord, and deceives his companion in regard to a deposit or a security entrusted to him, or through robbery, or if he has extorted from his companion, or has found what was lost and lied about it and sworn falsely, so that he sins in regard to any one of the things a man may do; then it shall be, when he sins and becomes guilty, that he shall restore what he took by robbery or what he got by extortion, or the deposit which was entrusted to him or the lost thing which he found, or anything about which he swore falsely; he shall make restitution for it in full and add to it one-fifth more. He shall give it to the one to whom it belongs on the day he presents his guilt offering. Then he shall bring to the priest his guilt offering to the Lord, a ram without defect from the flock, according to your valuation, for a guilt offering, and the priest shall make atonement for him before the Lord, and he will be forgiven for any one of the things which he may have done to incur guilt."

— LEVITICUS 6:1–7 NASB

Just as we desire to be made whole when someone offends us, steals from us, or slanders us, so we the nations of the world need to realize how we are indebted to the blessed people of Israel. The promise of Genesis 12:3 still stands, "I will bless those who bless you and the one who curses you I will curse."

The Global Re-Education Initiative (GRI), led by Apostle Dominiquae Bierman, is not only *necessary*, but *urgent!* For the sick who will die shall be numbered in the millions amidst plagues that will scourge the earth without end, unless THE LORD finds someone who fully understands what it is to restore honor to Israel. Restitution is more than asking for forgiveness! Truly, asking for forgiveness is the first thing we must do when we know we have done a wrong, but to *restore the honor to someone* we must do more than just apologize.

In history, we find that when a man was questioned about his *honor*, they made an appointment to settle the dispute and they said, "I challenge in a duel the knight who has questioned my honor." Then it people knew that whoever came to defend his honor showed that his *honor* was greater than all the slander against him.

We, the nations of the world, have committed a great dishonor by using slanderous and lying words against Israel, staining her honor. So, it is time to repent, ask for forgiveness and restore *His* honor.

In Leviticus 6:5, when an offering was made for the guilt of slander, the person acknowledged the damage, and asked for forgiveness with his atonement offering to THE LORD. Afterwards, it was time to *restore*, as it is written.

> ... he shall make restitution for it in full and add to it one fifth more; he shall give it to the one who belongs to him on the day he presents his guilt offering.

— LEVITICUS 6:5

In Leviticus 6:6, God adds that the offering should be given to the priest.

> Then he shall bring to the priest his guilt offering to THE LORD.

— LEVITICUS 6:6 NASB

Besides repenting, making restitution for the damage and adding the fifth part (equivalent to 20%), it was necessary to give it to the priest—so we must present it to the minister who can pray for us so we may get mercy from the Eternal.

Sometimes we rise against the *only person who will hear*. Do you know who has the doors open to ask ADONAI to have mercy on us? Yes, the answer is *the Jewish people of today*. They are His chosen ones, the light of the nations—they are our priests who will open the way for ADONAI to forgive us and for the refreshment of His presence to come (Acts 3:19).

The Hebrew words *shuv* and *shalem* clarify the concept of restitution. The word "will restitute" (Lev. 6:4) is the Hebrew word *shuv*, from which we derive the word *teshuvah*, meaning, "turn or return," or "repentance for a great restoration." And the word "restore" in Leviticus 6:5 is the word *shalam*, whose meaning here is "to make payments" and from the word *leshalem* which means, "to make a payment." So, to make peace, you need to make *a payment of restitution*. Yeshua mentioned this in Matthew 5, verses 21 through 26.

> "You have heard that the ancients were told, 'YOU SHALL NOT COMMIT MURDER' and 'Whoever commits murder shall be liable to the court.' But I say to you that everyone who is angry with his brother shall be guilty before the court; and whoever says to his brother, 'You good-for-nothing,' shall be guilty before the supreme court; and whoever says, 'You fool,' shall be guilty enough to go into the fiery hell. Therefore if you are presenting your offering at the altar, and there remember that your brother has something against you, leave your offering there before the altar and go; first be reconciled to your brother, and then come and present your offering. Make friends quickly with your opponent at law while you are with him on the way, so that your opponent may not hand you over to the judge, and the judge to the officer, and you be thrown into prison. Truly, I say to you, you will not come out of there until you have paid up the last cent."
>
> — MATTHEW 5:21–26

This entire Scripture speaks about the power of restitution, but lets go a little deeper into the way anti-Judaism works. It has been because of anti-Semitism that there have been deaths, hatred, and armies against the Jewish people. Much of this hatred is "under the mask of Christianity," which claims to give and claim Sunday offerings to God. But my question is this: Will the Eternal YHVH of Israel look with favor upon those offerings, which with one hand are offered to Him, and with the other hand have a knife of hate, anger, and even a death wish against the people of Israel? The answer is simple—He is not receiving those offerings! So Yeshua's advice is to reconcile with your brother Judah first and make peace. So restore and make peace.

This is All About Restoring Honor to Israel!

In every kingdom, we know that the king's son is the crown prince— he will one day become king. It is true in any of the kingdoms we still know, and it is very interesting that YHVH is the King, and that he called one of Abraham's descendants *"My first-born"* (Ex. 4:22). The one known as *My prince* was originally called Jacob, but ADONAI decided that his name would be known as Israel, the meaning of which is "Prince from ELOHIM." What a difference—what a substantial difference! But what an abysmal difference in how the nations of the world speak to Israel—they say it is just one more nation on earth, like any of our nations. In the eyes of the Living ELOHIM, however, they are not just any nation—it is *"His prince."*

Today I find many people talking about the Kingdom of God: the manifestation of the Kingdom of God, how they seek the Kingdom of God, and about their job being to extend the Kingdom of YHVH. But they stumble over this *principle.* That's why they turn the wheel continually like hamsters, just words and more words without results. And we do not see the establishment of the Kingdom of YHVH. Why? Because they stumble on the rock of stumbling—but, he that believes the Word of ELOHIM shall love and embrace this Prince, which is Israel. For them it will be "like the shade of a huge rock in a parched land" (Isa. 32:2); while for him who takes it lightly, "will be broken to pieces... scattered like dust." (Mat. 21:44)

Conclusion

The nations of the world are indebted to the people of Israel, for they gave us the Torah, the covenants, the promises, the revelation of the Living ELOHIM, and gave us Yeshua HaMashiach ('the Messiah' in Hebrew).

Today we must turn completely to *Him*, loving His Torah, (which is Yeshua incarnate), and restoring honor to Israel, their Prince. I am a witness of His goodness, for surely THE LORD means what He says.

I will bless those who bless you, and the one who curses you, I will curse.

— **GENESIS 12:3**

With all my love in Yeshua HaMashiach;
—**Pastor César Silva, Rio Bravo, Tamaulipas, México**
National Delegate for Mexico, *The United Nations for Israel (UNIFY)*
www.UnitedNationsForIsrael.org

APPENDIX II

MORE INFORMATION

Take the Online Course GRI Against Anti-Semitism

Take the Global Re-Education Initiative (GRI) Against Anti-Semitism online course that comes with purchasing this book by going to www.against-antisemitism.com and logging in with the credentials used to purchase this book. Purchasing this book from another website, such as Amazon, will not unlock course access. To unlock course access, you will need to get an E-Book with a minimum donation of $17 from our website.

Other Books By Archbishop Dr. Dominiquae Bierman

Order online: www.kad-esh.org/shop/

Restoring the Glory – Volume I: The Original Way
The Ancient Paths Rediscovered

The MAP Revolution (Free E-Book)
Find Out Why Revival Does Not Come... Yet!

The Healing Power of the Roots
It's a Matter of Life or Death!

Grafted In
The Return to Greatness

Sheep Nations
It's Time to Take the Nations!

Stormy Weather
Judgment Has Already Begun, Revival is Knocking at the Door

Yeshua is the Name
The Important Restoration of the Original Hebrew Name of the
Messiah

The Bible Cure for Africa and the Nations
The Key to the Restoration of All Africa

The Key of Abraham
The Blessing... or the Curse?"

"Yes!"
Archbishop Dominiquae Bierman's Dramatic Testimony of
Salvation

Eradicating the Cancer of Religion
Hint: All People Have It

Restoration of Holy Giving
Releasing the True 1,000 Fold Blessing

Vision Negev
The Awesome Restoration of the Sephardic Jews

Defeating Depression
This Book is a Kiss from Heaven

From Sickology to a Healthy Logic
The Product of 18 Years Walking Through Psychiatric Hospitals

ATG: Addicts Turning to God
The biblical Way to Handle Addicts and Addictions

The Woman Factor by Rabbi Baruch Bierman
Freedom From Womanphobia

The Spider That Survived Hurricane Irma
God's Call for America to Repent

The Revival of the Third Day (Free E-Book)
The Return to Yeshua the Jewish Messiah

Get Equipped & Partner With Us

Music Albums
www.kad-esh.org/shop/
The Key of Abraham
Abba Shebashamayim
Uru
Retorno

Global Revival MAP (GRM) Israeli Bible School
Take the most comprehensive video Bible school online that focuses
on dismantling replacement theology.
For more information or to order, please contact us:
www.grmbibleschool.com
grm@dominiquaebierman.com

United Nations for Israel Movement

We invite you to join us as a member and partner with $25
a month, which supports the advancing of this End time vision that
will bring true unity to the body of the Messiah. We will see the One
New Man form, witness the restoration of Israel, and take part in the
birthing of Sheep Nations. Today is an exciting time to be serving
Him!

www.unitednationsforisrael.org

info@unitednationsforisrael.org

Join Our Annual Israel Tours

Travel through the Holy Land and watch
the Hebrew Holy Scriptures come alive.

www.kad-esh.org/tours-and-events/

Send Offerings to Support our Work

Your help keeps this mission of restoration going far and wide.

www.kad-esh.org/donations

CONTACT US

Archbishop Dr. Dominiquae & Rabbi Baruch Bierman

Kad-Esh MAP Ministries | www.kad-esh.org | info@kad-esh.org

United Nations for Israel | www.unitednationsforisrael.org

info@unitednationsforisrael.org

Zion's Gospel Press | shalom@zionsgospel.com

52 Tuscan Way STE 202-412, St. Augustine, Florida, 32092, USA

+1-972-301-7087

THE ANTI-AMALEK PRAYER

As you did not obey Yahveh and did not execute His fierce wrath on Amalek, so Yahveh has done this thing to you this day.

—1 SAMUEL 28:18

Declare this prayer morning and night and as many times as you feel led to during the day. It has brought much freedom to my team and I since we started declaring this anti-Amalek prayer aloud. I pray and hope it may do the same for you!

Abba Shebashamayim (Father in Heaven) Mighty ELOHIM, YHVH Tzva'ot (Lord of Hosts) we declare that You have a battle with Amalek from generation to generation and we ask You to do this battle today in our generation, that You may blot out the name of Amalek from under heaven!

Hineni (here I am) Yahveh to wage war against Amalek that has been very wicked in attacking our lives and Israel from the rear and sneaking against the weak, the children, the women, and all our weak places. Our battle is not against flesh and blood and we wage Your war against Amalek with the spiritual weapons of prayer, fasting, and praise. You are fighting this battle and we say, 'let Yahveh arise and let all Your enemies, the Amalekites, and all their friends and allies be scattered seven ways away from us, from Your bride and from Israel in Yeshua's mighty name!' YHVH we ask You to execute Your fierce wrath against Amalek today and we execute Your fierce wrath against Amalek today. We totally annihilate and destroy you Amalek from all of our lives, families, affairs, finances ministries, congregations, and all of Israel in Yeshua's name! We declare that we will pursue and we will surely overtake and recover all that you have stolen Amalek! With the two-edged sword (the Word of God) in our hands and the High Praises of ELOHIM in our mouths, we bind you Amalek with chains and all your friends and allies with fetters of iron – we inflict the punishment and execute the judgment and vengeance that is already written against you Amalek, today! In Yeshua's name. We recover all the souls that have fallen prey to you Amalek in replacement theology Christianity! We recover all the Land of Israel that has been stolen through the false Oslo Accords and "Land for peace" agreements – for You YHVH have a Land Covenant with Israel up to 1,000 generations! We recover all the wealth that has been stolen due to anti-Semitism, anti-Judaism, and persecution against the Jews through Christian Crusades, Spanish Inquisition, Pogroms, the Nazi Shoa (Holocaust) and the like!

We pursue, we overtake and we recover all territory stolen in our lives, our families, and our ministries, (name your ministry), UNIFY and Kad-Esh MAP Ministries. We break your power

Amalek in every congregation of the living YHVH in Israel and in all nations due to the deception of replacement theology! We uproot replacement theology in all of our lives, ministries, and all over the body of Messiah that the very name of Amalek and replacement theology will be blotted out of the face of the earth and under heaven. We recover all the believers captive in replacement theology in Yeshua's mighty name!

We uproot and destroy you Amalek in our finances, our health, our children, and our marriages! We execute YHVH's fierce wrath against you Amalek in every area of our lives and ministries! We execute YHVH's fierce wrath and total annihilation on all Amalek-induced diseases such as Lyme disease, fibromyalgia, cancer, heart disease, blood pressure, diabetes, dementia, MS, Parkinson's, depression, bipolar disorder, ADHD, schizophrenia (and all their derivatives) that attack the weak places of the human being!

We execute the fierce wrath of YHVH against you Amalek throughout the Land of Israel (and my city and nation) uprooting all terror, hidden terror, terror cells in Gaza, Samaria, Judea and all Israeli territory from the River Nile in Egypt to the Great Euphrates River in Iraq to the Mediterranean Sea.

YHVH, You pursue Amalek and all his friends with Your storm and fill their faces with shame that everyone will know that Your name, YHVH ELOHIM, is the Most High over all the earth! We execute Your fierce wrath against Amalek in the government of the Church and of our Nation [your country], and every nation represented in the United Nations for Israel and we take back our governments and nations to become Sheep Nations, worshippers of Yeshua and lovers of Israel!

We execute Your fierce wrath against Amalek in the United Nations and we blot out the very name of Amalek and all his friends within every council and every officer anti-Israel or anti-Zionist in Yeshua's mighty name. YHVH, You execute Your fierce wrath against Amalek in Islam and uproot and blot out the memory of Islam from under heaven and we take back all the souls that have been captives to Amalek-Islam in Yeshua's mighty name.

YHVH, You execute Your fierce wrath against Amalek in all persecutors of the Messianic, Apostolic, Prophetic Jews and Grafted-in ones (gentiles) in Israel and in all nations especially from other Christians or Messianic believers that oppose Your End time Move of Restoration – including the Yad L'achim organization that seeks to destroy the Messianic Jews that are true followers of Messiah. We execute Your fierce wrath YHVH against Amalek and every spirit of anti-Messiah in Judaism, Christianity, Islam, and every religion and religious system in Yeshua's mighty name!

We break your power Amalek in the Negev, Beer Sheva, Eilat, the Mountains of Edom, Mevaseret Zyon, Yerushalayim, Herzlya, Raanana, Kfar Saba, St. Augustine Florida (name your city here) and all over Israel and we leave no remnant! In Yeshua's mighty name we pray, declare, execute, uproot and recover all that has been stolen by you Amalek in our lives, our families, ministries, finances, relationships, affairs, congregations, nations and all of Israel and we take much plunder to advance the Kingdom of

YHVH with abundant vision, provision, health, favor, and success in Yeshua HaMashiach's mighty powerful name!

If you would like to see the scriptural foundation of this prayer, see Genesis 36:12,16; Exodus 17:8-16; Numbers 13:29, 24:20; Deuteronomy 25:17-20, Joshua 1:4; Judges 3:13; 5:14; 1 Samuel 15:2-20; 28:18; 1 Samuel 30; Psalms 83:7; Psalms 105:8-11; Psalms 149:5-9; Matthew 18:18-20; Luke 10:19; Ephesians 6:10-18

Israel, hear the Word of your ELOHIM who says to you "Though you search for your enemies, you will not find them. Those who wage war against you will be as nothing at all. For I am YHVH, your ELOHIM, who takes hold of your right hand and says to you, 'Do not fear; I will help you. Do not be afraid, O little Israel, for I Myself will help you,' declares YHVH, your Redeemer, the Holy One of Israel."

— ISAIAH 41:12–16

BIBLIOGRAPHY

24NYT. *New Danish Bible translation purges Israel | 24NYT*. 19 April 2020. 18 May 2020. <https://24nyt.dk/ new-danish-bible-translation-removes-israel/>.

Aipac.org Editors. *Israel's Achievements*. 2013. The American Israel Public Affairs Committee. 19 May 2020. <https://www.aipac. org/resources/about-israel/israels-achievements>.

Amadeo, Kimberly. *Hurricane Irma Facts, Damage, and Costs*. 8 September 2017. The Balance. 19 May 2020. <https://www.thebalance. com/hurricane-irma-facts-timeline-damage-costs-4150395>.

Anti-Defamation League. *Extremist "Zoombombing" Hijacks Meetings; Swastika hits Sanders Campaign Office; Antisemitic Pastor Blames Jews for COVID-19*. https://www.adl.org/blog/ extremist-zoombombing-hijacks-meetings-swastika-hits-sanders-campaign-office-antisemitic 2020. ADL. 18 May 2020.

Anti-Defemation Leauge. *2017 Audit of Anti-Semitic Incidents*. 2020. Anti-Defamation League. 20 5 2020. <https://www.adl.org/resources/ reports/2017-audit-of-anti-semitic-incidents#major-findings>.

Avraham, Samantha Ben. *The First Aliyah to Israel*. 14 April 2016. 18 May 2020. <https://www.samanthaisraeltours.com/ the-first-aliyah-to-israel/>.

Avrutin, Eugene M., Jonathan Dekel-Chen and Robert Weinburg. "Ritual Murder in Russia, Eastern Europe, and Beyond: New Histories of an Old Accusation." Avrutin, Eugene M. *Ritual Murder in Russia, Eastern Europe, and Beyond: New Histories of an Old Accusation.* Bloomington: Indiana University Press, 2017. 39-40.

Büssow, Johann. "The Ottoman Empire and its Heritage: Hamidian Palestine." *Hamidian Palestine: Politics and Society in the District of Jerusalem 1872-1908.* Vol. 46. BRILL, 2011. 195.

Bachner, Michael. *Polish crowd beats, burns Judas effigy with hat, sidelocks of ultra-Orthodox Jew.* 21 April 2019. 18 May 2020. <https://www.timesofisrael.com/polish-crowd-beats-burns-judas-effigy-featuring-anti-semitic-tropes/>.

—. *Spanish Inquisition | Definition, History, & Facts | Britannica.* 2020. 18 May 2020. <https://www.britannica.com/topic/Spanish-Inquisition>.

Berkowitz, Adam Eliyahu. *Scary Divine Connections Between Gush Katif and Hurricane Katrina Revealed On 10 Year Anniversary.* 24 August 2015. 18 May 2020. <https://www.breakingisraelnews.com/47546/10-year-anniversary-scary-connections-between-gush-katif-hurricane-katrina-revealed-jewish-world/>.

Bernstein, Deborah S. "SUNY series in Israeli Studies: Constructing Boundaries." *Constructing Boundaries: Jewish and Arab Workers in Mandatory Palestine.* 2000, SUNY Press. 20-21.

Bickerton, Ian J. and Verity Elizabeth Irvine. *Jordan.* 2 May 2020. Encyclopædia Britannica, inc. 18 May 2020. <https://www.britannica.com/place/Jordan>.

Burleigh, Michael and Wolfgang Wippermann. "The Racial State." Burleigh, Michael. *The Racial State*. Reprint. Cambridge University Press, 1991. 40.

Cline, Austin. *Adolf Hitler on God: Quotes Expressing Belief and Faith*. 7 August 2007. Learn Religions. 18 May 2020. <https://www.learnreligions.com/adolf-hitler-on-god-quotes-248193>.

Cohen, Philip J. "Eugenia & Hugh M. Stewart '26 Series: Serbia's Secret War." *Serbia's Secret War: Propaganda and the Deceit of History*. Reprint. Vol. 2. Texas A&M University Press, 1996. 123.

Encyclopaedia Britannica. *The Colonial and Postcolonial Middle East*. Ed. Bailey Maxim. First. Rosen Publishing, 2016.

Fassihi, Farnaz. *Fourteen of 15 Security Council Members Denounce US Stance on Jerusalem*. 9 December 2017. The Wall Street Journal. 24 May 2020. <https://www.wsj.com/articles/fourteen-of-15-security-council-members-denounce-u-s-stance-on-jerusalem-1512777971>.

Florida Center for Instructional Technology. *Map of Jewish expulsions and resettlement areas in Europe*. 2013. 18 May 2020.

Fordham University. *Internet History Sourcebooks Project | Medieval Sourcebook: Constantine I: On the Keeping of Easter*. 1996. Paul Halsall. 18 May 2020. <https://sourcebooks.fordham.edu/source/const1-easter.asp>.

Gaines, Adrienne S. *Todd Bentley's New Wife Breaks Silence*. 2009. Charisma Magazine. 18 May 2020. <https://www.charismamag.com/site-archives/570-news/featured-news/7046-todd-bentleys-new-wife-breaks-silence>.

Gerstenfeld, Manfred. *The Origins of Christian Anti-Semitism*. 25 November 2012. 18 May 2020. <https://jcpa.org/article/the-origins-of-christian-anti-semitism/>.

Goldhagen, Daniel J. *Hitler's Willing Executioners: Ordinary Germans and the Holocaust*. Vintage, 2007.

Gottesman, Itzik. *When Christmas Was a Time of Fear for Jews*. 18 December 2019. 18 May 2020. <https://forward.com/yiddish/436870/when-christmas-was-a-time-of-fear-for-jews/>.

Haaretz.com. *Hundreds of Jews Massacred in Prague on Easter*. 2019. 18 May 2020. <https://www.haaretz.com/hblocked?returnTo=https%3A%2F%2Fwww.haaretz.com%2Fjewish%2F.premium-1389-hundreds-of-jews-massacred-in-prague-on-easter-1.5432665>.

Harries, Richard. *After the Evil: Christianity and Judaism in the Shadow of the Holocaust*. Oxford University Press, 2003.

Hay, Malcolm. *Roots of Christian Anti Semitism*. Anti Defamation League of Bnai, 1984.

Heschel, Susannah. "The Aryan Jesus." Heschel, Susannah. *The Aryan Jesus: Christian Theologians and the Bible in Nazi Germany*. Princeton University Press, 2010. 20.

History.com Editors. *Balfour Declaration letter written*. 16 November 2009. 18 May 2020. <https://www.history.com/this-day-in-history/the-balfour-declaration>.

—. *Pogroms*. 21 August 2018. A&E Television Networks. 18 May 2020. <https://www.history.com/topics/russia/pogroms>.

Hitler, Adolf. "Mein Kampf." *Mein Kampf*. 1926. 60.

Ireland, Corydon. *The pogrom that transformed 20th century Jewry*. 9 April 2009. Harvard Gazette. 18 May 2020.

<https://news.harvard.edu/gazette/story/2009/04/
the-pogrom-that-transformed-20th-century-jewry/>.

Israel Ministry of Foreign Affairs. *Israel's humanitarian aid efforts.*
2014. 19 May 2020. <https://mfa.gov.il/MFA/ForeignPolicy/
Aid/Pages/Israel_humanitarian_aid.aspx>.

Joslyn-Siemiatkoski, Daniel. *Why Good Friday was dangerous for Jews
in the Middle Ages and how that changed.* 15 April 2019. 18
May 2020. <https://theconversation.com/why-good-friday-
was-dangerous-for-jews-in-the-middle-ages-and-how-that-
changed-114896>.

Keter Books. "Israel Pocket Library: Anti-Semitism." *Israel Pocket
Library: Anti-Semitism.* Jerusalem: Keter Books, 1974.

Koyzis, Nancy Calvert. *Paul, Monotheism and the People of God.* Con-
tinuum International Publishing Group, 2004.

Liardon, Roberts. *God's Generals: Smith Wigglesworth.* Whitaker
House, 2001.

Luther, Martin. *On The Jews and Their Lies.* Ed. Coleman Rydie. Trans.
Martin H. Bertram. Coleman Rydie, 2008.

—. *On The Jews and Their Lies, Luthers Works.* Trans. Martin H. Bertram. Vol. 47. Fortress Press, 1971.

MacCulloch, Diarmaid. *Reformation: Europe's House Divided 1490-
1700.* Penguin UK, 2004.

Marans, Noam E. *On Luther and his lies.* 11 October 2017. 18
May 2020. <https://www.christiancentury.org/article/
critical-essay/on-luther-and-lies>.

McNeil, Sam. *Israel treating thousands of Syrians injured in war.* 8 April
2017. The Independent. 19 May 2020. <https://www.indepen-
dent.co.uk/news/world/middle-east/israel-syria-assad-treat-
ing-airstrikes-military-wounded-injured-war-a7673771.html>.

Merry, Sidney. "How the State Controls Society." *How the State Controls Society*. Null. Lulu.com, 2008. 220.

Michael, Robert. *A History of Catholic Antisemitism: The Dark Side of the Church*. 1. Palgrave Macmillan US, 2011.

Morris, Benny. *What caused the Palestinian refugee crisis?* 14 January 2004. The Guardian. 19 May 2020. <https://www.theguardian.com/world/2004/jan/14/israel>.

NBC News. Ed. Janelle Griffith. NBC News. 28 January 2020. Talk Show.

Nicholls, William. "Christian Antisemitism: A History of Hate." Nicholls, William. *Christian Antisemitism: A History of Hate*. 1. Lanham, Maryland, Boulder, Colorado, New York City, New York, Toronto, Ontario, and Oxford, England: Rowman & Littlefield Publishers, Inc., 1993. 178-187.

Nirenburg, David. "The Rhineland Massacres of Jews in the First Crusade." Nirenburg, David. *The Rhineland Massacres of Jews in the First Crusade: Memories Medieval and Modern*. Cambridge University Press, 2002. 279-310.

Outler, Albert C. "Augustine: Confessions Newly translated and edited." *Augustine: Confessions Newly translated and edited*. 1. Prod. Texas Southern Methodist University Dallas. Dallas, n.d. 18 May 2020. <https://www.ling.upenn.edu/courses/hum100/augustinconf.pdf>.

"Pantheon (Religion)." Wikipedia, Wikimedia Foundation, 31 July 2020, <https://en.wikipedia.org/wiki/Pantheon_(religion)>.

Percival, Henry R. "The Nicaean & Post-Nicaen Fathers." *The Nicaean & Post-Nicaen Fathers*. Vol. XIV. T. & T. Clark Publishers, 1979. 54-55.

Rohrer, Sam. *4/8/20 - Connecting COVID-19 and God's Message to the World*. 8 April 2020. 19 May 2020. <https://subsplash.com/americanpastors/lb/mi/+hjfspf6>.

Süss, René and Martin Luther. *Luthers theologisch testament*. 2. VU University Press, 2010, n.d.

Sandhu, Serina. *The 32 countries that support the US embassy moving to Jerusalem*. 15 May 2018. inews. 19 May 2020. <https://inews.co.uk/news/world/the-32-countries-that-support-the-us-embassy-moving-to-jerusalem-291611>.

Sasse, Martin. *Martin Luther and the Jews*. CPA Books, 1998.

Seltman, Muriel. *The Changing Faces of Antisemitism*. Troubador Publishing Ltd, 2015.

Telegraph.co.uk. *Centuries of Christian anti-Semitism led to Holocaust, landmark Church of England report concludes*. The Telegraph. 5 May 2020. November 21 2019. < https://www.telegraph.co.uk news/2019/11/21/centuries-christian-anti-semitism-led-hol caust-landmark-church/>

Text of the Balfour Declaration. 2020. 24 May 2020. <https://www.jewishvirtuallibrary.org/text-of-the-balfour-declaration>.

The Darker Side of Martin Luther. *Constructing the Past: The Darker Side of Martin Luther*. n.d. Emily Paras. <https://www.iwu.edu/history/constructingthepastvol9/Paras.pdf>.

The Editors of Encyclopaedia Britannica. *Haskala | Judaic movement | Britannica*. 2020. 18 May 2020. <https://www.britannica.com/topic/Haskala>.

The Jerusalem Post. *An American Holocaust? Antisemitism in the 21st Century, Part One of Three*. 16 March 2014. David Turner. 18 May 2020. <https://www.jpost.com/Blogs/The-Jewish-Problem---From-anti-Judaism-to-anti-Semitism/

An-American-Holocaust-Antisemitism-in-the-21st-Century-Part-One-of-Three-363922>.

—. *World Council of Churches trainees use antisemitic rhetoric, advocate BDS.* 14 January 2019. Lahav Harkov. 18 May 2020. <https://www.jpost.com/diaspora/antisemitism/world-council-of-churches-trainees-use-antisemitic-rhetoric-advocate-bds-577256>.

The Librarians. *Mark Twain in Palestine - "A Hopeless, Dreary, Heart-Broken Land."* 5 November 2018. 18 May 2020. <https://blog.nli.org.il/en/mark-twain-in-palestine/>.

The Sabbath Sentinel. "Council of Laodicea – 364 AD." *The Sabbath Sentinel*, The Sabbath Sentinel, 10 Nov. 2016, sabbathsentinel.org/2016/11/10/council-of-laodicea-364-ad/amp/.

TIME.com. *Religion: Luther Is to Blame.* 6 November 1944. 18 May 2020. <http://content.time.com/time/magazine/article/0,9171,803412,00.html>.

UN Watch. *2019 UN General Assembly Resolutions Singling Out Israel – Texts, Votes, Analysis - UN Watch.* 19 November 2019. 18 May 2020. <https://unwatch.org/2019-un-general-assembly-resolutions-singling-out-israel-texts-votes-analysis/>.

United States Department of State. *Defining Anti-Semitism - United States Department of State.* 6 March 2020. 18 May 2020. <https://www.state.gov/defining-anti-semitism/>.

VU University Press. *Luthers theologisch testament.* 2018. 18 May 2020. <https://www.vuuniversitypress.com/product/luthers-theologisch-testament/>.

Wikipedia Contributors. *Aliyah Bet.* 14 April 2020. Wikimedia Foundation. 18 May 2020. <https://en.wikipedia.org/wiki/Aliyah_Bet>.

—. *Antisemitism in Christianity.* 3 May 2020. 18 May 2020. <https://en.wikipedia.org/wiki/Antisemitism_in_Christianity#Church_Fathers>.

—. *Benjamin Disraeli.* 15 May 2020. Wikimedia Foundation. 18 May 2020. <https://en.wikipedia.org/wiki/Benjamin_Disraeli>.

—. *Big lie.* 2 May 2020. Wikimedia Foundation. 18 May 2020. <https://en.wikipedia.org/wiki/Big_lie>.

—. *Demographic history of Palestine (region).* 2 May 2020. Wikimedia Foundation. 18 May 2020. <https://en.wikipedia.org/wiki/Demographic_history_of_Palestine_(region)#cite_ref-44>.

—. *First Crusade.* 16 May 2020. 18 May 2020. <https://en.wikipedia.org/wiki/First_Crusade>.

—. *Identity Theft.* 4 May 2020. Wikimedia Foundation. 18 May 2020. <https://en.wikipedia.org/wiki/Identity_theft>.

—. *Jewish deicide.* 12 April 2020. Wikimedia Foundation. 24 May 2020. <https://en.wikipedia.org/wiki/Jewish_deicide>.

—. *Jewish National Fund.* 3 March 2020. Wikimedia Foundation. 2020 May 2020. <https://en.wikipedia.org/wiki/Jewish_National_Fund>.

—. *List of United Nations resolutions concerning Israel.* 17 March 2020. Wikimedia Foundation. 18 May 2020. <https://en.wikipedia.org/wiki/List_of_United_Nations_resolutions_concerning_Israel>.

William, Koenig R. *Eye to Eye: Facing the Consequences of Dividing Israel.* Revised. Christian Publications, 2017.

Wood, Christopher S. "Albrecht Altdorfer and the Origins of Landscape." Wood, Christopher S. *Albrecht Altdorfer and the Origins of Landscape.* London: Reaktion Books, 1993. 251.

World Israel News. *WZO report: 18% spike in global anti-Semitism*. 20 April 2020. <https://worldisraelnews.com/wzo-report-18-spike-in-global-anti-semitism/>.

YashaNet. *Anti-Semitism of the "Church Fathers."* 2019. 18 May 2020. <http://www.yashanet.com/library/fathers.htm>.

Zionism-Israel. *Zionism & Israel Information*. 2020. 14 April 2020. <http://www.zionism-israel.com/bio/E_Ben_Yehuda_biography.htm>.

—. *Zionism & Israel Resources*. 2020. 14 April 2020. <http://www.zionism-israel.com/bio/echad_haam.htm>.